MAIN CURRENTS OF WEST AFRICAN
HISTORY 1940–1978

By the same author

WEST AFRICA
ECONOMIC GEOGRAPHY OF WEST AFRICA
THE LION AND THE UNICORN IN AFRICA:
   THE UNITED AFRICA COMPANY 1787–1931

MAIN CURRENTS OF WEST AFRICAN HISTORY 1940–1978

Frederick Pedler

Honorary Fellow of the School of Oriental and African Studies, University of London

First published 1979 by
THE MACMILLAN PRESS LTD
London and Basingstoke
Associated companies in Delhi
Dublin Hong Kong Johannesburg Lagos
Melbourne New York Singapore Tokyo

Printed in Great Britain by
Billing & Sons Limited,
Guildford, London and Worcester

British Library Cataloguing in Publication Data

Pedler, *Sir* Frederick
    Main currents of West African history, 1940–1978
    1. Africa, West – History
    I. Title
    966   DT475

    ISBN 0–333–25870–3
    ISBN 0–333–26637–4 Pbk

Contents

PART IV CONCLUSION

List of Maps

Acknowledgements

The publisher and author wish to express their thanks to Elliot Berg, Professor of Economics at the University of Michigan Center for Research on Economic Development for permission to use the figures on p. 88; to Dr Lewis Gann, Senior Fellow of the Hoover Institution on War, Revolution and Peace, and to Virginia Thompson and Richard Adloff for permission to use the figures on p. 95; and to Theodore Geiger, Vice-President of the National Planning Association, Washington D.C., for permission to use the figures on p. 96.

Preface

From 1940 to 1974 I was frequently in West Africa, living in various parts, and for the rest of the time visiting constantly. Many of the statesmen who are mentioned in the following pages were known to me; some have taken me into their confidence in long conversations; and more than one were (or still are) personal friends.

This is a book for students and general readers who want a simple narrative of what went on in West Africa during this exciting period, and therefore it has not been felt necessary to use footnotes. However, if any reader should discover facts which have not previously been published, the source is my own experience, which in most cases rests upon diaries or notes, so that I am not at the mercy of memory. For example, I was within earshot when Lamine Gueye challenged De Gaulle in 1944, and Lamine Gueye and I had a laugh over the memory when I reminded him of it years later at the Senegal embassy in London. I was present at the interviews between Lord Hailey and Dr Joseph Danquah in 1940, I was in the Gold Coast through the main part of 1948, I was in the northern province of Sierra Leone when the disorders occurred, I have been in Cotonou during a coup, and I had long conversations with Sir Tafawa Balewa and with the Sardauna of Sokoto a few days before their tragic deaths. My wife and I were (we believe) the first tourists to hire a launch for a holiday trip up the Gambia river to Fatatunda. The story of how Kwame Nkrumah secured American help for the Volta project was told to me by Chad Calhoun and Robert Jackson, who were in the best positions to know what went on, and I am indebted to Nigel Cooke for various particulars about Kano and Sokoto.

However, though the help of friends and personal experience may cover a few events, in the main it is necessary to rely on reading, and first of all I must acknowledge my debt to *West Africa*, and express my admiration for the record of contemporary events which is found in that journal. I have used *The Annual Register* (Longman) and for francophone countries I have drawn on the bulletins of the *Association pour l'Etude des problèmes d'Outremer*. I have also read books, and I have acknowledged my reading in every case by including the publication in the biography. I wish to express my thanks to my wife, who is the first to read the typescript pages, calling attention to obscurities, polishing the style, and detecting typing errors.

December 1978   F.P.

Introduction: the Scope of the Book

This book takes up the West African story in 1940, the year of which it may be said that the process of colonisation ended and decolonisation began. With the exception of small coastal and riverain areas which had been in European hands since the sixteenth or seventeenth centuries, the British, French, and German territories were all occupied in the period between 1884 and 1910. In 1940 therefore the political geography was not very old. Many people remembered the time before the white man came. Yet the colonial settlement had met with remarkable acceptance. The significance of 1940 is that it was the year in which the war began to make an impact, and that impact was to hasten the change of attitudes which made people think that the colonial system was not acceptable. At just the same time the population, which had been static in numbers or even in decline for many years, began to increase very rapidly.

The area of this study runs from Saint Louis to Calabar, that is to say, from the north-west frontier of Senegal to the south-east frontier of Nigeria. Mauretania in the west and Cameroon in the east are excluded, despite the fact that both have been associated with West African affairs, because they also have affinities with other regions, which cannot be taken into account in a short book. Here follows a list of the countries in the area, showing on the left the names by which they were known in 1940, and on the right their present titles.

Colony of Senegal	Republic of Senegal
French Sudan	Republic of Mali
Gambia	The Gambia
Portuguese Guinea	Republic of Guinea-Bissau
French Guinea	Republic of Guinea
Sierra Leone	Sierra Leone
Liberia	Liberia
Ivory Coast	Ivory Coast

Upper Volta, an administrative area forming part of Ivory Coast	Upper Volta, or sometimes Voltaic Republic
Gold Coast	Ghana
Togo Mandated Territory	Togo Republic
Dahomey	Republic of Benin
Niger Colony	Niger Republic
Nigeria	Nigeria

Events of economic and social importance will be mentioned in the chapters dealing with these countries; but social and economic trends are treated in Part II (Chapters 10–12).

PART I

THE LAST YEARS OF COLONIAL RULE

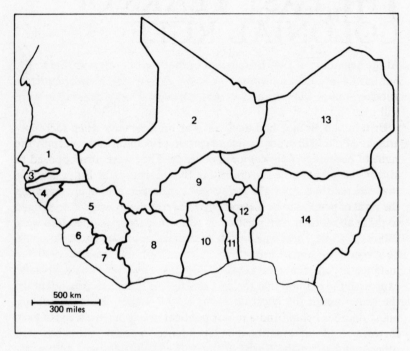

1 Senegal	8 Ivory Coast
2 Mali	9 Upper Volta
3 The Gambia	10 Ghana
4 Guinea-Bissau	11 Togo
5 Guinea	12 Benin
6 Sierra Leone	13 Niger
7 Liberia	14 Nigeria

Map 1   States of West Africa

1 The Year 1940

At the beginning of 1940 Britain and France were at war with Germany, but hardly any fighting was taking place. Poland had been completely knocked out in 1939. Italy, the United States, Russia, and Japan were still neutral.

Britain and France had declared war on Germany when Germany attacked Poland in order to defend certain principles, and especially the right of nations to political independence. They were also opposed to Hitler's view about the superiority of the German race. But in denying that one race had any right to overpower another, and in championing the right of peoples to be independent, the colonial powers were obliged to think about their own position in relation to those peoples who were subject to them. There was a ferment of ideas, and many examples could be cited both from Europe and from Africa. In January 1940 for instance a conference in London, organised by the Fabian Society, expressed the opinion that the colonies should become independent. In the same month the *Nigerian Eastern Mail* wrote, 'Although we are many decades behind India in our political development, we also look forward to ultimate national independence in equal fellowship with other members of the British Commonwealth of Nations, and in the meantime we expect honest, pertinent, and reasonably speedy progress towards that ideal.' The first appointment of a Nigerian to commissioned rank in the army took place. Professor W. M. Macmillan, author of *Africa Emergent*, was a leader of liberal opinion in Britain, while in Parliament Dr Haden Guest said that Britain must offer to the peoples of the colonies 'a real share in the new world', and that 'we should abolish colonial status altogether'. In the following year Clement Attlee, the Deputy Prime Minister in the British Government, said in a speech to the West African Students' Union that the principles of the Atlantic Charter regarding self-determination applied to all races in the world, coloured as well as white.

In the first quarter of 1940 it seemed to be a lazy war, and a long way from West Africa; but the Secretary of State for the Colonies, Malcolm MacDonald, did not expect things to continue like that, and believed that Africa would become more involved. He asked Lord Hailey to visit the African colonies, to identify any matters which might cause discontent, and recommend how to deal with them. He also wished to have advice which would help in considering any proposals which might be made for political changes in Africa during or immediately after the war.

The influence of Lord Hailey was of importance. William Malcolm Hailey was born in 1872, the son of a country doctor. He entered the Indian civil service and had a successful career in India, from which he retired in 1935 at the age of 63. Upon his retirement he was raised to the peerage as Lord Hailey.

A South African, General Smuts, had pointed out in a public lecture that Africa was developing under the control of a number of European powers, that different and often conflicting principles were being applied by them, and that there was no survey of what was taking place in Africa as a whole. He pleaded for the compilation of such a survey, and a committee was formed to carry the project into execution. The Carnegie Corporation and the Rhodes Trustees provided funds, and Lord Hailey was invited to undertake the work. The first edition of *An African Survey*, published in 1938, incorporated the results of work by Hailey and numerous helpers. It was a unique concentration of informed opinion. It stimulated and influenced action and further study.

The British colonial governments in West Africa were following the policy of 'Indirect Rule'. This policy was the subject of controversy within the colonial service. Many devoted men argued that the native authorities should be developed as the basis of a central political authority which, in due course, would take over the government of the country. Hailey however did not share that view. He described the native authorities as 'executive powers for the purpose of local government', and saw no future for them as a basis for central political institutions. It followed that if the native authorities could not be used as the basis of political evolution, another basis must be found; and that could only mean the development of parliamentary institutions. He wrote, 'Africans must before long be given a material addition to their very limited representation in the legislative councils' (*Survey*, p. 252). Hailey's influence was powerful in persuading British public opinion to accept that view.

Reference has already been made to Hailey's visit to Africa in 1940. At Kumasi he identified one of those problems which he had been asked to bring to light and lay to rest. It was the question of the Kumasi Clan

Lands, four square miles which had been taken away from the Asantehene by the government after the war of 1900. There had been agitation for the return of these symbolical areas. The governor wanted to agree that the land should again be vested in the Golden Stool, but he was at a loss to see how he could unravel all the leases and he feared that the return of the land might hinder the orderly development of Kumasi as a 'garden city'. Hailey convinced the governor and his advisers that the thing had to be done, and that the difficulties must be overcome. The decision to return the land to the Golden Stool was announced at once.

There was much discussion as to whether Africans ought to be appointed to the Colonial Administrative Service. As recently as 1939 the Chief Secretary of Nigeria had said that it would be contrary to policy. There were many enthusiasts for the idea of building up the native authorities as a basis for a federal government, and the supporters of that idea could see that if the best Africans were placed in the central government services, the native authorities would stand little chance of development. However, Hailey's advice to the Secretary of State was that the future political institutions of these countries could not be based on native authorities. He went on to say that Africans ought to be appointed to the Colonial Administrative Service, and that the best place to begin would be the Gold Coast. This recommendation was adopted.

From French West Africa 65,000 African soldiers were moved in 1939 and 1940 to France and other distant destinations. In connection with these arrangements Galandou Diouf, who represented Senegal as a deputy in the French parliament, made a speech in which he said, 'If by some ill-luck the allies lose the war, it will not be Paris that Germany will demand. It will not be Bordeaux or Marseilles. It will be the Colonies. And it is to defend them that we are fighting now.' Within a few weeks, France appeared to have lost the war, and the African troops who had gone to Europe were mostly prisoners of war.

The military forces in the British colonies were not so large, a mere 8000 professional soldiers of the Royal West African Frontier Force. Since West Africa seemed secure, the majority of these were moved to East Africa, where the possibility of an Italian intervention in the war made it advisable to strengthen the defences.

Freetown was already seeing much activity as a base for anti-submarine operations, and as an assembly port for north-bound convoys.

In 1940 the British parliament passed the Colonial Development and Welfare Act, which inaugurated a new era in colonial policy. It is true that there had been a Colonial Development Act since 1929; its sponsors had hoped that it would both help the colonies and provide employment in Britain. Some schemes conveniently served both these aims; but the use of the money was hindered by rules which were based on the idea that colonies ought to be financially self-sufficient. Therefore, colonies had to guarantee that they could meet the recurrent charges on any new schemes, and while the wealthier colonies such as the Gold Coast were able to do so, poorer colonies such as Nigeria were unable to submit many schemes.

In 1939 the Governor of Nigeria, Sir Bernard Bourdillon, asked the Secretary of State for a new deal. He wrote that his subject was the economic development of the African colonies, and that he raised it with less diffidence than he would have done a year earlier, because he noted evidence that the British public was awakening from its complacency. He quoted Hailey and W. M. Macmillan. He asked for 'soft' loans, and also proposed that the British government 'should accept responsibility for financing the operations of the agricultural, forestry, geological survey, veterinary and co-operative departments'. About this time a Royal Commission reported on the West Indies and made recommendations about aid. A report by Sir Alan Pim on Northern Rhodesia (now Zambia) exerted influence in the same direction. Responding to these pressures, the British government, by the Act of 1940, made available £5,500,000 annually, of which half a million pounds were for research. The rules which prevented the money from being used to assist poor colonies in their annual expenditure were relaxed.

The main economic aspect of the war in West Africa, so far, was the difficulty in selling cocoa. Important markets in Germany and central Europe had been lost, and since cocoa was not essential for fighting the war, it seemed unlikely that Britain would take as much as in peacetime. There were still plenty of neutral countries, but the only way of persuading them to take more cocoa would be to accept low prices. In order to avoid distress in the cocoa areas, the British government decided to buy all cocoa offered for sale, at a fixed price which was about the current market level. This was introduced as a temporary wartime measure, but in fact it was the end of the free marketing of cocoa. The government asked producers to deliver their cocoa to the shippers already established (mostly Europeans, but including some Africans and a few Lebanese) who would act as agents for the government. The agents' remuneration was fixed, and each agent was to handle a proportion of the total shipment based on his business in recent years.

The cocoa exporters had been generally accused of paying too little, especially during the cocoa hold-up of 1937, and now that the government fixed the price, the criticism was immediately transferred to the government. The principal spokesman for the farmers was the West African Students' Union (WASU) in London, who submitted a memorandum to the British government. They developed the suggestion that the cocoa price ought to take account of the sharp increase in the prices of European manufactured goods which had occurred as a result of the war. Groundnuts and palm produce were brought into the argument, and the British government was faced with the difficulty which was to embarrass it throughout the war and the years of scarcity which followed the war, namely, that any attempt to relate the prices paid for produce to the prices of manufactured articles was doomed to fail, because the supplies of manufactured goods were simply not available. However, the Colonial Office returned a reasoned reply to WASU. The main things which came out of this discussion were, first, a promise from the British government that if any profit was made out of its trading in West African produce, that profit would be made over to the West African governments; and secondly, the West African Produce Control Board was appointed, to take over the purchase of cocoa and oilseeds from the British Ministry of Food. The Board was intended to safeguard the interests of producers; it could sell to the Ministry of Food what was required in Britain, and market the balance elsewhere as advantageously as possible. In spite of fears that quantities of cocoa might have to be burned, the Board managed to keep the crop moving in the worst years of the war.

British air communications with Africa and Asia depended on flying-boats, which used strips of water in Italy on their journey between Britain and Egypt, since they were not able to fly long distances without refuelling. Passengers for West Africa travelled by the South African service of flying-boats as far as Khartoum, where the aircraft alighted on the river Nile. From there, a seven-seater plane flew via the Chad Colony (French) to Nigeria and the Gold Coast. On 10 June 1940 Italy entered the war on the German side, and the British air route to Asia, Africa, and Australia was cut. At the same time it became impossible for merchant ships to sail from Britain to the Far East through the Mediterranean. Emergency steps were taken to develop air and sea routes to Asia, using airfields and ports in West Africa.

The Germans occupied Belgium, a neutral country. There was grave anxiety lest German elements might appear in the Belgian Congo, and Lord Hailey was asked to go there and to establish a British Mission in friendly consultation with the Belgian Governor-General. France was utterly defeated and made an armistice with Germany. The head of the French government was now Marshal Pétain, and since the Germans held Paris Pétain set up his headquarters at Vichy, a town in that part of France which the Germans, under the terms of the armistice, had agreed not to occupy. The British government were on bad terms with the French Vichy government, because they supported General De Gaulle, who refused to follow Pétain or to accept the armistice, and also because they sank some French naval vessels in order to prevent them from falling into German hands. Among these was the battleship *Richelieu*, which was attacked by the Royal Navy in the harbour at Dakar. A couple of months later, a force of Gaullist French with British assistance attempted to capture Dakar, but the attack was repulsed by the Vichy French. There was fear in the British West African colonies lest the Vichy French might attack them in retaliation.

The war had now become very real for West Africa, and the *Nigerian Daily Times* wrote, 'We are fighting so as to maintain our connection with the only Empire under whose protection the full realisation of our natural aspirations as a people is possible.'

To the immense relief of everyone in British West Africa, the Governor of the Chad Colony threw off the command of Vichy and accepted the leadership of De Gaulle. This preserved for the Free French, and therefore also for Britain, an air-and-land corridor from West Africa to the east, and it established a buffer state between the Italian colony of Libya and the Belgian Congo, to which (as explained above) the Germans might have hoped to penetrate. The Governor of the Chad Colony who made this outstanding contribution was Félix Eboué. He came from Guyana, and was black. A graduate of the Sorbonne and a Rugby football player, he entered the colonial service and rose, after serving as Governor of Chad, to be the Governor-General of French Equatorial Africa.

The West African troops who had been moved to Kenya were now in action against the Italians in Ethiopia, where they made an important contribution to the conquest of that country. In February 1941 the British government made it clear that Ethiopia would be re-established as an independent state. This marked the turn of the tide in two senses. It was the end of the unbroken series of Nazi-Fascist victories, and the first success of the British and their allies. Even more significantly for Africa in the long run, the tide of colonisation, which had reached its furthest advance when Italy took possession of Ethiopia, now began to retreat.

In British West Africa, service personnel of all arms began to arrive from Europe. The construction of airfields and of naval and military installations created a great deal of employment, drawing people to towns and stimulating the formation of trade unions. During the course of the war the British enlisted 372,000 Africans for the army; 166,000 served outside their own territories. Two West African divisions fought against the Japanese in Burma alongside British and Indian forces.

In addition to all the unexpected events of 1940, it was a year of advances in social policy. The government of the Gold Coast provided low-cost housing at Labadi for people whose homes had been destroyed in the earthquake of 1939; a piped water supply was inaugurated at Ibadan; and the Kumasi Public Health Board instituted a scheme to provide pensions for its employees.

2 The Gold Coast, 1940-51

At the beginning of the period the Gold Coast had about 65,000 children in schools, and this was about 2 per cent of the total population of all ages. Small though this percentage was, it was much above the percentage in any other West African country. There were several good secondary schools, and the government college at Achimota had developed studies at university degree level, presenting candidates for the external degree in engineering of the University of London. This kind of relationship with London University was a normal step in the growth of university institutions at that time, both in Britain and in the empire.

The Gold Coast was unique in another respect. The chiefs and their councils, in the Colony and Ashanti, had not been incorporated in the system of government, in accordance with the 'native authority policy', to the same extent as the traditional authorities of Nigeria and Sierra Leone. In the Northern Territories of the Gold Coast, on the other hand, the Nigerian model had been followed. The Colony and Ashanti chiefs were capable of acting independently of government, beating gong-gong to make their wishes known, and enforcing those wishes through their own courts. Thus, they could support the cocoa hold-up of 1937 and the boycott of imported goods in 1948. This would have been inconceivable elsewhere. Furthermore, no direct tax was imposed by the government on the inhabitants of the Colony and Ashanti. This was the only area in British Africa where such a situation existed, and it was due to the robust resistance which the inhabitants had always shown when the government had considered the imposition of taxation. In the Northern Territories, on the other hand, the people were taxed; but since it would have been unfair for the central government to use this revenue so long as no direct tax was raised from the Colony and Ashanti, the whole of the tax collected in the Northern Territories was credited to the native authorities and was used by them locally in providing schools, including school farms, cattle insurance schemes, and other services. Income tax was introduced during the war, but that was direct taxation of a completely different kind.

The number of Africans who were actively working for independence in 1940 was small. The most impressive figure was Dr Joseph Buachie Danquah, PhD. He had recently organised the Gold Coast Youth Conference, of which he was the secretary in spite of his 45 years and the peppering of grey in his hair. The programme of the Youth Conference envisaged dominion status as the political objective and proposed that steps should be taken immediately to move towards that goal. Accompanied by three younger colleagues (Akiwume, Hansen, and Osei) Danquah presented a memorandum to Hailey, setting out what those steps should be. He proposed that the legislative council should be made more democratic. At that time it consisted of 29 members of whom only nine were elected Africans, six being elected by the chiefs and three being directly elected in the towns of Accra, Cape Coast, and Sekondi on a property qualification. Danquah proposed that there should be two houses in the legislature. In the lower house he asked for a majority of members directly elected on manhood suffrage. The upper house should consist of chiefs and it should have power of veto. To facilitate this, and to render it acceptable to liberal minds, Danquah advocated important reforms in the chiefdoms. In discussion with Hailey, the younger men who accompanied Danquah did not share his view that an assembly of chiefs should exercise power of veto over a house in which elected representatives of the people commanded a majority. In this it is possible to see Danquah's personal problem of reconciling his two positions, the position of a democratic leader and the position of a member of a distinguished chiefly family.

The other important request which Danquah presented to Hailey was that Africans should be appointed as members of the administrative service; Hailey's favourable reaction to this proposal has been mentioned above.

On the day following his first talk with Hailey, Danquah went to Akropong to attend a gathering of the Youth Conference. The speakers included people who were to be famous names – Harry Sawyerr, Amishadai Adu, Daniel Chapman, and William Ofori-Atta. The meeting attracted attention, and put the independence movement on the map. Danquah described its proceedings in a talk on the Accra radio. (Radio-diffusion had recently been introduced on the initiative of the governor, Sir Arnold Hodson. He had been governor of the Falkland Islands, Sierra Leone, and now Gold Coast, and had established radio-diffusion at each of those places in turn.) Danquah then led a delegation to speak with the governor; but to Sir Arnold's surprise they did not use the occasion to present any proposals for political reform; they spoke about the development of agricultural resources and industrial manufactures.

Sir Alan Burns was appointed as governor of Gold Coast in 1941; a man of liberal opinions with experience of Nigeria and of the Caribbean. He was sensitive to African opinion and quickly adopted the suggestion, made by Hailey, that Africans should be appointed to the administrative service. Furthermore, he insisted that he must have some African members of his executive council. It was a step which could be taken quickly without a great deal of public argument (always inconvenient in wartime). The Secretary of State, though surprised at the vehemence of Burns' representations, agreed, so Nana Sir Ofori Atta and Mr K. A. Korsah were appointed to the executive council. Burns' initiative had results elsewhere in West Africa, for it was felt that this dramatic step, associating Africans with the innermost workings of colonial government, must be taken in Nigeria and Sierra Leone at the same time.

In 1943 new arrangements were introduced for the municipality of Accra, and the town council was given an elected majority.

The construction of airfields and other military works brought together large numbers of workers in circumstances which favoured the formation of trade unions, and in order to assist this process the government recruited a British trade unionist in 1942. By 1947 there were 28 registered trade unions with paid-up membership of 12,000. The leaders of the trade unions added their voices to the demand for constitutional reform, and introduced a new element into the movement which hitherto had belonged to the middle class.

As soon as the war was over, Gold Coast became the first colony in Africa to have an elected majority in its legislative council. The membership is shown in Table 2.1.

TABLE 2.1 Gold Coast legislative council, 1946

President: the governor	
6	government officers
6	persons nominated by the governor
9	members elected by the provincial councils of chiefs
4	members elected by the Ashanti confederacy council
5	members elected by four municipalities (Accra, Cape Coast, Sekondi, and Kumasi)
31	(9 British, 22 Africans)

This change was of tremendous importance. Eighteen of the 31 members of the legislature were elected. Although the elections were not based on universal suffrage, there was no reason to suppose that persons representing the chiefs or the property-holders of the four towns would be yes-men in the hand of the government. The government could not now enact any law, nor secure the passage of the annual budget, without persuading some of these people to vote for the bill. The finance committee of the legislative council became the place where the financial implications of government policy were considered and, in effect, decided.

Shortly after the new constitution was inaugurated the United Gold Coast Convention (UGCC) was formed, to demand more concessions in the direction of self-government. The leaders proclaimed that the UGCC was not a political party, but a national movement. The president of the UGCC, 'Pa' Grant, was a wealthy timber merchant. He said, 'Our aim is self-government in the shortest possible time, and to my mind the time is at hand. This is a national movement, and when we move we must move together, not separately, but as one great mass towards the great foe – the great master who now dominates our country.' Danquah brought the support of those elements whom he had previously rallied in the Youth Conference. He formed a shadow cabinet, ready to take power at an early date.

Nana Sir Ofori Atta I of Akim Abuakwa died in 1943, and his second funeral 'custom' was observed after an interval. About the time of the celebrations a minor chief disappeared, and eight men were convicted of the murder of this person. Danquah (who was a barrister, and also the half-brother of Ofori Atta) organised the defence. It was alleged by the prosecution that the murder had been carried out in fulfilment of the custom of human sacrifice which had in earlier days been 'an inseparable part' of the obsequies of great chiefs, as Danquah himself had written in his book, *Akan Laws and Customs*. The defence took advantage of all the possibilities of appeal but the conviction was upheld. The governor commuted the death sentences which had been passed on the two youngest of the accused, but the others faced the death penalty. Danquah then succeeded in postponing the executions by initiating a new legal proceeding, waiting on each occasion until the eleventh hour. Under the principle that sentence may not be carried out while legal proceedings are pending, the executions were on each occasion postponed. Danquah did not hesitate to use this circumstance to awaken the sympathy of highly-placed persons in London for his clients, on the ground of the mental anguish to which they had been subjected by facing imminent execution on several occasions. In the British parliament both those who were opposed to capital punishment and the anti-colonial lobby lent him their aid. The defence of the condemned men became mixed up in a macabre way with the constitutional dispute. Danquah came under criticism for unprofessional behaviour but the final outcome was that three more of the six who were under sentence had their penalty commuted; only three were executed.

The country was menaced by a serious threat to its prosperity. Cocoa trees were attacked by a disease called swollen shoot. It affected particularly those areas where cocoa had been first developed. The only known way of checking the disease was to destroy the trees, but it was difficult to secure the co-operation of farmers because diseased trees were still capable of yielding valuable crops. Shortly after the end of the war a programme of destroying affected trees was adopted. This strained the relations between the government and the cocoa community, and disposed the farmers to support those who were bringing pressure on the government to adopt a democratic constitution.

Ako Adjei returned to the Gold Coast from studies in the USA and Britain and became active in the UGCC. The part which he played was critical. He had been with Nkrumah in America at the University of Pennsylvania, where they had co-operated in publishing a newspaper. Now he suggested to the UGCC that they should appoint Nkrumah as secretary. Danquah wrote a letter to Nkrumah (who was in London) inviting him to take the job, and George (Pa) Grant, president of the UGCC, sent to Nkrumah the money for his fare. Nkrumah arrived in the Gold Coast in the last days of 1947 and set up a secretariat for the Convention.

He arrived just as the people of the country were beginning a great demonstration of public protest, of the kind which had been a feature of Gold Coast affairs in colonial times. The subject was high prices. The movement was organised by Kwamina Taylor, a successful import merchant aged 60, who bore the title of Nii Kwabena Bonne III in his capacity as Osu Alata Mantse, one of the chiefs of the Ga tribe in Accra. He was (as he wrote) 'horrified at the unbearably high price which Africans had to pay for European goods, particularly textiles'. He decided that the only way to remedy the situation was to force the importers 'to alter their trading system by constitutional means'. He approached the Joint Provincial Council of Chiefs, and that body approved the campaign. Nii Bonne then gave a courteous warning to the Accra Chamber of Commerce that unless the importers reduced their prices a boycott would start on 26 January. The boycott was very effective. The government called the two sides together. The European merchants argued that on various imported commodities, including essential foodstuffs, their margins were as low as 12 per cent, and therefore it was reasonable for them to take a margin as high as 75 per cent on printed textiles of the best quality, to average things out. Furthermore, they maintained that the high prices of which the people complained were not the prices charged in the importers' warehouses, but the prices charged by African retailers in the markets. After negotiation an agreement was reached, which Nii Bonne and his friends declared to be satisfactory. The boycott was therefore called off, and on the morning of Saturday 28 February 1948 trade resumed.

It was however the lull before the storm. There was much discontent among ex-servicemen. Demobilisation was by now complete, but the economy was unable to provide employment for the disbanded soldiers at the levels to which they had become accustomed in the army. On that very day, Saturday 28 February, they held a rally in Accra, and about midday they marched towards the governor's residence, with the intention of presenting their requests to the governor in person. The police barred the route and required the advancing column to stop. The order was not obeyed and shots were fired by the police, causing a number of casualties. The furious ex-servicemen rushed back into the trading quarter, and were joined by the worst elements of the population; looting and arson broke out. The damage in Accra was considerable, and there was also some damage in other towns, which presumably was started by men who were returning from the rally. The casualty roll mounted to 15 deaths and 115 wounded.

The looting and burning removed practically all the commercial stocks in Accra, as well as a number of old buildings which were in need of redevelopment. The stocks consisted almost entirely of unsuitable goods which had accumulated during the years of scarcity during and after the war; for the buyers employed by the importing companies had too often sent out the 'nearest substitute' when they could not supply what was really wanted – and African customers proved to be very discriminating. Those firms which were well insured replaced their stocks in the new conditions of plenty which had just set in, and the rebuilding of the burned premises was the inauguration of modern Accra. However, the insurance companies suffered severely and they decided that they did not want any more business of that kind, so that it became impossible, in effect, to insure against riot risks.

The UGCC had taken no part in the boycott, and there is no reason to think that they bore any responsibility for the march of the ex-servicemen or for the rioting; nevertheless, they took advantage of the situation to send a telegram to the British government in London saying: 'Civil Government Gold Coast broken down. Unless Colonial Government is changed and a new Government of the people and their chiefs installed at the centre immediately the conduct of the masses now completely out of control . . . will continue and result in worse violent and irresponsible acts by uncontrolled people. Working Committee United Gold Coast Convention declare they are prepared and ready to take over interim government . . . We speak in the name of inherent residual sovereignty in chiefs and people in free partnership with British Commonwealth . . .'

The government, to reassert its authority, arrested six leaders of the Convention, including Danquah and Nkrumah. They were, however, soon released and a Commission of Inquiry investigated the affair. Following the consideration of that Commission's report, the governor appointed a committee on constitutional reform under the chairman-ship of Mr Justice (later Sir Henley) Coussey. The committee included nine chiefs and three ministers of the gospel. Eight members of the UGCC were included, and there were representatives of Ashanti and of the Northern Territories.

The UGCC's attacks upon the government became bitter and violent. The lawyers, traders, and other leading citizens, who had brought the Convention into existence, were not happy to be associated with this vitriolic agitation, which was the work of the new secretary, Nkrumah, and his friends.

A conference of African legislative councillors was held in London towards the end of 1948, and Danquah attended it. The strength of the sympathy which was felt in England for African aspirations was plain to those who took part in this gathering, and after returning to the Gold Coast Danquah wrote, 'If so great a country as Britain offers us friendship we must lift up ourselves and ensure that we become worthy of it.'

Nkrumah and his circle, however, did not share the view that independence could be achieved in friendly co-operation with Britain. In June 1949 they split off and formed the Convention People's Party (CPP). Its object was announced as 'self-government this year'. The organisation of the CPP was a brilliant achievement. It went with such speed and was so thorough. The whole nation was mobilised for action. Tribal and social divisions were overcome. It was no longer possible for anyone to suppose that nationalism was a sentiment felt only by a small intelligentsia.

The British government accepted the recommendations of the Coussey committee. The legislature was now to be composed of 75 Africans and nine Europeans, chosen as follows:

5 members for urban constituencies elected directly
33 members for rural constituencies elected indirectly
12 members selected by Colony chiefs
6 members selected by Ashanti chiefs
19 members chosen by the electoral college of the Northern
    Territories (a gathering of notables)
3 Europeans elected by the chambers of commerce
3 Europeans elected by the chamber of mines
3 European government officials.

The work of the government was to be carried on by eleven ministers. Three of them were the officials who were members of the legislature. The other eight were Africans. The African ministers, but not the officials, were dismissible by an adverse vote of two-thirds of the members of the legislature. The governor had 'reserve powers' which made it legal for him to enact a measure without the consent of the legislature if he considered it to be essential in the interests of good government, and he also had the power of veto. During the life of this constitution, that is to say up to 1957, the reserve power and the veto were never used. Much of the report was devoted to a system of local government, in which features of the English system were combined with the traditional institutions of the Gold Coast.

This constitution was a great step towards self-government, but it did not satisfy the CPP. They described it as 'bogus and fraudulent' and maintained that 'Freedom had never been handed over to any colonial territory on a silver platter.' They called upon the people to support 'Positive Action', which Nkrumah described in a book written some years later as 'all legitimate and constitutional means by which we could attack the forces of imperialism in the country. The weapons were legitimate political agitation, newspaper and educational campaigns and, as a last resort, the constitutional application of strikes, boycotts and non-cooperation based on the principle of absolute non-violence, as used by Gandhi in India.' Nkrumah was ably supported by Gbedemah, Botsio, Welbeck, Plange, Baako, and Edusei, and they created a tremendous popular movement. Despite what Nkrumah had said about non-violence, there were some riots, and in January 1950 the government took action to preserve public order. Nkrumah and several members of his party were charged with offences against the peace, and Nkrumah received a long sentence; but the others were soon out of prison, wearing hats embroidered PG for Prison Graduate, and addressing public meetings. Nkrumah in prison was the perfect martyr-figure, and Gbedemah out of prison was a most competent organiser of victory. The CPP gained all the places in the municipal elections at Accra, Cape Coast, and Kumasi. It claimed to have 203 branches and 45,000 members. Party committee-rooms were seen in remote towns and villages, flying the party flag, and people shouted 'FreeDOM' to passers-by. Politics were carried to the common people in a way which had never been seen in Africa before. The CPP called a general strike. This was not supported by all the trade unions, and it did not succeed in paralysing the economy; but it was unnecessary because the testimony of the ballot boxes, in the election held at the beginning of 1951, was conclusive. By order of the governor Kwame Nkrumah was released from gaol and was invited to be the Leader of Government Business, under the constitution which he had described as 'bogus and fraudulent'. With statesmanlike moderation he agreed to accept, and the governor asked him to form a government; that is to say, to choose the African ministers who were to serve with him. In his own account of that historic meeting, Nkrumah wrote of the governor, Sir Charles Arden-Clarke, 'He was a man with a strong sense of justice and fair play, with whom I could easily be friends even though I looked upon him as a symbol of British imperialism.' Nkrumah was a superb tactician, capable of great flexibility. He had seen that the way to win the support of simple people was to attack the British government and its colonial offshoot. Now, with much achieved, he reversed his tactics and for the next six years he devoted his best efforts to winning the support of the British people and of their government.

The African ministers were agreeably surprised to find that they had real power and that the British gave them every help in using it. Almost the first thing that claimed attention was the swollen shoot disease of cocoa. The government offered to the farmers a 'New Deal for Cocoa'. Diseased trees would be destroyed, but there were new provisions regarding financial compensation, and replanting was to be encouraged by the payment of a subsidy. Nkrumah personally sponsored this proposal and explained it to the farmers. His reputation was greatly enhanced by this statesmanlike action and by the response which he received from a farming community which had previously refused to agree that their diseased trees should be destroyed. There were however other matters connected with cocoa. After the war the West African Produce Control Board was wound up, and the Gold Coast government created a Cocoa Marketing Board to take over its functions as regards cocoa. The board fixed the price which should be paid to farmers. Nkrumah's government adopted a policy of fixing low prices, leaving plenty of profit in the hands of the board when the cocoa was sold on the international markets; and the government made arrangements that most of this margin should pass into its hands as revenue. The board had continued to employ agents to buy the cocoa for it, and most of these were foreign companies. Now Nkrumah created a Cocoa Purchasing Company, which was owned by the government, and which acted as an agent for the marketing board; at first alongside the old-established agents, but eventually replacing them. Unfortunately corrupt practices became a feature of the Cocoa Purchasing Company's activities; and even more regrettably, when an attempt was made (by various people including members of the CPP) to expose these practices, Nkrumah's government hushed up the affair and whitewashed the offenders (1956).

When Nkrumah became the Leader of Government Business (1951) the Gold Coast had a ten-year development plan which had run about half its course. It provided for the expenditure of £11½ million. The CPP government scrapped it and adopted a five-year plan in which they proposed to spend £120 million. The ensuing five years witnessed major developments. The roads were greatly improved and the bridge across the Volta at Adomi was constructed. The Akyease–Kotoku railway was built, Takoradi harbour was extended, and a new harbour at Tema was begun. Free compulsory primary education for children between the ages of six and twelve was introduced. Important improvements were made at the secondary stage of education, in teacher training, and at Legon Hill university college. A new college of Arts Science and Technology was built at Kumasi.

In the reform of local government Nkrumah and his ministers went farther than the Coussey committee had recommended in abolishing the native authorities and setting up urban and district councils in which nearly all the members were elected. They acted with such speed that it was possible to hold elections in 1952, and the CPP swept the polls. Thus the chiefs were supplanted by party men, of whom many were young and few had any connection with the stoolworthy families. It was a social revolution at the grass roots.

In 1952 Nkrumah was accorded the title of Prime Minister. The minimum daily wage of unskilled labourers in government employment was increased by 50 per cent. Salaries in the civil service were also raised, though not by such a large percentage. Private employers fell into line.

The year 1953 was a happy one. The country was prosperous. Nkrumah's prestige stood high with the people of the Gold Coast and also with the people of Britain. There was a small opposition party in the legislative assembly, remnants of the UGCC renamed Congress Party, but it had little support. The CPP brought forward proposals for a new constitution, and in placing the proposals before the legislature Nkrumah moved what he called his 'Motion of Destiny', a motion which asked the British government to declare the Gold Coast a sovereign and independent state within the Commonwealth. In this speech Nkrumah said that on becoming independent the country would be known as Ghana. The constitutional changes were rapidly agreed by the British government, and arrangements were made to hold elections in 104 constituencies on the basis of adult suffrage, all men and women being entitled to vote. CPP won 72 seats, and when a number of 'independents' made up their minds about party affiliation, CPP had increased its representation to 79 seats. The next largest group was the Northern People's Party, with 12 members. It had been formed only weeks before the election, when chiefs and educated people in the Northern Territories realised that CPP, with its organisation, was likely to win all the northern seats unless local interests went into politics in an organised way.

After the election the three British civil servants who had continued to hold ministerial portfolios since 1951 withdrew, and Nkrumah formed a government in which all the ministers were members of the legislature and answerable to it.

Before taking the final step to declare the country independent, the British government had to make arrangements regarding that part of Togoland which had been combined with the Gold Coast since 1919. It was administered as a Trust Territory under the supervision of the United Nations, and therefore the consent of the UN was required for the termination of the Trust and for the incorporation of the area in the independent state of Ghana. The UN took some time to reach a decision, sending a mission to the area in 1955 and requiring that a plebiscite should be held in 1956.

Had it not been for this delay, Nkrumah might have secured independence within a few weeks of the election of 1954; but with the suddenness of a tornado a new opposition party came into existence. It raised strong-arm gangs to challenge the CPP 'on the streets' and in Ashanti it gained such strength that many CPP members fled to the south, and ministers dared not visit the area. The new party described itself as the National Liberation Movement (NLM), and when they spoke of liberty, they meant emancipation from the bondage laid upon them by Nkrumah and his CPP! It was to happen many times again in Africa, that on the eve of independence a bitter struggle broke out between rival claimants for the prize of victory. The rewards to be gained by forming the first government of a newly-independent country were so enormous that the situation almost inevitably stimulated a struggle in which the two sides resorted to every means of contest, including armed force. It was fortunate that when it happened in Ghana, the army and police were in good shape, and were commanded by 'neutrals'.

The NLM gained much support from cocoa farmers who were angry with the CPP for breaking promises which had been made during the election campaign. Many CPP candidates had promised a price of 100 shillings a load; it was said that Nkrumah himself had used that figure, though there seems to be some doubt about it, but as soon as the election was over the price was fixed at 72 shillings, not only for one year, but for the life of the newly-elected legislature. The cocoa farmers had shown their temper in the hold-up of 1937, and that temper was now turned upon the CPP.

The local government reforms provoked resistance in Ashanti. The stoolworthy families of Ashanti were an ancient aristocracy much practised in the art of rule, of which the first principle is of course to secure the loyalty of the common people. However, under the custom of the country the rulers had not had things all their own way, because the common men were organised in *asafo* companies which would some-times assert a popular point of view. The CPP reforms deprived the chiefs of their power and left them with mere ceremonial functions; but Ashanti was not ready for that and the customary rulers with their supporters rallied to the NLM.

In any case, to the proud Ashanti it was inconceivable that independence could mean anything else than the restoration of the Ashanti kingdom. Many people still alive remembered Ashanti as an independent state before its conquest in 1900. They did not want to be ruled from Accra. This feeling was enhanced by anger over the allocation of seats in the legislature, for Ashanti had claimed 30, but had received only 21. The NLM programme therefore demanded a federal constitution in which Ashanti should enjoy autonomy. Propagandists however went farther than that, adopting as a war-cry the word *mate*, which implied secession. To the Fantis and other neighbouring tribes who had suffered much in past times from Ashanti invasions, the thought of a revived Ashanti kingdom was not agreeable, and as this agitation developed, the NLM lost much of the support which it had initially enjoyed in the Colony.

There were two other separatist movements which, while not joining the NLM, co-operated with it. The Northern People's Party, already mentioned, was of that mind. The other was the Togoland Congress, who wanted an all-Ewe state in which the Ewes of the Gold Coast would be united with the Ewes of the French Trust territory.

The British government sent a commissioner to inquire into the advisability of adopting a federal constitution, but he advised against it. However, since the support for the NLM appeared to be very strong, the British government felt that it must know to which party the people of the country wished it to hand over power; and therefore, much to the chagrin of Nkrumah, another election was held in 1956. He had no reason to fear, for the mass of the people were still for him, and his party won 71 of the 104 seats. Independence was proclaimed on 6 March 1957.

Ghana became independent as a sovereign state within the British Commonwealth of Nations, achieving the same status as Canada, Australia, New Zealand, the Union of South Africa, India, and Pakistan. The constitution provided that (as in Canada, Australia, and New Zealand) the Queen of England should be the sovereign of Ghana; and the Queen was represented in Ghana by a governor-general who was the Earl of Listowel, a British nobleman. Three years later, Ghana adopted a republican constitution, whereby the Queen of England ceased to be the sovereign of Ghana, and the office of governor-general ceased to exist: but Ghana continued to belong to the Commonwealth, as India had done after becoming a republic. The Commonwealth provided a piece of constitutional machinery which was useful in enabling colonies to become independent in a way which the people of Britain felt able to accept and approve. Nigeria, Sierra Leone, and Gambia followed Ghana's example in due course, but in those countries, during the period between independence and the declaration of a republic, the governor-general, representing the Queen, was a native of the country.

3 Nigeria

Nigeria in 1940 was believed to have 20,000,000 inhabitants. Its area, over 370,000 square miles, was as large as Britain, France and Belgium. There were more than forty main tribes and many languages. This area and these millions were ruled by 1800 British officials, and that figure included not only administrative officers but technical services such as medicine and agriculture.

The ratio of children in schools of western type to total population was a little over 1 per cent. However, more than half the population was in the Northern provinces, where there were few schools of western type. In Nigeria's Western and Eastern provinces the ratio was at least as high as Gold Coast's 2 per cent. Among the northern Muslims all little boys and many little girls attended koranic schools where they chanted the Koran. There was one government secondary school, at Katsina, attended by sons of chiefs and other distinguished people, and in 1940 many of the men who were to lead independent Nigeria were there at their lessons. No university nor any other facilities for post-secondary education existed in Nigeria.

Many experiments were being tried out in the native authorities, and in them the beginnings of political activity were seen. In the east a new system of government had been inaugurated after the riots of 1929, and the immense work of research into tribal institutions, and of creating new native authorities on the basis of family clans, was still in progress. Lagos newspapers devoted much attention to the affairs of native authorities.

The leading personality in the press was Dr Nnamdi Azikiwe. After years in America and in Gold Coast he had returned to Nigeria with the avowed intent of encouraging in his countrymen a disposition to resist foreign rule. The tone of his newspapers was therefore vigorously anti-British. He began with *West African Pilot* in Lagos in 1937, and as his business prospered he launched newspapers in other towns, *Eastern Nigerian Guardian* in 1940, *Nigerian Spokesman* in 1943, *Southern Nigerian Defender* also in 1943, *Daily Comet* in 1944, *Eastern Sentinel* in 1955, and *Nigerian Monitor* in 1960. Thus he overcame the difficulty of distributing one newspaper over the long distances of Nigeria. Azikiwe was the outstanding former of opinion against colonial rule.

In the Western provinces it had been normal for the Obas (chiefs) to be gazetted as sole native authorities, but by 1940 it was felt by educated Nigerians and by British civil servants that this was an out-of-date formula, and that the Obas ought to act in accordance with the advice of councils. In 1940 the change from Oba alone to Oba-in-council was made in several native authorities, and in the following years the others followed suit. There was pressure for this change from the Nigerian Youth Movement. It had been founded in 1933 by Ernest Ikoli and Dr. J. C. Vaughan, and had been strengthened by the support of Azikiwe and by the return of H. O. Davies from his studies in London. It had a membership of about 10,000, of whom three-quarters were in Yorubaland. The Motor Union with 2000 members also took part in politics, while local associations in several towns were active in native authority affairs.

At Ilaro the progressive element was demanding that the chief should be chosen by a secret ballot of taxpayers. In this year the Awujale of Ijebu Ode agreed to admit to his council persons nominated by the Youth Movement. At Ijebu-Remo a council was established which was a blend of old title-holders and young educated men. In Ondo province all the authorities were gazetted as chief-in-council by the end of 1940. At Ife a new Oni (chief) had just taken office, and he had previously been the secretary of the Ife Progressive Society. In Ibadan, following custom, the native authority had from the first been the Olubadan-in-Council, and the council consisted of 33 chiefs; now it included two representatives of the educated people, chosen by the Ibadan Progressive Union; but the educated people were dissatisfied with this arrangement, and the numerous 'stranger' community felt that they should have representation on the council. In the Abeokuta province nine native authorities were gazetted as chief-in-council, though at Abeokuta itself the Alake had so far resisted changes in the constitution of the state. He had however taken a bold initiative and won much admiration by appointing a barrister as the president of the native court.

At Benin the Oba agreed that the native authority should be gazetted as Oba-in-council, and the council was then constituted of 16 traditional title-holders, 23 town councillors, and 26 representatives elected at meetings held in the rural districts. At Ilesha the affairs of the native authority attracted a great deal of criticism, and the local political organisation, known as Egbe Omo Ibile, exposed the corrupt practices of the chief and his assistants. This was not the only instance of an attack on the chief by the educated people. At Ogbomosho for instance the Progressive Union instituted legal proceedings against the Bale, alleging that his appointment was irregular, and they won their case on appeal to the Privy Council.

In Eastern Nigeria the most noteworthy developments were among the Ibibio people. In 1928 the educated members of the community formed an Ibibio Union, but unlike most of the progressive societies at that time it was not limited to the educated, for it acquired a large membership among the people of the villages. The Union collected money for objects of general interest, including the award of scholarships to young men enabling them to study in England. It acquired sufficient standing for the Governor to invite it to suggest a name for nomination as a Member of Legislative Council, and this person was shown on the council list as 'Member for the Ibibio division'. Nearly all the native authority councils in Ibibio country included members of the Union. There was an active Ibo Union with branches in the towns – Onitsha, Enugu, Port Harcourt, Warri, and Lagos. Although it did not command the same authority as the Ibibio Union, and though it did not seem to have extended its influence among the village people, one of its members had been nominated by the Governor as 'Member of Legislative Council for the Ibo division'. The nomination of the Ibibio and Ibo members was welcomed by popular sentiment.

In the North the majority of the population were Muslims and they were in 38 native states, each with its chief, known outside Northern Nigeria as Emir, but always described in the North as *Sarki* (plural *Sarakuna*); for the language here was Hausa, spoken by Europeans as well as by Africans. This created a barrier against the infiltration of political ideas which were expressed in English. A conference of Emirs and Residents had recently been instituted, and at its meetings one of the favourite subjects was whether there was any advantage for the North in being associated with Eastern and Western Nigeria. The native authorities were under no pressure to change their constitutions; yet the year 1940 brought one change which was fraught with consequences for the future. Africans from the South had been migrating to Northern Nigeria in large numbers, especially since the railway began to run to Kano in 1911, to secure employment as clerks and labourers in the railway, the public works department, and the expatriate firms, and to engage in trade. Hausamen were not interested at that time in salaried or wage-earning employment. The social stigma of slavery still lay heavily on any form of service. So the Southerners had all the employment, and they lived in New Towns (*sabon gari*) which were situated outside the walls of the ancient Hausa cities. Hitherto these new urban areas had been ruled directly by the British administration, but in 1940 they were placed under the native authorities. Each *sabon gari* was provided with a representative board, and the chairman of the board had the right of access to the *sarki*.

The grass roots of political activity were in the native authorities, and it was the view of the British government that 'if the mass of the people are to play an effective part in the constitutional scheme, it will be necessary to foster more resolutely the formal meetings of village, district, and, in some cases, Provincial Councils as part of the system of Native Administration. It is in these Councils that the habit of political thought will be inculcated so as to make possible the wise choice of the provincial members of the Houses of Assembly' (Cmd 6599, *Proposals for the Revision of the Constitution of Nigeria*, para. 25).

There existed a Legislative Council meeting from time to time in Lagos. Since 1928 it had had 50 members, of whom 31 were European government officers. Lagos elected three members and Calabar elected one member, the franchise being open to males with an income qualification of £100. The other members included a number of persons nominated by the Governor to represent African opinion, of whom the members for the Ibibio and Ibo divisions, referred to above, were examples. In the elections held in Lagos for three members of the Legislative Council, the Nigerian Youth Movement (led by Azikiwe and H. O. Davies) had recently defeated the Nigerian National Democratic Party led by Herbert Macaulay. The Nigerian Youth Movement was of course backed by the *West African Pilot*, a daily newspaper founded by Azikiwe. In 1940 they had a shock. Ernest Ikoli, who had helped to found the Youth Movement, but who had fallen out with Azikiwe and Davies, founded a rival paper, *Daily Service*. The antagonists contested a by-election in Lagos, and Ikoli won. This led to the resignation of Azikiwe and Davies from the Youth Movement; but, as mentioned above, its largest membership was in Yorubaland, and the leadership was taken over by Chief Obafemi Awolowo, a lawyer and journalist in Ibadan. The efforts of these groups were directed towards securing more rapid economic development, education, and the employment of more Nigerians in the higher branches of the government; there was little interest in constitutional reform. Azikiwe in his paper expressed the desire for a federation of the British colonies of West Africa, as a basis for constitutional advance. It is easy to appreciate how a democrat like Azikiwe must have felt the need for support from the other colonies in contending with the massive conservative elements in the Nigerian interior.

As mentioned above, when Africans were appointed as members of the Executive Council in the Gold Coast (1942) a similar step was taken in Nigeria. Another important event of this year was the commencement of a Ten Year Educational Plan, under which it was proposed to increase the provision of schools of all types throughout the country, especially in the Western and Eastern provinces.

In the same year 1942 Governor Sir Bernard Bourdillon put forward for discussion a scheme of reform. He proposed to bring the Northern provinces within the scope of the Legislative Council, which hitherto had been supposed to deal only with the Western and Eastern provinces. The scheme provided for a regional council in each group of provinces; the membership of these councils was to be drawn partly from the native authorities and partly from electoral constituencies; it was hoped to replace the practice of nomination by the governor with a system of election.

Bauchi province, in the so-called 'Middle Belt', had presented exceptional difficulties to the colonial government in its efforts to organise native authorities. It was reported in 1938 that the area consisted of 'a multiplicity of small village units without traditional sanction'. However, in 1943 the Bauchi General Improvement Union was formed, and it provided a basis of activity for Tafawa Balewa, who later became prime minister, and for Aminu Kano, who played a part in politics as a radical leader.

In Nigeria (in contrast to Gold Coast) direct tax was collected from all men throughout the country. The tax was gathered by the native authorities, and these authorities kept for their own treasuries a portion of the tax, 75 per cent for 'fully organised' authorities and 50 per cent for the others. In 1944 the native authorities were told that they might keep the whole of the tax, and since this increased their main source of revenue by 100 per cent or by 33 per cent, as the case might be, it added greatly to their strength, enabling them to provide more local services, to improve the remuneration of their staffs, and to become more interesting to those progressive elements who might wish to participate in running them.

The native authorities had more vitality in the North than in the West, and hardly any vigour in the East. This is illustrated by the contrast between the native authority revenues in 1953–4 (which, for reasons to be explained, was the last year of native authorities in parts of the country) when the totals were £5$\frac{3}{4}$ million in the North, a little less than two million pounds in the West, and £950,000 in the East.

Although there had been much talk about building up the strength of the native authorities, it had been too easily assumed that they could discharge their functions without employing competent people at competitive rates. No arrangements existed for a native authority service with approved conditions of employment and prospects of promotion. The inevitable result was inefficiency and corruption. However, one of the earliest trade unions was a Federal Union of Native Administration Staffs, and in response to its representations the government set up two committees in 1941 to review the conditions of service of native authority staffs in the Western and Eastern provinces respectively. The committees recommended that the qualifications required of new entrants should be the same as those specified for corresponding places in the service of the central government, and that the remuneration and conditions of service should be the same as those provided by the government. The native authorities complied with these suggestions and the improvement of their financial position in 1944 (as noted above) accelerated the process. In 1946 a pension scheme was provided for native authority staffs. It was high time, for not only had government servants enjoyed pension privileges for some time, but in 1943 the principal commercial companies, led by John Holt and the United Africa Company, had introduced arrangements to provide their staffs with retirement pensions.

Azikiwe hardly engaged in political activity for some time. It was a wise attitude in wartime. But in 1944, when the end of the war seemed to be near, he called a meeting in Lagos in the hope of persuading the various small political groups to unite. Herbert Macaulay joined with him to form the National Council of Nigeria, which soon added 'and the Cameroons' to its title, and became known as NCNC. The Nigerian Youth Movement however declined to join. The NYM continued to find its most numerous members among the Yoruba, and the NCNC was most vigorously supported by the Ibo; although both parties aimed at nationwide membership, they unhappily acquired these tribal labels.

War activities stimulated a demand for labour in Lagos. The population of the city grew, with overcrowding and discontent. Trade unions were formed and their leaders were more radical than any others in West Africa. Nduka Eze especially was a man who wanted to fight the whole colonial system, and who was not concerned to distinguish between industrial action against an employer and political action directed against the government. In June 1945, immediately after the end of the war against Germany but before the final defeat of Japan, seventeen unions called out on strike about thirty thousand workers of the government, including the railway and the postal system. Azikiwe's newspapers gave support to the strikers. The editors were fined and imprisoned for libel and sedition and two of the newspapers were temporarily banned.

These events changed the political atmosphere. The government's response was given in the form of a new constitution, enacted in 1946 and put into operation in 1947. It was known as the Richards constitution, named after Governor Sir Arthur Richards (later Lord Milverton) though its provisions were similar to the proposals circulated by his predecessor Sir Bernard Bourdillon as explained above. The Legislative Council became the legislature for the whole country. The word Region now came into use, and in each of the Regions, North, West, and East, a House of Assembly was set up. In addition the Northern Region had a House of Chiefs. The new Legislative Council consisted of 17 official members and 28 non-official members. Of the latter, four were elected in the two towns of Lagos and Calabar as before. Eighteen were elected by the Regional Houses of Assembly (and, in the North, by the House of Chiefs). The Regional Houses all had a majority of members selected by the native authorities. The Regional Houses had no legislative powers; their functions were consultative and members could put questions to the Regional governments. Six members of the Legislative Council were nominated by the governor to represent special interests.

This was an attempt to integrate the native authorities into the political system by making them the basis for the selection of the most numerous element in the legislature. The great achievement of this constitution was to bring in the Northern Region, and it is difficult to see on what other basis, at that time, this could have been done. In announcing the reforms, the government suggested that they should remain inforce for nine years and should then be reviewed.

In 1946 a ten-year development plan was promulgated, and brief particulars of it will be given in Chapter 11. In 1948 a Commissioner for Africanisation was appointed, and the policy was established that no expatriate should be posted to any position for which a qualified African was available. The complementary step was to educate Nigerians to become qualified, and this same year saw the foundation of the University of Ibadan. Shortly afterwards the Nigerian College of Arts Science and Technology (CAST) was set up, with branches at Yaba (Lagos), Ibadan, Enugu, and Zaria, to cater for a range of practical subjects. The University of Ibadan has been much lampooned through the years for being an ivory tower, lacking contact with the real problems of Nigera; but a review of its record and of the men whom it has produced proves the contrary. It was blamed for being 'like Oxford and Cambridge'; in fact, there could be no higher compliment, for they were the best examples to follow at the time, and Nigerians would not have been content with less.

1948 was a critical year in the growth of indigenous banking. The National Bank of Nigeria had existed since 1933 and had already gained a sound reputation, but in the years 1946 to 1951 it enlarged its business, increasing deposits from £17,000 to £871,000. The Nigerian Farmers' and Commercial Bank was founded in 1947 and in 1948 it was opening branches in many towns; but it went into liquidation in 1951. The Agbonmagbe Bank had been founded in 1945 and it went along soundly for 14 years, at which point it was raised to a position of importance by receiving the custom of the Western Region Marketing Board. The African Continental Bank began operations in 1948 under the leadership of Azikiwe, and it worked in close connection with the Eastern Regional Government and the various boards and corporations which that government sponsored.

In political circles in the South the Richards constitution of 1946 provoked uproarious protest. The politicians were determined that the native authorities should not be allowed to choose members of the legislature. Politicians who were ambitious for power viewed the native authorities as competitors. Some educated people in the progressive societies regarded the native authorities as being too conservative, and too much under the influence of the colonial government. There was a demand for the rapid extension of direct elections, with a much more democratic franchise qualification. The fact that the government was not in any way responsible to the legislature, and the failure to introduce even the beginnings of a ministerial system, were much criticised. There was dissatisfaction over the limited function of the Regional Assemblies, and the suggestion that everyone should be patient for nine years was received with disgust and derision. The government was also criticised for promulgating the constitution without sufficient consultation with the people.

The trade unions again played a part in the political contest, and this time an assault was directed against the largest expatriate business, the United Africa Company. The operation began in 1948 with a strike of labourers employed by the company in Lagos, and continued through 1949 and 1950 with more extensive stoppages. Nduka Eze was no doubt sincere in believing that the company was part of a monolithic 'colonial system', but in fact the government was not embarrassed by the company's troubles, and after a couple of years the company's employees grew weary of being moved as pawns in a political game, and most of them resigned from the trade union. For nine years after this nothing was heard of trade unionism among the company's staff.

The government agreed as early as 1948 to revise the constitution without waiting nine years, and on receiving this assurance, Azikiwe announced that he was prepared to co-operate in discussing a new constitution. Some younger members of his party refused to follow his lead, believing that only violent revolution could achieve what they desired; and they described themselves as the Zikist Movement. They were active at Enugu during a strike of miners in the government-owned colliery, which led to violence and shooting by the police. Then they were responsible for an attempt to assassinate the Chief Secretary, upon which the government arrested them and banned the Zikist Movement. This was well received by the responsible political parties, and it was the end of revolutionary violence in Nigeria.

Azikiwe's party continued to be the NCNC, but Awolowo had ceased to work under the name of the Youth Movement and was now leader of the Action Group. This had developed as a political wing of a Yoruba cultural society Egbe Omo Oduduwa. Its slogan was 'self-government in five years'.

In view of what had been said about consulting the people, arrangements were made for discussion to take place in village units, and then in larger units, and then in the Regions, and finally in a conference which assembled at Ibadan in 1950. A new constitution was promulgated in 1951. It was of federal form, and it introduced a ministerial system.

A council of ministers was set up as the 'principal instrument of policy in and for Nigeria'. Presided over by the governor, it consisted of six government officers and twelve ministers, four from each Region. Nine of the ministers had departmental responsibilities, but the five departments of defence, external affairs, public service, finance, and justice were held by government officers who were members of the council of ministers. Regional Executive Councils were created with important powers. Each was presided over by the lieutenant-governor of the Region, and comprised from six to nine regional ministers, three government officers who were members by virtue of the offices which they held, and not more that two other officials.

The central legislature, now known as the House of Representatives, was enlarged. It had six *ex officio* members, 136 representative members, and six special members nominated by the governor to speak for interests which in his opinion would not otherwise have a voice. Of the 136 representative members, 68 were chosen by the joint councils of the Northern Region, 31 by the Western House of Assembly, three by the Western House of Chiefs, and 34 by the Eastern House of Assembly. A House of Chiefs was now added to the House of Assembly in the Western Region. In all the Regional Assemblies the great majority of members were chosen by local electoral colleges, that is to say by meetings of notables; it was not at that time considered possible to hold elections.

In 1948 the Colonial Office (London) instructed all the colonial governments in Africa to encourage the development of 'efficient democratic local government'. The Nigerian government endeavoured to comply with this policy by establishing a three-tier system of local government councils in the Eastern Region; County Councils, District Councils, and Local (usually Village) Councils. All were directly elected, and this was an important decision because it was the first introduction into Nigeria of the machinery of elections with a wide democratic franchise, and it prepared the way for the big constitutional change of 1954. The Nigerian government proposed to introduce the new arrangements gradually, but the Regional Executive of the East, established under the constitution of 1951, embraced the policy with enthusiasm and speedily extended it throughout the Region. That was the end of the laborious effort to identify and activate the traditional authorities of Eastern Nigeria, which had started in 1930.

In the Western Region a law was enacted in 1953 which authorised the establishment of local, district, and divisional councils based on the model of the British local government bodies, including powers of raising money by rating property. However, the break from the native authority system was not so complete as in the East. Up to one-fourth of the new councils might consist of 'traditional members', the rest being elected.

The North was resistant to the democratisation of local administration. There was just a little widening of the membership of the councils which advised the *sarakuna*, by the inclusion of educated people and of representatives of non-Muslim communities.

A census was made in the years 1950 to 1953 and people were amazed to learn that 31,168,000 inhabitants had been counted. The rapidity of the growth of the population had not been appreciated, and the report of the census commissioners helped to prove the health and vigour of Nigeria.

Unfortunately the constitution of 1951 did not work well, at any rate at the centre. The ministers were less interested in carrying on the central government than in promoting the interests of the Regions from which they were drawn.

In March 1953 Anthony Enahoro, a member of the NCNC, proposed a motion in the House of Representatives that 'this House accepts as a primary objective the attainment of self-government by Nigeria in 1956'. The motion was supported by both the NCNC and the AG, but the leader of the Northern delegation, the Sardauna of Sokoto, proposed that the phrase 'self-government as soon as possible' should be substituted for 'self-government in 1956'. 'The Northern Region', said the Sardauna, 'does not intend to accept the invitation to commit suicide.' This reflected the feeling that they were happier with the British than they expected to be under a government dominated by Southerners. For adopting this attitude the Northern leaders were subjected to such abuse that they began to talk about secession. In an attempt to win support for 'self-government in 1956' among the common people, the Action Group sent a delegation to some of the Northern towns, but this intervention was not welcomed and it provoked riots in Kano where a Hausa mob attacked the Southerners. At least 36 people were killed and casualties would have been more numerous but for the reinforcement of the police by members of the expatriate community, who were sworn as special constables.

The attitude of the Muslim North was seldom understood by people who lived a long way off, whether in Lagos or in London – for the good reason that the Northern people took no steps to make their views known except by speaking in the Hausa language to people who could understand it. In Lagos and London they were described as 'primitive', 'backward', and 'not interested in politics'. Nothing could have been further from the truth. Politics were the subject of discussion every evening round the barbecue sticks in the eating houses, and the daily news broadcasts were widely known. But every reference to the South was accompanied by the Hausa jingle, '*Ba su son mu ba mu son su*' ('They don't like us and we don't like them') and British friends were embarrassed by being told that they did not know how to deal with Southerners and that all problems would be solved if the Hausa were allowed to take charge at Lagos.

In these circumstances the Secretary of State, now Oliver Lyttelton, convened a constitutional conference in London in 1953. He announced that in view of the attitude of the North, the British government could not grant self-government to the whole country in 1956, but that they would be willing to grant 'full internal self-government' to any Region which wished to have it in 1956. Azikiwe declared that this was 'the first time . . . that Britain had offered self-government to a colonial people on a platter of gold'. Well might he rejoice. The British government conceded the critical principle that all representatives should be elected directly by the people. Men and women were to vote in the West and the East, men only in the North.

The constitution was to enter into force in October 1954, and elections had to be held before that date. It became urgently necessary for the Northern leaders to form a political party which would be able to contest the election, and this they did by creating the Northern People's Congress, with the Sardauna of Sokoto as president, and as vice-president Abubakar Tafawa Balewa, who was mentioned above in connection with the Bauchi General Improvement Union. The *sara-kuna* all supported this party and the Hausa people followed their lead. Aminu Kano, Tafawa Balewa's former colleague in the Bauchi Union, founded a radical party under the title Northern Elements Progressive Union, but its support was practically confined to the Middle Belt and was not very significant even there.

The constitution of 1954 formally established a Federation of Nigeria under a governor-general. The heads of the regions now bore the title of governor. The regions received a greater measure of autonomy. Certain subjects were allocated to the federal government, leaving all others to the regions, except for 'concurrent' matters, on which both federal and regional legislatures were entitled to make laws. Political scientists have divided federal constitutions into two varieties, 'loose' federations in which the federal government has defined powers and residuary powers are with the constituent units, and 'tight' federations in which the units have defined powers and residuary powers are with the central authority. In this context, Nigeria became a loose federation.

The position of Lagos proved controversial, and it was decided that it should be the capital and should become a federal territory, separated from the Western region. The Southern Cameroons were separated from the Eastern region, and were provided with a legislature and executive, which made them to all intents another region, albeit a small one compared with the others. Arrangements were made for the allocation of revenue necessitated by these changes.

The central legislature had 194 members; 92 elected from the Northern region, 42 from the Western, 42 from the Eastern, six from the Southern Cameroons, and two from Lagos. In addition there were a Speaker, three *ex officio* members, and special members up to six in number to be nominated by the governor-general to represent interests not otherwise adequately represented.

The central council of ministers was composed of ten ministers (three from each region and one from the Southern Cameroons), three *ex officio* members, and the governor-general as president.

In 1957 a further step was taken towards responsible government, when a prime minister was appointed to be the leader of the government. The choice fell upon Tafawa Balewa. He was 45 years of age. He was the son of the district head of Lere in Bauchi, and he had completed the course at the government secondary school, Katsina College. For some years he worked as a teacher, but after studying in 1945 at the Institute of Education in London he was appointed as education officer of the native authority in his home area. He was a devout Muslim and liked to discuss matters of religious principle with friends, including Christian friends. He had natural dignity and could never be suspected of dishonesty.

For the next three years the NCNC was in alliance with the Northern People's Congress (NPC) in the legislature, anxious to dispose of the talk about secession by the North; while the Action Group stood alone. In 1957 the East and the West were granted 'full internal' self-government. In that year also the Northern leaders announced that the North would be ready for 'full internal' self-government in 1959. The years of the 'Lyttelton constitution', 1954 to 1960, were a time when everyone saw that independence was coming soon, and under the inspiration of that idea a great deal of work was done to make ready, preparing the civil services both at the centre and in the regions, and pressing ahead with education and training.

Following the announcement that the North would be ready for internal self-government in 1959, the Action Group joined the coalition of the NCNC and NPC in order to give an appearance of national solidarity which might strengthen the hand of the Nigerian delegation in negotiating with the British government for independence. The negotiations revolved mainly round the question whether new regions should be created. Minority populations put in claims for states in their areas, and the Action Group spoke in favour of the creation of more regions. The NPC and NCNC however were opposed to any division of the regions from which they drew their main support. As time dragged on the Secretary of State, Sir Alan Lennox-Boyd, put it to the delegates that the creation of new regions would take a long time; they must make their choice between independence in 1960 on a basis of the existing regions, or an indefinite postponement. Faced with these alternatives, the Action Group opted for early independence, so the negotiations ended with unanimous agreement.

In preparation for independence, the control of the military forces was handed over to the federal government in 1958 and a navy was created. In 1959 a central bank was formed and a Nigerian currency was issued, replacing the West African currency. In December 1959 there were federal elections for an enlarged House of Representatives, and members of a new senate were appointed. The federal election was hard-fought, but it was a triumph of organisation and nobody challenged the fairness of the results. The ballot was secret and techniques had been adopted which ensured that illiterates could vote as secretly as those who could read and write. There were clear rules for the settlement of disputes. It has been described as 'the last great act of the British Raj'.

All was now prepared for the handover of sovereignty. The British, in relinquishing power, transferred it to men who had nearly all been in high political office since 1952. The British colonial officials and the nationalist leaders had worked side by side with the object of ensuring that independence could be taken in the best possible conditions. The Federation of Nigeria became independent on 1 October 1960.

4 Sierra Leone

The population of Sierra Leone in 1940 was believed to be about 1,800,000. About 100,000 lived in the Colony (Freetown and the rural districts adjoining) and the others in the Protectorate. The inhabitants of the Colony were sharply divided into two groups, about 30,000 Creoles and about 70,000 tribesmen who had moved in from the Protectorate.

The Colony was, by contemporary African standards, well provided with schools. There were 44 primary schools, with an enrolment of 7200, and eight secondary schools. For higher education there was Fourah Bay College, affiliated to Durham University, and students were prepared for the Durham degree. In the Protectorate, on the other hand, only 8200 children were on the school rolls – about half of 1 per cent of the population. There was a government secondary school at Bo, the principal town of the Protectorate. It had begun as a school for the sons of chiefs, but shortly before 1940 a wider entry had been permitted.

The main problem in Freetown was the influx of people from the Protectorate. Some came to meet the wartime demand for labour, but many more were there just to avoid paying their tax in the Protectorate chiefdom, or for the sake of adventure. They begged and did odd jobs, and some engaged in vice and crime; and they lived in squalor. There was a 'chief' in Freetown for every tribal group, and people from the Protectorate were supposed to report to their 'chief' on arrival. With the help of the 'chiefs' the government rounded up undesirables and put them on the train for the Protectorate, but many of them left the train at the first station and walked back to Freetown. The situation urgently called for the institution of a pass system, but the evil reputation of that system in South Africa made it impossible to introduce it in Freetown, the traditional home of liberty. An ingenious solution was found in the form of a Compulsory Service Ordinance, which was presented as a wartime measure, under which all persons between the ages of 18 and 55, of whatever colour or race, were required to register. The system was introduced in 1942, and 117,000 persons registered.

The administration of the Protectorate was in the hands of 216 paramount chiefs, ruling small chiefdoms with an average population of 8000. The chief had to be chosen from a limited number of 'crowning families', but candidates presented themselves at a public meeting of the tribe, which made its choice known by that informal consensus of opinion which was a feature of tribal gatherings. The chief acted in consultation with a council which normally consisted of from 60 to 90 persons, including village headmen. Sierra Leone was therefore fortunate in having native authorities which were in close touch with the people. The chiefs collected the tax, which although described as a hut tax was in fact a poll tax of 5 shillings for every adult male. Apart from that, they had until 1937 carried on with their court-work and other functions in a traditional way; but in that year, laws had been passed for the reorganisation of the chiefdoms. The government's intention was to persuade the chiefdoms to undergo reorganisation, and to proceed as and when agreement could be secured. In 1940 the process was in full swing.

On the financial side, reorganisation involved starting an account book and buying a safe to keep the cash. The government then paid $1\frac{1}{4}$ shillings for every tax (5 shillings) collected. Under custom, chiefs had been entitled to various dues, presents, and services from their subjects. The main feature of reorganisation was that all these were commuted for a single annual payment. So far, the government had only sanctioned reorganisation if the chief agreed to commute his dues and services for 4 shillings a year from each male subject. (Some were standing out for 7 shillings.) The commuted tribute was taken by the tribal treasury, and in return the chief received a salary from the treasury. The amount of this had to be negotiated. A feature of the new system was the regularisation of dues such as fees for cutting timber, for making palm wine, for clearing mangroves to plant rice, and for setting fish traps. It became possible to use local revenues to provide services. With this scheme, the Sierra Leone government had found a way to increase revenue while at the same time arranging that ordinary people should pay less – an achievement which has been granted to few governments; needless to say, it was popular with the people but less enthusiastically welcomed by the chiefs. Tribal meetings where proposals were discussed to spend the new money on local services were well attended.

In Freetown the legislative council met briefly twice a year. It consisted mainly of officials and government nominees, but three members were elected by the people of the Colony, on a property-or-income qualification which produced 5164 voters. Three of the nominated members were chiefs from the Protectorate.

There was a good deal of active political interest among the Creole people of Freetown, and at this period it was expressed mainly through the Sierra Leone National Congress. I. T. A. Wallace-Johnson, a journalist, was a radical. He disapproved of the colonial system, and attributed the worst motives to everybody who was connected with it; and he was not afraid to publish his views. In 1978 a memorial was erected to him outside the new City Hall in Freetown. It is a bronze bust, seven feet high, and it describes him as 'Indomitable freedom fighter, vanguard politician, pioneer trade unionist, fearless journalist and pan-Africanist'. However, like many pioneers, he had little following at that time in his home country, and much of his activity took place in the Gold Coast and London. The majority of the National Congress, led by Dr Bankole-Bright, a medical practitioner, stood for the interests of the Creoles. They would have liked to acquire more influence with the government, but what they wanted most was that Britain should continue to protect them, especially against the people of the Protectorate.

In March 1940 Lord Hailey visited Sierra Leone and he discussed the affairs of the country with eleven paramount chiefs. They saw him individually and separately, but they took the occasion to hold a meeting. Five of them expressed to Lord Hailey the hope that such meetings might continue to be held. Paramount chief Caulker of Bumpe (a member of the legislative council) said that the chiefs would like to meet in conference to discuss the business of that council. Paramount chief Soloku of Sembehun (who, among the services which he provided for his people, ran a mail between Sembehun and Moyamba) wanted to meet other chiefs so that they could tell the member of the legislative council what to say, and Paramount chief Kajue of Dasse suggested that the chiefs should form a union. Paramount chief Kunafoi of Fakunya said, 'It would be a fine thing to have meetings such as has taken place today.' Later in the year regular meetings of chiefs commenced, with the assistance of Dr Milton Margai, a medical practitioner, son of a well-to-do trader; and this was the beginning of organised political activity in the Protectorate.

Following the example of Gold Coast and Nigeria, the government of Sierra Leone invited two Africans to be members of the executive council in 1943. In 1946 a Protectorate assembly was inaugurated, in which there were 26 Paramount chiefs and two persons nominated to represent the educated. The functions of the assembly were mainly consultative. In that same year the Sierra Leone Organisation Society

(SLOS) was formed; Dr Milton Margai and his lawyer half-brother Albert were among the founders; they belonged to the Mende tribe and attracted support from the southern area of the protectorate which was occupied by that tribe. Another founder member was Siaka Stevens, a Limba from the North, formerly employed by the iron mine at Marampa and now a trade union leader. The main purpose of the SLOS was to protest against the preponderance of chiefs in the Protectorate assembly, and to seek more power for the educated section of the Protectorate population.

In 1947 a new constitution was introduced, establishing a legislature with an unofficial majority. The Creole people were furious that more places had been allocated to the Protectorate than to Freetown, and four years of bitter conflict ensued. At one stage, briefly, SLOS formed an alliance with the National Congress to protest against the important place which the constitution reserved for the chiefs in the legislature. In 1950 however SLOS joined with the chiefs in launching a new party, the Sierra Leone People's Party (SLPP) under the leadership of Milton Margai. He referred to the thirty thousand Creoles as 'foreigners'.

A new constitution came in 1951. The legislative council consisted of seven British officials, 21 elected members (seven elected in the Colony on a low property franchise, 12 elected among the district councils of the Protectorate, and two elected by the Protectorate assembly) and two members nominated by the governor to represent trade and the mining industry. There was thus a large African majority. At the same time the executive council was reconstituted with four British officials and four members appointed by the governor from among the elected members of the legislative council. In 1952 the legislative council adopted a motion urging the allocation of portfolios to members of the executive council, and in 1953 this was done. Milton Margai was given the title of Chief Minister.

The excitements of this period led to several outbreaks of mob violence in the southern (Mende) area. There was some mystery about how they were organised, but there was no doubt that they were intended to support the claims of SLOS. There were two important traditional societies, the Porro for men and the Bundu for women. Everyone was initiated into one of these societies at an early age. There was no secret about their existence and the areas of bush where they carried on their affairs were made known by decorated arches and other signs; but the exact purpose of the societies, the identity of their leaders, and the character of their ceremonies, were jealously guarded secrets. It was widely supposed that the Porro had some connection with the disorders.

Other disorders arose from another cause in 1952–3. Extensive deposits of diamonds were discovered in gravels near the surface. They were in an area where the Sierra Leone Selection Trust held an exclusive mining licence from the government, but local Africans were not restrained by that. It was estimated that 50,000 of them engaged in digging diamonds. Several stones of exceptional size were found. Since the digging was illegal, the stones had to be sold into the smugglers' market, and constant clashes occurred with the police. It took many years to work out a legal basis for this industry, but it was done by curtailing the Selection Trust's area, by licensing African diggers, and by providing an official buying organisation.

In 1956 a step was taken which is probably always the most critical change in a series of constitutional developments leading to independence: direct elections for the legislature were extended to the whole country. Thus 25 members were directly elected and 12 were elected by the chiefs. Milton Margai received the title of premier. In 1958 and 1959, in two stages, an African minister took over financial control from the British financial secretary.

Sierra Leone followed in the wake of Ghana and Nigeria, and everything seemed to be moving smoothly towards independence, when (as so often happens) the near approach of that event gave rise to a struggle between rival contenders for power. Milton Margai adroitly secured the support of several small parties by forming a coalition government under the name United National Front (UNF) but Siaka Stevens led a hostile group. His side bore the name Election Before Independence Movement (EBIM). His followers were numerous among the trade unions, and there was also a tribal aspect, for the Temne people did not like the predominance of the Mende in the UNF and many of them therefore favoured Siaka Stevens. The EBIM was transformed into a political party, the All People's Congress (APC). In support of it there were large gatherings of people in the northern districts, in which the Porro of those parts may have played a role. Thousands of people assembled around the palaver trees and they remained in permanent session for some days. They sent out bands of strong young men to set up road blocks, especially at the ferries. It was their intention to deny the use of the roads to members of the opposing faction, but they were scrupulous in allowing normal traffic to pass, even when it was carrying loads of cash with no protection. It was difficult to understand what was the aim of all this, but there was a good deal of adverse comment on politicians generally, and people were saying that they did not want the British to go.

More serious disturbances occurred in Freetown where there was fighting, and the government dealt with the situation by arresting Siaka Stevens and a number of his associates. They were still in detention when independence was granted on 27 April 1961.

5 The Gambia

The Gambia is a narrow strip of land on both sides of the river, with Senegal adjoining both to the north and to the south. In 1940 its population was about 300,000, of whom 21,000 lived in the capital city, then known as Bathurst, but after independence renamed Banjul. During the war of 1939–45 the Gambia government adopted a ten-year plan for general development. It was largely the work of a devoted civil servant named Kenneth Blackburn, and it was the first plan for general development adopted by any British colony in Africa.

In the 1940s no one thought of the Gambia as a candidate for independence, but following the general British policy of giving the people of the colonies more opportunity to participate in their own affairs, certain steps were taken. For the population of Bathurst, sophisticated and largely Christian, a town council with elected members was provided in progressive stages between 1946 and 1951.

The Protectorate – which comprised the whole country save for a small area around Bathurst – was peopled by several ethnic groups, speaking different languages, but nearly all the inhabitants were Muslims. For administrative purposes there were 35 districts, each under a ruler with the title *seyfu*. A few of these were traditional chiefs, but more were men who had secured appointment either because the government had selected them, or because they had a local following in the district and for that reason had been accepted by the government. In 1944 and 1945 in each district a council was created and the *seyfu* became its president; it had power to establish a treasury and to impose a local rate. The membership of the council consisted of a representative of every village in the district, normally the village headman or someone deputising for him. The Councils were charged by law with the administration of lands, and it therefore lay within their competence to grant leases whether to residents or strangers.

In 1946 Bathurst and the adjacent area of Kombo were each permitted to elect one representative for the legislative council, and this proved to be the first of a series of moves in the direction of democratic government at the centre. All these measures were taken on the

43

initiative of the government, and by 1951 they had produced a situation in which there was a majority of non-officials in the legislative council and four non-official members in the executive council.

Although in the years 1946 to 1951 there was little interest in politics, there was considerable interest in the egg farm, a project of the Colonial Development Corporation. It started by removing all the trees and bushes from a flat area near Bathurst which was exposed to the Atlantic gales, regardless of the experience which the colonial service had gained in the matter of precautions against erosion. It then raised a great many chickens; but refused to sell them to merchants in Africa (who were importing poultry, expensively, from Britain and France), saying that it was necessary to accumulate stock in order to fulfil large orders from Britain. The accumulation filled all the cold storage accommodation and birds were then held in large fields, where they had to be kept quiet under sedatives. Barhadian women were employed to watch these fowls, and to administer an injection with a syringe to any bird that seemed to wish to wake up. Needless to say, disease came in and the fantasy ended.

The political changes of 1951 created an interest in politics and three parties were formed, the Democratic Party, the Muslim Party, and the United Party. There was now, in the legislature, an exact balance between the Colony and the Protectorate, seven members from each. The Colony members were elected (some by rather complicated procedure) and the Protectorate members were chosen by an electoral body which consisted largely of *seyfolu*. In 1953 three African members of the legislature were invited to sit in the executive council with the title of minister, but they bore no responsibility for any department of state.

These arrangements inevitably provoked objections. Protectorate people thought that they ought to have more representatives, seeing that they were much more numerous than the Colony people. The educated elements, whether in the Colony or in the Protectorate, objected to the position of the *seyfolu*, whom they regarded as being conservative and subject to the influence of the government. This led all the parties to demand that the representatives of the Protectorate should be chosen by direct election by universal adult suffrage. Finally, the logic of democratic principle required that there should be executive ministers responsible to the legislature.

However, the British government could not believe that the tiny Gambia was a candidate for independence, and there were discussions with a view to merging the Gambia with Senegal. The United Nations became involved in these negotiations, but they led nowhere. In view of the difference in size between the Gambia and Senegal, it was difficult to see how there could be a union without Gambia losing its identity. Gambians were proud of their Englishry and did not want French culture. Furthermore, the Gambia had always been a country of low customs tariffs and Senegal had high tariffs. Goods moved into the Gambia plentifully and cheaply, and much of what came in found its way into Senegal by local routes without paying customs dues. If there were a union this state of affairs would be stopped; no one in the Gambia wanted that to happen and certain interests in Senegal shared that view. The Gambia would have had to accept a steep increase in prices of nearly everything. It all ended with a vague agreement to try to co-ordinate policies in matters of common interest.

Universal adult suffrage was introduced in 1960, and at the same time a ministerial system of government was established, with a cabinet consisting of the governor, four British departmental heads, and six African ministers. A new party was formed, based on the Protectorate; the Progressive People's Party (PPP). Its leader was David Jawara, a veterinarian with a degree from Edinburgh university. As he said himself, it was a good thing to have a vet at the head of affairs because the country had more cattle than people. David Jawara was in no doubt that he wanted complete independence and no complications with Senegal. His party was successful in the elections. The *seyfolu* (who still had eight members of the legislature) made an alliance with P. S. N'Jie, leader of the United Party, to keep Jawara out of power. Jawara retaliated with a vigorous campaign demanding independence, and for reducing the number of members chosen by the *seyfolu*. His influence was increased by the action of the Gambia Workers' Union, which in 1960 called a strike which led to disturbances; and the Gambia government was not well organised to deal with that kind of situation, for the country had always been so peaceful. The Union leaders were not exactly supporters of Jawara, but they were highly critical of the existing constitution, and all in favour of independence. General elections in May 1962 brought Jawara into office with the title of chief minister. He conducted the final discussions with the British government, and the Gambia became an independent country within the Commonwealth on 18 February 1965.

6 Federation of French West Africa, 1940–46

The Federation of French West Africa and Togo had an area of 1,844,828 square miles and in 1940 it was believed that their population amounted to about 16 million people, giving an average density of less than nine persons per square mile; although no census had ever been taken.

In the French attitude towards colonies, the permanence of the association was never doubted: there was no idea of eventual self-government, such as formed a basis of English thought. The French had at one time believed that the colonies could be 'assimilated' with France, and in that phase of policy citizenship had been extended to the four communes of Senegal, together with the right to elect a deputy to the French parliament. Later however, when French rule was extended over large areas, the policy of assimilation was seen to be impracticable, so a new philosophy of 'association' was evolved, and this formed the basis of the relationship between France and her West African colonies (apart from the four communes) in 1940. The inhabitants did not enjoy the privileges of citizenship unless they were able to show special qualifications, and they were not represented in the French parliament. They were therefore not citizens but subjects, and as such they were placed under a law known as the *indigénat*. This empowered administrative officers to order subjects to perform a number of days of work on public enterprises such as roads. The system was in harmony with the customs of tribal areas where the people had always been been liable to perform unpaid labour as a service to their chief, but it was unsuitable when subjects were educated people, or when they depended for livelihood on working for wages; and by 1940 the *indigénat* was beginning to be bitterly resented and stigmatised as forced labour.

A personal tax was imposed without discrimination of race or sex on all persons above the age of 14 years; but exemptions were granted to soldiers and their families, students, and indigent and aged persons. The tax was collected at rates adjusted to capacity to pay, and most Africans paid the minimum. This varied from colony to colony, from 50 francs in Niger to 410 francs in Dahomey; the rate was related to the cash income which it was possible for the inhabitants to earn; it was intended to act as a stimulus to people to sell produce in the markets or to work for wages.

The proportion of children who attended school was 0.45 per cent of the population, which was low even by African standards. The schools were under the control of the state in the highest degree. The essence of the curriculum was to teach the French language and French civilisation. There were some institutions of advanced education, and their purpose was to form an African élite and to train them to occupy posts in the government services. There was for instance a college for medical auxiliaries, a college for schoolteachers, another training agricultural extension workers, and a four-year course to prepare technicians for the public works. Africans frequently pursued university studies in France, where they were welcomed. In two secondary schools, one at Dakar and the other at Saint Louis, children of Africans attended the same classes as the children of European residents.

The African élite had been described as partners of France in her civilising mission, and the deputy who represented the four communes in 1940, Galandou Diouf, probably accepted that view. He had clearly enjoyed becoming a member of the French establishment. He had been vigorously (but unsuccessfully) opposed in the election by a lawyer named Lamine Gueye, founder of the Senegalese socialist party, Africa's first political party organised on modern lines. Gueye and his associates saw themselves as the leaders of the mass. Probably no one then visualised independence for colonies, but there were more immediate aspirations, such as the abolition of the *indigénat* and the extension of the right to elect deputies to the French parliament.

When Pétain became the head of the government at Vichy in 1940 he appointed Pierre Boisson as the governor-general of French West Africa. Boisson had lost a leg at Verdun in the First World War but had nevertheless followed a successful career in the colonial service. He was now faced with a widespread movement to continue the war in alliance with the British, but when Dakar was attacked by a mixed force of British and Gaullist French (as mentioned above) the failure of the attack provided the occasion for the arrest of those who had dared to declare their support for De Gaulle. Boisson however had no intention of saving the territory from the Gaullists for the purpose of handing it over to the Germans. He refused to have any Germans or Italians in the place. At the same time, British sailors who fell into his power while escaping from sinking ships were interned in an unhealthy camp far inland.

Trade with France continued by sea, and there was a weekly air service for mail and passengers. The demand in France for African produce was heavy, and although shipments were slow the price of commodities continually rose so that merchants made profits. Imports of consumer goods almost ceased. Smuggling went on over the frontiers of the British colonies, and was encouraged by the British army who wanted meat-on-the-hoof from French territory, for which they were prepared to exchange consumer goods. Vast quantities of 'refugee capital' sought investment in the Federation. It was the springboard for French capital into the free world – the freest territory which they could reach. Patriotic Frenchmen were trying to push their capital out of reach of the Germans. Collaborationist financiers were given facilities by the Germans to place part of their rake-off in Africa. While consumer goods were terribly scarce, there was considerable importation of capital goods.

Since Africans were not interested in earning money if they could not use it to buy what they wanted, production was only maintained by the imposition of forced labour and by devices such as making it compulsory in certain areas for people to bring to market a quota of rubber or palm kernels. Into these conditions came the fascist corporative philosophy of Vichy. Racialism was accepted as a political creed. Elections ceased to be held. The newspapers owned by Africans were suppressed. All economic activity was brought within the organisation of sydicates modelled on Italian principles.

In an effort to keep prices under control everything was either taxed or subsidised. This was the system of *peréquation*. Nearly everything had to bear perequation taxes in order to finance subsidies for basic essentials such as rice and bread. Since the importation of petroleum had ceased, civilian road transport was converted to producer gas. This involved the attachment to the side of the vehicle of an oven in which charcoal was burned, releasing a gas which rose through a pipe to fill a balloon which was held in a frame on the roof of the vehicle.

The landings of the British and Americans in Morocco and Algeria in November 1942 changed all this. Admiral Darlan established himself as the head of the French administration at Algiers and Boisson declared his adhesion to Darlan. He tried to make an arrangement with General Eisenhower (commander of the allied forces in Africa) under which he would receive an American mission, while having nothing to do with the British. He was told that the Americans and British were in the war together as allies and that he would have to show equal favour to both.

In order to facilitate quick decisions and inter-departmental co-ordination in wartime, the British had posted a cabinet minister, Lord Swinton, at Accra. He met Boisson on 17 January 1943 at Porto Novo in Dahomey and laid the basis for better relations. Nevertheless, when Boisson received British representatives there was on his desk, between himself and his visitors, a large piece of steel with jagged edges. 'That is what your countrymen threw into my garden in 1940', he said, and the tone of his voice sounded a little unfriendly. However, Boisson soon found reason to change his mind about the British. He became aware that the British were fighting the Germans vigorously, and this was something which he had not appreciated. The presence of the Royal Air Force at Dakar and Port Etienne, from which point they maintained the anti-submarine patrol across the Atlantic to Brazil, worked wonders. Furthermore, the British supplied French West Africa with petroleum, coal, lorries, and textiles of West African design; and they bought and shipped sisal, rubber, palm products, and diamonds. The shrapnel disappeared from Boisson's desk.

By this time the Gaullist French were in power at Algiers, and they wanted to keep African produce in store so that at the appropriate time they could pour it into metropolitan France. Boisson was instructed not to sell to the British, but then he was confronted with the fact that if the British did not get his produce they could not be expected to maintain his supplies of petrol and so on. He tried to make a judgment of Solomon.

The most urgent wartime requirement of the British was rubber. In the rubber-collecting areas the French had previously made it compulsory for every man to bring in a quota. This system was continued, and a standard price was paid for the quota; but a much higher price was paid for any quantity delivered voluntarily in excess of the quota. Men engaged in rubber production had a prior claim on incentive goods, and what they most wanted were shot-gun cartridges and trapping wire; clearly they combined their visits to the forest with some hunting. Following intensive research, latex was accepted from various vines which had not previously been used commercially, and this made it easier for the collectors to fill their quotas. In the season 1943–44 3325 tons were secured, an excellent achievement.

Groundnuts were an essential war commodity. There had been crops as large as 600,000 tons in shell, but in 1942–3 only 130,000 tons had been marketed; there had been no consumer goods to attract the interest of groundnut growers, and since rice and flour could not be imported, groundnuts had been used as food. The quantity marketed in 1943–4 was 310,000 tons, two-and-a-half times what had been secured in the previous year. It represented a great effort by the Senegalese, and owed much to the arrival of supplies from America – trucks, loco-motives, rice, and textiles.

On 30 June 1943 Boisson resigned; he was placed under arrest and never regained liberty, for he died in confinement in 1947. In the office of governor-general he was succeeded by a Gaullist, and in 1944 Charles De Gaulle visited Dakar on his way to the famous conference at Braz-zaville. De Gaulle was not pleased with his visit. On the road from the airport the patriotic slogans were mixed with 'Equal pay for equal work' (referring not to men and women but to white and black) and 'Down with race discrimination'. At the reception where hundreds of people filed past De Gaulle to shake hands, Lamine Gueye was in the line, and when he came face to face with the great man, he asked him in a loud voice what he proposed to do for Africans. The great Charles drew himself up to his full height and said something sibylline in which justice was linked with discipline.

De Gaulle flew to Brazzaville for the conference, accompanied by the governor-general and all the governors, but without any African representatives. The conference adopted a resolution that the empire should be known as the French Union. Each constituent of that Union would develop in its own way. The loyalty of individuals to the Union was to be given through their own units. The economic policy of the colonies should be directed towards the advantage of the inhabitants. There should be established 'in the colonies representative institutions effectively associating the subject peoples in the conduct of public affairs'. On the other hand, the conference stood firmly against any idea of independence: 'The civilising work of France in her colonies rules out all ideas of autonomy, and any possibility of evolution outside the French empire.' A more liberal political atmosphere followed upon these events, and a chief in Ivory Coast named Houphouet-Boigny took advantage of it to organise an African Farmers' Union (*Syndicat Africain Agricole*). Later it changed its name to *Parti Démocratique de la Côte d'Ivoire*. This leader and his party were to have great influence in shaping the future.

Lamine Gueye championed the cause of the ex-servicemen. Some were returning from the exciting experiences of a victorious war, while others had endured years in German labour camps. As happens often when troops are in process of disbandment, the men in a camp at

Tiaroye near Dakar became impatient and angry, and there was a mutiny which resulted in numerous casualties. The deaths caused public indignation which strengthened the support for Gueye who had shown that he would speak out for the rights of Africans. In a general election (1946) Lamine Gueye secured election as deputy for the four communes, and he was appointed to a ministerial post in the cabinet formed by Léon Blum.

It was not until after the close of hostilities that the government felt able to bring compulsory labour to an end. For some months it was hard to secure any labour, and some of the ports had to close. The railways and other services suffered from strikes. Wages were far too low, and in November 1945 the government grasped the nettle and doubled all its rates of pay. The commercial employers immediately followed.

The Pan African Trade Union Conference met in Dakar and demanded that Africans should receive equal pay for equal work, and social insurance on the same basis as in France. To back these demands railway workers throughout French West Africa went on strike at the opening of the produce season 1947–8, and they remained on strike for six months.

In October 1945 elections were held for a constituent assembly for the French empire, and arrangements were made for six spokesmen to be elected for West Africa for this constituent assembly. Of the six, four were to play leading roles in the following decades: they were Lamine Gueye and Léopold Senghor in Senegal; Felix Houphouet-Boigny in Ivory Coast; and Maurice Apithy in Dahomey. Senghor was a Roman Catholic and a professor at the Sorbonne university in Paris; also a poet in the French language. Houphouet-Boigny was a medical doctor, a customary chief, and a landowner growing crops on a plantation scale. Gueye and Senghor joined the French socialist party, while Houphouet-Boigny and Apithy associated with the communists. (It is perhaps as well to bear in mind that the communists were participating in the coalition which provided the government of France.)

This first constituent assembly was unable to agree on the text of a constitution, and so it dispersed, and a second constituent assembly was elected; West Africa sent forward the same six members.

In the first constituent assembly the African members had plenty to say and they made large claims for democratic institutions and for equality with France. They were disappointed when the assembly dispersed without reaching any conclusions, and the frustration born of that experience led to the formation, at Bamako in 1946, of the

Rassemblement Démocratique Africain (RDA), a federation-wide association of local parties, which was to be the most important force in French African politics in the 14 years following.

7 French Union, French Community

The French possessions now ceased to be colonies and became parts of a Republic, of which another part was France.

The second constituent assembly produced the constitution of 1946. It employed the phrase French Union, but defined it in a different way from that which had been contemplated at Brazzaville. The Union now consisted of the Republic on the one hand, and of the associated states and territories on the other. The Republic *included* the oversea territories, and this phrase covered French West Africa. The associated states which belonged to the Union but did not form part of the Republic were such places as Morocco and Tunis; the associated territories were the trusteeship territories, of which Togo was one. French West Africa was part of the Republic, and had seventeen deputies and twenty-two senators in parliament at Paris. There was a large extension of the franchise. African women, and many persons who were illiterate and knew no French, could now claim voting rights. The status of 'subject' was suppressed and with it went the hated *indigénat*. The former subjects became citizens of the Union, though not citizens of the Republic. It is strange that this title was applied to inhabitants of the oversea territories at the time when their countries were declared to be part of the Republic: it was done out of respect for those people in the oversea territories who did not wish to have the civil law status which belonged to citizens of the Republic. The citizen of the Union regulated his marriage, inheritance, and other personal matters according to the rules of the community in which he had grown up, but the citizen of the Republic had his affairs regulated by the French civil code. In elections for the chamber of deputies the two kinds of citizens voted together without distinction.

In each of the units of West Africa the constitution set up a general council, which was to reflect local opinion and advise the governor; but the general councils had no power of legislation, being closely modelled on the *conseils généraux* of departments in France. In elections for these general councils Union citizens and Republic citizens voted on separate lists, save only in Senegal where a single list served for all purposes. In Soudan, Ivory Coast, Guinea, Niger, and Dahomey, the voting for the local assembly was carried out in two colleges, one for Republic citizens and the other for Union citizens. This was important because the local assemblies chose the senators for the upper house (senate) in Paris. Under these arrangements, Republic citizens had more generous representation than Union citizens in relation to their numbers; even so, the places reserved for Union citizens exceeded the places reserved for Republic citizens. It was clear that if Republic citizens resident in Africa did not have some places in the senate reserved for them, they would have no representatives, but would be in the same position as any other small minority in a large democracy; but the separate voting college for Republic citizens caused indignation among Africans.

In the constituent assembly much bargaining took place. There were many who wanted a federal solution following the resolutions of the Brazzaville conference. They wanted the oversea representatives to sit in a federal legislature, and logically then the Paris parliament would have confined its activities to metropolitan France, and no deputies nor senators from overseas would have belonged to it. However, the assimilationists carried the day, so the parliament in Paris continued to be the supreme law-making body of the Union. As a concession to the federalists, an Assembly of the French Union was established; but its functions were purely advisory. It brought together in equal numbers representatives from France and representatives from the oversea parts of the Union, for by a fortunate coincidence the population of the Union overseas was approximately equal to that of France. The election of members of the Assembly of the French Union was based on a common roll in which Republic citizens and Union citizens had equal rights.

This constitution of 1946 was very complicated. Mention has been made of three assemblies in Paris to which Africans were elected – chamber of deputies, senate, and assembly of the French Union. The general councils in each of the units have also been referred to. Between the units and Paris was another level, the Federation of French West Africa with headquarters at Dakar. The head of the federation exchanged the name of governor-general for the title of high commissioner of the Republic. He had the advice of a grand council. The general council of each unit sent five members to this body. However, it never counted for much. Three levels of deliberative assemblies, unit, Dakar, and Paris, were too many.

The successful candidates in the elections of 1946 and 1947 belonged to three groups. One, led by Lamine Gueye, received support mainly in Senegal and was affiliated with the socialist party in France. This group wanted a centralised federation of West Africa with its centre at Dakar. Lamine Gueye secured ministerial office at Paris. He won acclaim by proposing the law which abolished the *indigénat* and in 1950 he secured the adoption of the 'second Lamine Gueye law' which made the conditions of African civil servants identical with those of Europeans. Gueye's influence with the government enabled him to arrange the appointment as governor of Senegal of a Guadeloupian named Wiltord, who shared Gueye's views. He introduced a system of popular elections for the choice of chiefs of villages, cantons, and provinces; and this enabled Gueye's party (which was well organised) to increase its influence in the rural areas. This was a welcome reinforcement of his political base, for he had lost the votes of organised workers by supporting the Government during the railway strike of 1947–48.

The second important political combination was the RDA (see above). It was affiliated with the French communist party, who created for it an impressive organisation, a hierarchy of committees in town and country. The RDA was radical but not secessionist. Its leader Houphouet-Boigny has already been mentioned; he was never a charismatic leader like Kwame Nkrumah and Sekou Touré, and he did not impress as an orator; but he may claim to be the best political operator that Africa has produced in this highly political age. The communist party, being in coalition with other parties to form the French government, secured the appointment of one of its members as governor of Ivory Coast. The communist governor did not hesitate to promote the interests of the RDA. However, in 1947 the communists ceased to participate in the French government, and thereafter the governor of Ivory Coast and his principal officers used their influence to hinder the activities of the RDA. For two years Ivory Coast was torn by conflict. Some RDA leaders were arrested and civil servants who belonged to that party were dismissed. Eight of the jailed leaders went on hunger-strike and there was a mass demonstration by women in sympathy. Houphouet-Boigny provided himself with a bodyguard at his home in Yamoussoukro. When the government sent a force to arrest him its way was barred by the bodyguard, and after a period of tension it retired without using its arms. At Dimbokro on the other hand the government forces opened fire upon a gathering of RDA supporters, of whom thirteen were killed. After this, meetings were banned. It occurred to Houphouet-Boigny however that he and his followers could gain nothing from this situation, and that they were really working for the communists. Despite the link with the communist party, it is hard to imagine anybody less like a communist than Houphouet-Boigny, a traditional chief and a successful businessman in the private sector. He was impressed by the second Lamine Gueye law, which showed what could be gained by co-operating with the government. So in 1950 the alliance with the communists was ended, and RDA made an alliance with a small party, *Union Démocratique et Sociale de la Résistance*, whose leader was Mitterand. With their support, in 1956 Houphouet-Boigny became a minister in the cabinet formed by Mollet; and he proved to be more stable than his prime minister, for he retained office in the next four governments, led by Bourges-Manoury, Gaillard, Pfimlin, and De Gaulle. Houphouet-Boigny and his RDA colleagues were prepared to support any government in power, in order to use their position to win economic and political advantages for Africa. They believed in co-operation with the government and with the leading companies in the private sector.

Finally, in these first elections some successful candidates were from parties not combined either with Lamine Gueye or with Houphouet-Boigny. They came together as the *Indépendants d'Outremer* (IOM) with Apithy and Senghor as leaders. The IOM did not affiliate with any party in France, and talked of autonomy for Africa, but within the French Union. In Senegal Senghor resigned from Lamine Gueye's socialist party and formed the *Bloc Démocratique Sénégalais*, which enjoyed the support of the marabouts, religious leaders in the Mohammedan community; an interesting situation for a party led by a Roman Catholic.

The first election (1946) yielded the following results:

	Socialists	RDA	Independents
Chamber of Deputies	5	6	6
Senate	7	4	11
Assembly of the French Union	7	5	16

At about the same time as the constitution was adopted in 1946 the French government established the Fund for Economic and Social Development (FIDES). The purpose of FIDES was to provide money for the oversea parts of the Union. In the administration of FIDES a useful function was found for the general councils (which, as explained above, had no power of legislation) because they were associated in the preparation of the plans under which the fund was invested. In 1948 a further step was taken to give financial help to Africa: the salaries of French officials serving in Africa were provided in the metropolitan budget. This arrangement had a lasting effect for it continued through all the changes which were to come, and many French civil servants stayed at their posts in Africa at the expense of the French government even after the African countries had become fully independent. By 1958 the equivalent of £400 million had been spent in West Africa on roads, railways, ports, aerodromes, agriculture, hospitals, and schools. Seventy per cent of public investment and over 30 per cent of recurrent expenditure came from France. This helped the African parts of the Republic but it also made them very dependent on the metropolitan country, and the effect of this can be observed in subsequent political developments.

The African deputies and senators, whatever their party, were not concerned to work for independence, but they were very insistent on equality, demanding that Africa should have exactly equal treatment with metropolitan France.

In 1947 Upper Volta, which had been part of Ivory Coast, became separate. About half of the inhabitants were Mossi people, who had a strong feeling of group identity. They were in a special position to make their wishes felt because many returning soldiers belonged to the Mossi tribe. The separatist movement was headed by the Mossi chief, the Moro Naba. The French administration was favourable because by removing Upper Volta from the orbit of Ivory Coast they reduced the influence of Houphouet-Boigny, regarded at that time as a dangerous left-winger.

Another event of 1947 deserves to be noted. The chiefs of Guinea drew up a manifesto asking for a definition of their status, and for a guarantee of their position as guardians of custom. Their request did not go unheeded, for a bill was submitted to parliament and eventually became law in 1953 'dealing with the status of customary chiefs who are auxiliaries of the administration'. This may indicate that the Guinea chiefs were capable of acting in their own interest without depending on the educated élite. Guinea, as will be seen, parted company from France and gave her chiefs short shrift.

Another event of 1947 concerned the *sociétés de prévoyance*. These so-called societies had long existed, and there was one in every administrative unit. It was under the control of the administrative officer. Membership was compulsory, and the small subscription was collected with the personal tax. The administrative officers used the 'societies' as a flexible local instrument of government, supplying seed

for sowing, constructing dams and wells, providing agricultural equipment, and furnishing transport for produce. Much useful work was
done, but the authoritarian methods were resented. So the *sociétés* were
abolished. To provide the local services for which they had been
responsible, it was proposed that co-operative societies should be set up.
Following this, no less than 253 co-operative societies were registered
in Senegal in the years 1948–52, but in other units there were not very
many.

In 1948 the African franc was devalued. At the same time the federal
government in Dakar instructed the unit governments to discontinue
the control of the selling prices of merchandise, which had lasted on
from wartime. They were instructed to permit freedom to sellers in the
pricing of goods. However, the governors all replied that they could not
remove the price control. It was a new experience for the governors to
decline to follow an instruction from the centre, and it showed that the
new councils had more influence with their governor, in a matter such as
this, than the federal authority. Merchants, large and small alike, were
horrified; it was obvious that after a massive devaluation of the
currency, they had to raise their prices or shut up shop. They pressed
hard to be allowed to increase their prices to cover replacement costs.
The reactions to these representations were different in each of the
units: the monolithic economic system of French West Africa had, for
the first time, broken up.

In 1948 the government accorded to farmers treatment com-
mensurate with the increases which had already been granted to wage-
earners, by increasing the prices to be paid for 'controlled' crops by
about 100 per cent. At the end of that year there was another large
devaluation of both the metropolitan and the African francs. These
frequent changes in the value of money made it difficult to operate
control schemes for produce, and one result was the lifting of control
from cocoa, which was restored to the free market.

The African deputies and senators devoted their efforts to securing
equality with France in political rights, social benefits, and economic
subsidies. The franchise was extended more widely in 1951, so much
that, whereas in 1947 939,000 persons had been entitled to vote, in 1952
the number of voters had increased to 3,200,000. In 1952 the proportion
of members of the general councils elected by Union citizens was
increased at the expense of the proportion elected by Republic citizens.

General elections took place, in 1951 for the Paris parliament and in
1952 for the general councils. In these elections the *Indépendants
d'Outremer* (Senghor and Apithy) were very successful. Their alliance

with the marabouts and peasants in Senegal enabled them to win many seats from Lamine Gueye's socialists, while in Ivory Coast the RDA had not yet won its way back into the favour of the government, so that it was embarrassed by every kind of difficulty in registering voters and in putting forward candidates.

The years from the end of the war through 1951 into 1952 were difficult ones for France and her colonies. The economic collapse of wartime was not made good without years of effort, and complications in Indo-China and Algeria did not help. Then in 1952 the economic tide turned. In Africa scarcity was followed by plenty. Competition was intensified by the arrival of merchant houses which had transferred from Indo-China. Prices fell dramatically. It was a bad time for merchants, but a good time for customers. Perhaps it was partly owing to the new feeling of prosperity and confidence that in 1953 the trade unions won their struggle for equal rates of pay. A new labour code took effect, for which the *Indépendants d'Outremer* were entitled to claim credit in the Paris parliament. It laid down rates of pay irrespective of whether the work was done by a European or by an African. The code included a forty-hour working week. It also introduced family allowances and leave pay on a scale which was higher than that which had previously obtained. The result was a change in the attitude of investors and employers to the ratio between capital and labour as factors of production. Everyone began to study how to use machinery to save labour.

A few statistics about the economic boom will be of interest. The tonnage of exports in 1956 was four times as large as in 1947. The tonnage of imports was three times as large. The prosperity of business, and the increase of government activity in economic and social services, attracted many more Europeans to French West Africa; their numbers increased from 17,000 in 1946 to 100,000 in 1960.

Early in 1953 the IOM held a congress at Bobo-Dioulasso and formulated a policy to strive for a federal French republic, in which West Africa would be one of the federating units, enjoying its own responsible legislature and ministerial government. Two years later in a congress at Conakry the RDA adopted the same policy, and at the same time expelled some left-wing elements. Thus IOM and RDA entered into close association; but even so, RDA deputies seemed to have reservations about a strong ministerial government in Dakar, and continued to show some preference in favour of ministerial governments in each of the units of West Africa.

The political strength of the African parties in the Paris parliament was important, for their votes were frequently decisive. Their loyalty was a moral asset to France during the very difficult days of the withdrawal from Indo-China, and then of the war in Algeria. It was in recognition of this that the metropolitan parliament in 1954 granted municipal self-government to the towns of Africa, with Union citizens and Republic citizens voting on a common roll.

In 1956 another general election took place and again the franchise was more widely extended. This time 6,054,300 voters were registered. The RDA made important gains at the expense of the IOM and of the socialists. This enhanced the influence of Houphouet-Boigny. He became a minister in the cabinet which Guy Mollet formed after the election, and in 1957 he achieved senior cabinet rank as Minister of Health and Population. He had a great deal to do with the next step in political evolution, which was the passing of the *loi cadre* (framework law) by the Paris parliament. It was a curious piece of legislation, an enabling act under which the French government was empowered to change the system of government in Africa without bothering the legislature further. It was perhaps a gesture of weariness by the metropolitan deputies; in the existing state of France, they did not wish to have time taken up by discussing the affairs of Africa.

The constitutional instruments were quickly completed, and as was to be expected in view of the influence which Houphouet-Boigny was able to exert, they followed the RDA pattern; new local legislatures and ministerial governments were set up in each of the units of West Africa. In each case the civil servant previously known as governor became the president of the government with the title *chef du territoire*, but the leading African politician was described as vice-president and acted effectively as prime minister. The principal architect of this settlement was Houphouet-Boigny, and although the advocates of union with France and the champions of a West African federation fought hard through the next three or four years, their efforts could make no headway against the local interests entrenched in their positions by Houphouet-Boigny.

All the units depended for their prosperity on large grants of money from France, and the new arrangements provided for increases in these subventions; so political autonomy was accompanied by an enhanced measure of economic dependence.

The IOM and the socialists were very upset by the action taken under the framework law. In January 1957 they both held meetings which supported the principle of a strong federation. Furthermore, a majority of the trade unionists met at Cotonou under the leadership of Sekou

Touré, a Guinea man who hitherto belonged to the RDA. Under his leadership organised workers formed the *Union Générale des Travailleurs d'Afrique Noire* (UGTAN) and it attacked the framework law, denouncing the action taken under its powers as divisive.

Elections for the new legislatures in Africa were held in 1957. The RDA won a majority, and formed the government, in Ivory Coast, Guinea, Upper Volta, and Soudan. In Senegal the IOM (now under the name *Convention Africaine*) gained control. In Niger a dissident faction of the RDA formed a coalition government in alliance with the socialists. In Dahomey Apithy won control with the support of his local organisation, *Parti Républicain du Dahomey*.

In September of that year, 1957, the RDA held a conference at Bamako, at which resolutions were passed favouring the establishment of a federal legislature and ministerial government at Dakar; but the RDA was after all a group of local parties, and its Ivory Coast constituent, which was the largest, temporised; but it was clear that they would have nothing to do with any government at Dakar, and that was, to all intents and purposes, the end of federation. However, in February 1958 all the African parties met in Paris and the federalists made a great effort to persuade them all to agree to support a strong federal government in Dakar. At this moment the African parts of the French Union were just becoming associated with the European Economic Community, and it was argued that they would be in a stronger position to negotiate favourable terms if they had a strong federal centre. On the other hand, Ghana was on the point of becoming independent, and her example was not without influence on people and politicians in neighbouring territories; it was an example that favoured independence in small unfederated units. In fact, during the last few months independence had become an issue in French Africa – really for the first time. At the Paris conference in 1958 a small Senegalese party demanded immediate independence, and was promptly expelled from the gathering. The three main parties were agreed that the right of each unit to independence should be acknowledged, in order that it might be clear that they remained within the French Union of their own free will. The Paris conference ended with a victory for the federalists, but the discussion was then transferred to the meeting of the grand council in Dakar in April 1958, and here again progress was stopped by the attitude of Ivory Coast. In the following month, May 1958, the Fourth Republic in France came to an end, and Charles De Gaulle acceded to power. This was to introduce a completely new train of events in the politics of West Africa.

De Gaulle almost immediately directed that the *chefs de territoire* should cease to preside over meetings of ministers, and that the leading African minister of each place should have the title of prime minister; but the territories still did not enjoy full independence, because the *chefs* retained responsibility for defence, foreign policy, customs, postal services, and civil service.

De Gaulle quickly prepared a constitution for his Fifth Republic. Houphouet-Boigny and Senghor were consulted in the preparation of the text, which basically reflected the principle that the French Union should be a federation, as De Gaulle had always wished since his Brazzaville days. French West Africa was no longer to have representatives in the parliament at Paris. Each oversea unit would be an autonomous member of the French Community. The Community would be governed by an executive council in which each member-country would be represented by its prime minister. There would be a legislature called a senate in which each member-country would have one senator for every 300,000 inhabitants. The government of the Community was to deal with certain common subjects including foreign affairs, defence, currency, economic policy, justice, university education, external transport and telecommunications. Thus the 'autonomy' of the constituent parts would be of limited character. As to what these constituent parts should be, in regard to West Africa the proposed constitution said nothing; there might be one federation, or eight units, or some intermediate grouping; the problem was left to be determined by the Africans.

Having drafted the new constitution, De Gaulle determined to submit it to the electors of the Union in September 1958; and he set out on a lightning tour of the French Union to explain his plans and to win support for them. People in the oversea territories were told that any country which rejected the constitution by a majority vote would forthwith be regarded as independent, 'with all the consequences'. This meant the withdrawal of French staff and French subsidies; but any country which accepted the constitution might subsequently, if it wished, negotiate its independence or arrange a special treaty relationship with France. As was to be expected, the situation stimulated heated discussion in Africa as to whether the opportunity should be seized to take full independence. However, the conference resolutions and verbal acrobatics are no longer of importance. The fateful vote took place, and most of the colonies of French West Africa approved De Gaulle's constitution by large majorities. There were two exceptions, Niger and Guinea.

In Niger two parties were fairly evenly balanced in the legislature. The UGTAN (see above) had a slight majority, and it declared in favour of voting 'No' and becoming independent. The opposition party used the name RDA, and it appealed for a vote of 'Yes'. The *chef de territoire* and his administrative officials, determined to secure a victory for De Gaulle's policy, used every means of influence to help the RDA, and this may well have assisted them to win the contest with about three-quarters of the votes cast; but it may be doubted whether the vast mass of the peasantry were very interested.

In Guinea however the situation was very different, Sekou Touré was the prime minister and he had organised his *Parti Démocratique de Guinée* (PDG) as effectively as Kwame Nkrumah had organised his CPP. Sekou Touré was a descendant of the famous chief Samory who fought against the French for many years; but his political affinities were not aristocratic but trade unionist, and he has been mentioned above as founder and leader of UGTAN. As recently as 1957 he had disposed of the chiefs in Guinea, replacing them by elected functionaries. Under the inspiration of his sparkling oratory, Guinea voted 'No'. Thus Guinea became independent. It was an event of outstanding importance, for it made it impossible for any political leader in Africa to settle for less. If the whole of West and Equatorial Africa had voted 'yes' in the referendum, it is possible that De Gaulle's hope of combining them in a 'Community' might have continued as a political possibility, at any rate for some years longer. Much more can be said about Guinea and Sekou Touré, but it will be convenient to reserve it for a later chapter.

As stated above, the constitution left it to the African countries to decide whether they would be members of the Community as separate units, or as one unit (i.e., a federation of West Africa), or in some intermediate grouping. Before the end of the year they had all declared themselves to be members of the Community as separate units. The federation disappeared; the grand council ceased to exist, and the last high commissioner left Dakar. Many people were sorry to see him go. Representatives of the governments of Senegal, Soudan, Upper Volta, and Dahomey (in spite of the fact that they had all just declared their intention to be members of the Community as separate states) met in January 1959 and declared that they would form a federation under the name Mali – the name of an ancient empire of West Africa. However, the legislative assemblies of Dahomey and Upper Volta refused to ratify this declaration, so the Federation of Mali was reduced to two members, Senegal and Soudan.

Upper Volta and Dahomey rejected the offer of a federal union with

Senegal and Soudan under pressure from Houphouet-Boigny, who was determined that Ivory Coast should not be placed in the comparatively minor role which it would play in a federation with headquarters in Dakar. However, Upper Volta and Dahomey were poor and lonely, and Houphouet-Boigny had to offer them something to take the place of the Mali Federation. This necessity seems to have been the original reason for forming the *Conseil de l'entente* in 1959. It brought together Ivory Coast, Upper Volta, Dahomey, and Niger in an association, the exact scope of which remained to be worked out. Houphouet-Boigny soon learned that it would not survive unless Ivory Coast accepted certain restraints on its freedom of action, for already in 1960 he was involved in a quarrel with Upper Volta. The cause was that Ivory Coast abolished the head tax without consulting its partners in the *entente*. This tax supplied only 4 per cent of Ivory Coast's revenue, and therefore Ivory Coast could afford to abolish it, thereby adding to the popularity of the government. In Upper Volta on the other hand head tax provided a quarter of the revenue, and it could not be dispensed with. In retaliation, Upper Volta abolished the organisation which recruited Mossi labourers for Ivory Coast's plantations. The two governments could not agree what should be done to replace (or continue) an arrangement which had existed in the federation of French West Africa by which Upper Volta received a percentage of import duties collected in the port of Abidjan. The percentage was supposed to represent the proportion of imported goods which found their way to Upper Volta. Ivory Coast, now that it had independent command of the customs collection, discontinued that practice and substituted the payment of a lump sum, which the government of Upper Volta did not consider to be sufficient. Houphouet-Boigny had to hold out an olive branch. He assured Upper Volta that an equitable arrangement would be worked out regarding customs duties, and he begged (successfully) that the arrangements for recruiting labourers should be restored. In order to avoid further collapses in the structure of the *entente* a secretariat was set up at Niamey in Niger, and it was agreed to hold regular meetings of the heads of the four states, who were to take the chair by annual rotation.

While all this had been going on in the eastern part of the area, at the western extremity the partners in the new Federation of Mali, Senegal and Soudan, had been setting up their combined government in Dakar. They did not find it easy to agree. Senghor with his liberal mind and strong links with France was out of sympathy with Modibo Keita, the radical man from Soudan, whose opinions were close to those of Sekou Touré. It was very important to France to make sure of the continuing goodwill of Senegal, and towards the end of 1959 De Gaulle paid a personal visit to Dakar to try to cement a cordial relationship. During this visit he had to recognise that the Federation of Mali would not be satisfied with anything less than complete independence, and he agreed to recognise that. Forthwith, the four states of the *entente* abandoned the thought of remaining in a special relationship with France as members of the Community. They decided to take complete independence, leaving any agreements with France to be concluded afterwards. The French government agreed, and the four countries declared their independence in June 1960.

In the decade 1950 to 1960 the population of the area had increased from 16,000,000 to 19,000,000. The principal towns grew in size, Dakar rising to 300,000 inhabitants and Abidjan to 128,000. The number of children attending school rose from 200,000 to 375,000.

8 Togo, 1940–60

Togo is a very small country, in area less than one fourth the size of Ghana, a narrow strip about 70 miles wide and 300 miles long from south to north. In 1940 there was no reliable count of its population, but it was probably about 780,000. Togo was a part of the former German colony of Togoland, which had been divided into two parts after the First World War. The part with which this chapter is concerned was administered by France as a mandated territory under the supervision of the League of Nations.

The southern part of Togo is inhabited by members of the Ewe tribe. The tribe is however not all contained within Togo; other Ewes lived in that part of the former German colony which had been placed under British mandate, an area which Britain administered as though it were part of the Gold Coast; and there were also Ewe people inside the boundaries of the Gold Coast, living in country which never formed part of the German colony. The Ewe people are enterprising and in 1940 the proportion of them who had a European style of education was high by African standards. Many of them had secured positions of responsibility in other countries. There was, in consequence, a tendency to think of Togoland as the land of the Ewes. It is therefore important to note that the people of the centre and north are ethnically different, and are more numerous than the Ewes.

In the early 1940s Togo was combined with Dahomey for administrative purposes, and this 'union' was operative in the elections to the French constituent assemblies in 1945 and 1946; so that Togo and Dahomey jointly elected one representative, who was Apithy, the deputy mayor of Porto Novo in Dahomey. However, the electoral laws of 1946 were more generous to Togo, which now elected one deputy, two senators, and one counsellor of the assembly of the French Union.

In the late 1930s, when Hitler was ruling Germany, that country revived its claims to its former colonies, of which Togo was one. A group of Togo inhabitants favoured the German claim, and expressed their opinion through a society with a German name, *Bund der Deutschen Togoländer*. The majority of educated people however preferred the

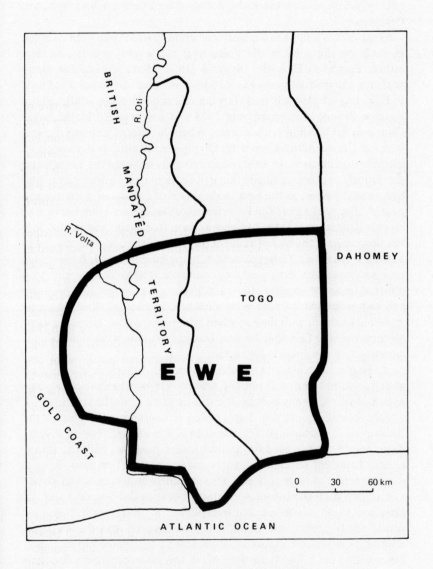

Map 2   The Home of the Ewe people

French connection, and the expression of this view brought into public activity men who were to be the leaders of political life for more than twenty years; and of these the outstanding character was Sylvanus Olympio.

Sylvanus Olympio was a member of a family which had been engaged in trade on the delta of the Volta river for several generations. His father, Epiphano Elphidio Olympio (1873–1968) worked for many years for a British company named Miller Brothers. Sylvanus was fluent in Ewe, English, French, and German. He completed his studies at the London School of Economics in 1923 and was engaged by the Niger Company for training as a manager. When the Niger Company merged into the United Africa Company, Olympio continued as a manager of the new organisation. In 1940, when relations between the French and the British became strained, the British manager had to leave, and Sylvanus Olympio, as the next in the chain of command, took the top post. At the end of 1942 the French authorities arrested him because of his pro-British sentiments, but he was soon free again, and he not only ran the company, but acted as agent for the British economic mission in French West Africa. Olympio's outstanding qualities made it inevitable that an important section of his countrymen should elect him as a political leader; though he often said that he never sought that position, and only accepted it under great pressure. In view of Olympio's hot-and-cold relations with the French in later years, it is of interest to draw attention to the fact that he first became prominent in politics as a champion of the French connection.

In Togo, as in other territories within the French orbit, political activity was prohibited during the war until 1944, when the conference at Brazzaville set many people off discussing new ideas. In May 1945 the French commissioner for Togo called a conference to discuss the Brazzaville resolutions: 45 Togolese and 17 Frenchmen. For some years Togo had been combined for administrative purposes with Dahomey, and the first thing which the Togolese made clear was that their status as a separate unit must be restored. This attitude was not caused by dislike of Dahomey; on the contrary, relations between the Togolese and the Dahomeans were cordial; but acceptance of union with Dahomey would imply absorption into the French empire, and the Togolese wished to retain the status .of a mandated or trusteeship territory, because they set value on the right which this gave them to express their national ambitions before the Trusteeship Council of UNO. From this time the possibility of independence began to be discussed in Togo, and although the French tried hard to persuade the Togolese to be happy within the French Union, they had to accept in the trusteeship agreement of 1950 the general formula required by the United Nations in concluding trusteeship agreements; and in that formula the French promised to promote 'progressive development towards self-government or independence'. The Togolese did not allow the French to overlook that commitment.

As already stated, the Ewes do not all live in Togo, and there were in fact more Ewes on the British side of the border than on the French side. In 1946 a demand for the unification of the tribe was voiced by an all-Ewe conference which met in Accra. The leader on the Gold Coast side was Daniel Chapman. A petition was placed before the Trusteeship Council of the United Nations (which had just been formed, and which took over the function of supervising the government of the trusteeship territories from the mandates commission of the league of nations) in 1947. Through the next decade the affairs of Togo frequently engaged the attention of that council, and attracted such interest that they were carried beyond the council to the general assembly of the United Nations. The issues were complex. There was the suggestion which inspired the petition of 1946, that all the Ewes should be united in a state. What, then, would happen to the rest of Togo? Another proposal was canvassed, namely that the two portions into which the former German colony had been divided should be reunited. As years went by, both these propositions tended to be submerged by the idea that the 'British' part of the trusteeship territory should become part of Gold Coast, soon to be independent; and this inevitably brought into the arena the proposal that 'French' Togo should become independent within its existing frontiers, including Ewes and nón-Ewes. Several missions were sent by UNO to visit Togo. Consultative commissions were set up, canvasses of public opinion were conducted, and plebiscites were held; but since all this activity, in so far as it related to proposals for adjusting frontiers, achieved nothing at all, it will not be described in detail. In the course of all this Sylvanus Olympio became known as the most experienced tactician in presenting a case to the Trusteeship Council. His outstanding linguistic attainments were helpful. Younger Africans who came to seek the support of the Trusteeship Council turned to Olympio for guidance, and he became the 'doyen' of African petitioners. Julius Nyerere of Tanganyika (which was, like Togo, a trust territory) particularly valued his friendship.

As in French West Africa, a territorial assembly was established in 1946. It had thirty members. From 1952 they were elected on a common roll in which citizens of metropolitan France and citizens of the Union voted together.

The first election for a local assembly (1946) was contested by two parties. Sylvanus Olympio and his friends acted under the name *Comité d'Unité Togolaise* (CUT) and their opponents were *Parti Togolais du Progrès* (PTP). It is difficult to detect any differences of principle between these two parties. The leaders of both were drawn from the same families, and there appeared to be no conflict regarding social objectives, nor on the subject of Ewe unification. Considering what happened over the next fifteen years, it may be that CUT was more inclined to use the opportunities of the UNO connection (which tended to antagonise the French government) whereas PTP was more inclined to seek its political objectives in close harmony with the French. Each party had a youth organisation, Juvento for CUT and *Rassemblement des Jeunes Togolais* for PTP, and these tended to be more radical in social policy than the senior parties. In 1954 Juvento, because of its interest in social reform, broke away from CUT. In the election of 1946 CUT gained an easy victory, but in spite of this the leader of PTP, Nicholas Grunitzky, secured election as the deputy for Togo, and this gave him considerable influence.

Until 1951 Olympio supported the policy of Ewe unification and gave little thought to the non-Ewe (majority) people of Togo. The advance of the Gold Coast towards self-rule however led him to reconsider his position, and in 1951 he abandoned the cause of Ewe union and made 'Unified Togo' his political goal. In 1951 some members of his party became involved in disorders at a place called Vogan, where ten persons were shot dead by the police. Tension increased when CUT refused to attend the celebration of France's national day, 14 July, rendering it a failure. Olympio's activities caused concern to the French government, and the French colonial minister brought pressure on the United Africa Company to prevent Olympio from going to America to present the Togo case before the United Nations. The United Africa Company however had no power to stop Olympio from going to America. The French government then appealed to the British government to restrain the United Africa Company from supporting the nationalist movement. They maintained that the unrest in Togo was due to Olympio, who used his position with the company to further his political activities. The company pointed out that if any action were taken against Olympio he would be regarded as a martyr to the cause, and might become more of a menace to the peace than he was said to be already. However, multinational companies have to take account of the wishes of the governments of the places where they operate, and to oblige the French government the company expressed its willingness to ask Olympio to accept employment in London or Paris for a period of twelve months. The French authorities thought that this would be a good solution, and Olympio readily agreed to work in Paris. It had not been foreseen by the French authorities that the United Nations Trusteeship Council would arrange its next meeting in Paris! They were aghast at having Olympio on UNO's doorstep, and asked the company to move him again. At that moment Olympio tendered his resignation to the company and decided to devote the whole of his time to politics.

In the elections of 1952 the PTP (Grunitzky) won a majority in the legislature. It continued to press the French to agree to constitutional changes leading in the direction of self-government. In 1955 therefore a council of government was created. It consisted of four members nominated by the French commissioner (i.e. governor) and four members elected by the legislature. Each member of the council had a sector of activity over which he exercised powers something like those of a minister. Thus Togo went ahead of French West Africa, because there the councils of government were not set up until 1956.

The PTP continued to request a greater measure of autonomy, and in August 1956 Togo was declared an autonomous republic. Nicholas Grunitzky was appointed prime minister. The events which were happening on the Gold Coast side of the frontier (Chapter 2) attracted great concern. Following the plebiscite which was held in 'British' Togoland the doubts about the future of that area were resolved since it was annexed to Gold Coast and the trust regime came to an end. The French government decided to reinforce their position by holding a referendum in 'French' Togo, in which the public were invited to declare in favour of ending the trust regime in their part of the country. The United Nations declined to have anything to do with this proposal, but the French proceeded with it, and the vote was affirmative by 313,000 to 22,000. In 1958 France granted a further constitutional advance, by which the prime minister was appointed by the legislature (instead of being nominated by the commissioner) and the council of government had control of all subjects save foreign affairs, defence, and currency. This was in essence the same status as that which the British had accorded to Gold Coast in the constitution of 1954.

The elections which followed the 1958 constitution were supervised by a commission from the United Nations. Olympio's CUT won complete victory with 190,000 votes, and PTP with only 40,000 votes was in third place, for second place (56,000 votes) was secured by a party speaking for the interests of the north, UCPN (*Union des chefs et des populations du nord*). Sylvanus Olympio was the new prime minister and he appointed seven ministers of whom two were northern men. He asked the French government for complete independence, and they asked the United Nations to terminate the trust agreement so that Togo might become an independent sovereign state. Doubts were entertained by several members of UNO whether so small a place as Togo could be successful as an independent country. However, once France had agreed with the Togolese on the grant of independence, UNO had no choice but to acquiesce.

Hardly had Olympio taken office when disorders broke out on the Gold Coast side of the frontier, and the government of Kwame Nkrumah took energetic steps to suppress the Ewe separatist movement. This upset the Ewe population in Togo, and Olympio was reflecting their sentiments when he resisted the invitation to join up with Ghana as related in Chapter 14. These incidents made it impossible for any Togolese politician to discuss union with Ghana. Kwame Nkrumah was therefore wasting his time in trying to persuade Olympio to 'join up'. If Nkrumah had been prepared to offer 'home rule for all the Ewes' within a Ghana confederacy, he might have secured a hearing; but of course he hated 'tribalism'. As it was, union with Ghana looked like ethnic suicide.

Between 1946 and 1960 there was an important increase in education; children in primary schools rose in the south from 33,000 to 60,000 and trebled in the north from 9000 to 27,000. In 1960 2800 scholars were in secondary schools, and 675 in technical schools.

Independence was celebrated in April 1960.

9 Portuguese Guinea

Portugal was the first European power in West Africa, and the last. While Britain and France made no use of military force to prolong colonial rule, Portugal declared that her oversea territories were all parts of Portugal, and fought for years to suppress the independence movements.

Portuguese Guinea was even smaller than Togo, but its shape was more compact, occupying the coast between Senegal and French Guinea. It had about half a million inhabitants, of whom (according to a census of 1950) 2263 were white, 4568 were half-caste, and 1478 were African *asimilados* enjoying full rights of citizenship. The capital town was Bissau. The crops were groundnuts, rice, cocoa, millet, cassava, sorghum, and sweet potatoes, and there were herds of cattle, sheep, and pigs. The country was represented by one member in the national assembly at Lisbon. In 1953, under the terms of a new law, an advisory council with elected members was to be provided. It was years before this intention was implemented in Guinea, but eventually an advisory council came into existence, in which eleven members were elected by the citizens and three members were nominated by the governor. Since only one political party was permitted to exist, elections were formalities.

Africans and children of mixed marriages could secure citizenship if they followed a European way of life. They had to be monogamous, to speak Portuguese, to have a trade or profession, and to perform military service. The first of these conditions was administered in a way which practically meant that the applicant had to be a Roman Catholic. Africans who were not citizens had to carry a pass known as a *cadernata*. It was used in the collection of tax, and the tax was regarded by the government as a method of obliging people to produce a marketable crop or to work for wages. The law empowered an administrative officer to direct a man to work if he could not produce a *cadernata* showing that tax had been paid for the current year. This practice was known as the *indigenato*.

In 1940 the Pope made an agreement with the Portuguese government by which Portuguese catholic missions secured an important position in the control of state schools for Africans. However, the number of Christian converts was no more than 2 per cent of the population (1950).

Portugal took no part in the war of 1939 to 1945, so that the exciting and disturbing influences which war brought to the British and French colonies made no impact on Portuguese Guinea.

In 1953 a young agronomist named Amilcar Cabral published a tract against the Portuguese regime. Cabral was born in the Cape Verde Islands, where the people have both African and European ancestry, being descended from Portuguese settlers and African slaves. He studied at Lisbon university from 1946 to 1950 and then received an appointment as a government agronomist in Guinea. He married a Portuguese wife. In the course of duty in Guinea he travelled all over the country and acquired local knowledge which proved valuable when he became the leader of the people in war.

As a consequence of his publication he had to live in exile and he was now committed to work for the independence of Guinea and Cape Verde. In 1956 he formed the *Partido africano da independencia da Guiné e Cabo Verde* (PAIGC). For the next three years the party tried to work by peaceful means but this proved to be impossible under the authoritarian regime of Portugal. In 1959 the dockers at Bissau went on strike, and this led to fighting in which the police killed fifty people. The public indignation which this incident provoked gave Cabral the opportunity to start a clandestine movement, in which he was assisted by the Russians and by Ghana. In 1961, on the anniversary of the massacre, he announced that his party would undertake sabotage and military action. He smuggled in arms and conducted propaganda among the peasants, establishing cells on communist lines.

Portugal made certain gestures. In 1961 the African inhabitants were declared to be full citizens of Portugal. This gave the Africans an improved status and involved the suppression of *cadernata* and *indigenato*, but since Portugal was ruled by a dictator, citizenship offered no satisfaction to those who wished to take part in the government of their country.

The independence movement suffered from lack of unity. While PAIGC enjoyed support from Ghana, from Sekou Touré's Guinea, and from Russia, there were two other groups, the Movement for the Liberation of Guinea (MLG) and the Guinea Popular Union (UPG). Both of these set up offices in Dakar and received encouragement from the government of Senegal, which broke off diplomatic relations with Portugal in 1961. At a meeting of the Organisation of African Unity (OAU) in Lagos in 1963 PAIGC was recognised as the independence movement, but in 1964 another OAU conference took place in Dakar, and was embarrassed by the hostility between PAIGC, supported by Guinea, and the freedom-fighters supported by Senegal, now described as *Front de Libération pour l'Indépendance de Guinée Portuguaise* (FLING). The foreign ministers of the OAU were unable to agree to whom they should give support.

Amilcar Cabral's published works show that he thought clearly about the problem of winning independence, and knew exactly how he should set about it. He employed the language of communist literature about classes, but he did not consider that the classes visualised in Marxist theory existed in Africa. For the purpose of revolutionary theory he wrote that his war was with the ruling class of the imperialist country, but he aimed at drawing to his side all the people of Guinea-Bissau, irrespective of class. The proletariat of wage-earners was too small to count for much, so his main intention was to stimulate armed resistance among the peasants. He recognised that peasants are not natural revolutionary material, but he worked upon their grievances. To conduct this propaganda he used the petty bourgeoisie, the small class of literate Africans employed by the Portuguese as clerks, storekeepers, and foremen. They had learned enough about government and business to organise the peasant armies and to run an administration in the areas from which the Portuguese had been driven. He set up a school for his adherents at Conakry in Sekou Touré's Guinea. They would have to identify themselves with the revolution, just as hitherto they had identified themselves with the colonisers. Cabral wrote of this as committing suicide as a class, but the phrase 'rebirth' might have been used. Cabral's programme of action was entirely military, including of course sabotage, but he did not use terrorist methods. He felt that the ancient culture of the people should be kept alive, and although it had been identified with tribes he optimistically believed that under the influence of the nationalist movement tribal differences would diminish and disappear.

In 1963 Cabral was strong enough to cease hit-and-run tactics, and to undertake military operations against the Portuguese. He occupied more than a third of the country, organising it as a state. The revolt had now assumed the scale of a war, and Portugal sent a large number of troops. By 1968 no less than 40,000 Portuguese soldiers were engaged, but in spite of them all Cabral's men carried out a dramatic attack with mortars on the airport of Bissau. The war in this little land had become of large importance in continental politics, for the Guineans were engaging forces which might otherwise have been deployed in Angola or Mozambique, Portugal's much larger colonies in the south. In 1970 the Portuguese attacked vigorously, and called upon Cabral to surrender; but he rejected the appeal. Portuguese forces were alleged to have crossed the Senegal border, and Senegal appealed to the Security Council of UNO to take action against Portugal. The independent state of Guinea (under Sekou Touré) was very active in helping Cabral, and in 1970 the Portuguese retaliated by assisting a force of Guinean dissidents who landed near Conakry, and tried (unsuccessfully) to overthrow Sekou Touré's government.

In 1972 PAIGC, claiming that it controlled three-quarters of the country, announced that it had held elections and established a government. Then a tragedy occurred; Amilcar Cabral was assassinated in Conakry by dissident members of his party. He had been greatly respected, and the secretary-general of UNO referred to him as 'a great African patriot and leader'. His work lived after him, for in 1973 the representatives who had been elected in 1972 met at Boe and proclaimed Guinea-Bissau as 'a sovereign, republican, democratic, anti-colonialist state'. The new state was immediately recognised by many others, and the general assembly of the United Nations welcomed Guinea-Bissau's accession to independence. A few months later, in 1974, the Portuguese dictatorship was overthrown by a revolution in Lisbon. Talks between the government of Guinea-Bissau and the revolutionary Portuguese government took place in London and established a cease-fire. The war had gone on for thirteen years, and for eleven years it had been a sustained military operation, a war between armies. Formal recognition by Portugal was not long delayed, and the Portuguese troops evacuated the country before the end of 1974.

PART II

SOCIAL AND ECONOMIC TRENDS

10 Population

In 1940 little was known about the statistics of population in West Africa. The British and French had conducted censuses but over large areas the results depended on estimates rather than counts. The figures which appear to be the best available are shown in the left hand column of Table 10.1, but their very unreliable character cannot be too strongly emphasised. They add up to 41,940,000. It was not known whether the population had been expanding or declining. In connection with Lord Hailey's *Survey* a demographer named Kuczinski was invited to make a special study, but he found little material and at the time of the publication of the *Survey* in 1938 he could not say whether the population had increased or diminished in the previous century. Statistics published by the League of Nations indicated that the populations of Nigeria and of Gambia declined in the five-year period 1931 to 1936; though the same source reported modest increases over those years in French West Africa, Gold Coast, and Sierra Leone. Probably the population had been fairly static, at a low level of density, with very high rates of births and deaths. There was much unoccupied land, and labour was often difficult to engage, especially when men were on their farms during the planting and harvesting seasons.

The second, third, and fourth columns of the table indicate the size of population in 1950, 1960, and 1970; but again it is necessary to say that the figures must be accepted with great caution. Counts of population continued to be subject to wide margins of error, and no country in the area maintained records of births, marriages, and deaths. (The Germans had begun the registration of births and deaths in four towns of Togo in 1909, and the French extended this initiative, but were never able to apply it to the whole country.) Sometimes people refused to be counted in order to avoid tax; at other times party politicians inflated figures in order to magnify their influence; one head of state observed, when he was asked why the figure of population in the UNO yearbook was larger than that which was being used in his own government departments, that it was advisable to 'put up a good show' for UNO. Even when such factors did not falsify statistics, the difficulty of counting large populations, illiterate and widely dispersed, meant that much was left to guesswork or to the opinions of enumerators, and these could not possibly have experience, for censuses came at rare intervals.

TABLE 10.1   Population in millions

	1940	1950	1960	1970
Gambia	0.19	0.29	0.26	0.33
Portuguese Guinea	0.50	0.51	0.51	0.52
Liberia	0.90	1.00	1.25	1.50
Togo	0.78	1.03	1.44	1.90
Sierra Leone	1.80	1.85	2.45	2.60
Dahomey (Benin)	1.28	1.61	1.70	2.70
Senegal	1.79	2.18	2.70	3.90
Niger	1.80	2.00	2.50	4.00
Guinea	2.06	2.20	2.49	4.00
Ivory Coast	3.98	2.10	2.48	4.90
Voltaic Republic		3.10	3.32	5.40
Mali	3.63	3.20	3.70	5
Ghana	3.23	4.11	6.80	8.50
Nigeria	20	31.10	40	55.10
Total	41.94	56.28	71.80	100.35

TABLE 10.2   Densities of population, 1970 (number of persons per km²)

Nigeria	61	Japan	283
Ghana	38	Britain	228
Dahomey	25	India	168
Senegal	20	France	94
Guinea	16	China	80
Ivory Coast	14	United States	22
Mali	4	USSR	11
Niger	3	Brazil	11
Voltaic Republic	20		

SOURCE: World Bank, *Trends in Developing Countries*, 1973.

However there is no doubt that about 1940 the population began to expand very rapidly, and that in thirty years it increased by about 150 per cent. The rate of growth in the area as a whole was higher than 2 per cent per annum. By way of comparison, in the decade 1960 to 1970 Britain's rate of growth was 0.6 per cent; in France and Japan population increased by 1 per cent per annum; in China the figure was 2 per cent, in India 2.3, and in Mexico 3.5. Table 10.2 gives the densities of population in West African countries in 1970. Remember that in 1970 the population was less than half as 'dense'! Figures for some other parts of the world are added for the sake of comparison. About half the people dwelt in the broad band of rolling savannah, dry for at least half the year, which lies between the parallels 10° and 17°, and which is far from the sea, save where it comes to the coast at Dakar. Nigeria recorded much higher density than any other West African country, due to the existence of several large towns, including Ibadan, Lagos, and Kano, and to concentrations of agricultural populations in the forest country of south-eastern Nigeria and in the Kano region, where intensive farming had long been practised with the assistance of manure.

The outstanding fact of the period 1940 to 1970 is, that the population increased by two-and-a-half times. This demographic explosion was new, unexpected, and to many observers astonishing.

It is hardly necessary to say that the principal factor supporting the increase of population was a great expansion of food supply. It is always difficult to express in figures what is happening about the production of food for local markets in Africa, but a serious study has been made of what happened in French territories between 1947 and 1954 (by Marcel Capet) and it reached the conclusion that production of the principal foods went up by about 50 per cent.

Once the conquest was complete, the colonial powers established secure peace. A man could drive a herd of beasts from Kano to Accra and fear no foe; a produce dealer could set out with 20,000 shillings in the back of his car, and never doubt that they would be safe. In such conditions farmers had confidence to plant in the knowledge that, if Allah granted, they would reap. Crops and cattle would not be stolen. The improvement of communications brought wide areas into the cash economy for the first time. The peasants responded in the main by traditional methods, and the hoe was still the principal tool for turning the soil; though some credit must be given to the colonial agricultural departments which encouraged ploughs, draft oxen, manure fertilisers, crop rotation, irrigation and catchment dams, new crops, and traps and poisons for vermin.

Under the systems of agriculture established in most parts of West Africa, an annual period of food shortage was normal. It came in the weeks before the first of the new harvest was ready, because the food stored from the previous harvest hardly ever lasted through plentifully until the next one was reaped. It needed no more than a slight misfortune to convert the normal temporary shortage into a serious famine. Either the rains failed, or they fell too copiously and washed away the stored food, or vermin (any size from elephants to termites) did more damage than usual. In such circumstances many people died and this was one factor which restrained the growth of population. In the last period of colonial rule, the governments distributed grain when famines occurred. The improvement of communications and especially the introduction of motor vehicles facilitated famine relief. This helped to spark off the population explosion.

In those areas which were most prone to temporary scarcities, every village was made to plant a special crop as a famine reserve; often it was manioc (cassava), which was not a favourite food but which would survive underground through very dry conditions. In order to speed up the harvest, people were persuaded to plant crops like sweet potatoes or feterita millet, which would provide food (once the rain had fallen) sooner than the traditional grains. Locusts, a plague which from time to time had spread famine through the continent, were brought under control, and after the great breakout of the migratory locust from its endemic home in the Niger marshes in 1933–34 that plague was not seen again.

In some parts of West Africa people lived on starchy food but were short of protein, and some of them, especially children, suffered from deficiency diseases. Peace and communications enabled cattle to be driven or railed from the northern savannahs to these areas.

However, although there was more local food, it did not satisfy the hunger of the growing population, and a great deal of food was imported. In 1953 (to take that year as an example) the British colonies imported food as follows:

	Gambia	Gold Coast	Sierra Leone	Nigeria
$ million	2.14	38.24	5.39	38.85

Between 1950 and 1960 Nigeria's imports of sugar increased five-fold, and the imports of fish increased ten-fold.

Water supplies improved. This was the first priority in Nigeria's ten-year plan of 1946 to 1956. In earlier times the women of the villages had sometimes been obliged, at the end of the dry season, to walk miles for water, carrying it in pots on their heads. With year-round wells near by, the strain on women was somewhat relieved. Purer water reduced the incidence of bilharzia and other waterborne diseases.

In certain respects the health problems of rural Africa were as serious in 1970 as in 1940, and particularly this was true of malaria. In townships, on the other hand, mosquito control was already efficient in

1940, and improved through the following two decades. Leprosy was a serious scourge at the beginning of the period; in Nigeria for example the incidence was 16 per thousand. This disease was energetically tackled, and much credit is due to the British Empire Leprosy Relief Association. Sufferers were concentrated into settlements where they were provided with work and wages, and the discovery of sulphone drugs greatly improved the situation. The use of DDT insecticides reduced the danger of plague. The incidence of sleeping sickness in Nigeria was reduced by clearing vegetation to prevent the tsetse flies from breeding, and by settlement schemes whereby people were brought into healthy locations where the density of population was sufficient to keep the bush (with its deadly tsetses) from encroaching. In Gold Coast after ten years of anti-tsetse measures from 1946 to 1956 human trypanosomiasis had ceased to claim many victims. Smallpox was checked by a certain amount of vaccination but no country of the area achieved universal vaccination. Tuberculosis yielded to sulpho-namide drugs though many sufferers failed to take advantage of the treatment because they did not take the correct dose, or they stopped too soon. The campaigns against yaws on the other hand generally secured co-operation from the patients, and they were sometimes a substantial proportion of the population. In 1954 for instance the World Health Organisation examined 250,000 people in Nigeria and 117,150 of them had signs of yaws. An attractive medal was awarded after the first inoculation, to be worn on a cord round the neck; and it was exchanged for another disc at each subsequent treatment. Yellow fever used to occur in epidemics, and an outbreak in the eastern region of Nigeria killed 600 people in 1951; but thanks to the Yellow Fever Research Institute at Yaba in Nigeria and to the Institut Pasteur at Dakar much was found out about yellow fever and prophylactic measures were developed. In all these ways improvements in the prevention and treatment of sickness enabled more people to survive; but probably the work of the maternity centres was even more important. Christian missionaries provided many such centres and their influence spread far beyond the women who visited the centres to have their babies. They disseminated the knowledge of how to manage the conditions of childbirth and infancy. The spread of the Christian and Islamic religions, both respectful of human life, suppressed practices such as human sacrifice and the killing of twins.

The growth of the population was accompanied by the concentration of people into towns, with all the social problems which were involved. For instance the population of Dakar increased from 94,000 in 1939 to

400,000 in 1960, and of Abidjan from 18,000 to 180,000 in the same period. Freetown's inhabitants increased from 44,000 in 1921 to 128,000 in 1963, and Lagos grew from 99,000 in 1936 to 675,000 in 1962. In 1940 the number of people working for wages was small, but by 1960 it was estimated to be two million in the whole of West Africa. In the first dozen or fifteen years of the period the traditional scarcity of labour for wage employment was still a factor, but from the middle of the decade of the fifties the situation changed to one in which unemployment was a problem in nearly all the towns. The rise in wage levels of the period 1945 to 1955 had encouraged many young people to leave the country and flock to the towns in search of employment. This was most frequently the case with school-leavers who expected to be paid for being literate, but saw no prospect of earning a premium for literacy in farm work.

The rapid growth of population made it difficult to achieve a growth of income per head. Gross national product might increase, but the number of claimants for a share in it also increased. 'Grow more food' campaigns were included in practically every development plan, but it is difficult to identify any place where food production kept pace with the increase in the number of mouths to feed. Saving was harder when each family had more bodies to clothe and nourish, and the expense of school fees was one which African parents eagerly incurred. If population is growing at the rate of 3 per cent per annum, it is said to be necessary to invest 10 per cent or more of the national income in order to maintain the standard of living, to prevent the rising generation from being poorer than its parents.

The expanding population provided a constantly increasing market which stimulated the development of manufactures, and which caused several crops previously exported to be entirely consumed by the local people.

It is difficult to be sure what effect the population explosion had on political development, but there can be little doubt that the increase in the numbers of young people provided massive support for the champions of independence. The increase of population provided proof of vitality which commanded international respect. The impressive growth of the population of Nigeria compelled the world to accept that country as an important power.

11 Prosperity, Depression, and Aid

The war of 1939 to 1945 caused acute shortage of imported goods. For instance stockfish from Norway, which had become a staple food in Eastern Nigeria, was not available. Dutch wax block prints ceased to arrive, and supplies of other textiles were reduced to a fraction of what was required. Shot-gun cartridges and trapping wire, essential for hunters, were very scarce. These conditions of scarcity stimulated a little local production to provide substitutes for imports, but it was inadequate to make good the shortages. The cost of goods landed at African ports increased considerably; but that increase was small, compared with the prices charged by retailers in the markets, where prices were several times as high as they had been before the war. All the governments tried to control prices, and they were able to impose their will to some extent on the importing companies; but no government was able to control prices in the markets. The sale of goods in importers' warehouses to market resellers at controlled prices was therefore like giving away gold. Many of the rural population responded to these conditions by doing without imported goods, and they ceased making the effort which was required to earn enough money to pay the high prices. This attitude hardened as time went on, and in the last years of the war some very low figures were recorded of crops offered for sale.

Unfortunately the shortages did not cease when the war came to an end. The principal manufacturing countries of the world took several years to recover from the war. In Africa the change from scarcity to plenty, when at last it happened, came suddenly; in 1948 in the British colonies, and four years later in the French territories.

Prices of food produced in Africa also increased, and wage-earners in the towns found their position very difficult. Strikes occurred in Nigeria and in Gold Coast in 1941–42, and the period 1945 to 1951 was a time of industrial unrest in most parts of West Africa, with many strikes.

Economists and statisticians were full of gloom. The bitter experiences of the period 1919 to 1939, between the two great wars, made people pessimistic. In addition to economic depression, it was generally

85

supposed that there would be a world shortage of food, and especially of edible fats. As a defence against this peril, the ill-starred groundnut scheme was started in East Africa, and West Africa had two smaller but still ambitious projects for growing groundnuts with mechanical tools, one at Kontagora in Nigeria, and the other at Gonja in Gold Coast.

These forebodings turned out to be wrong. Edible fats were so plentiful that stocks of butter piled up in Europe, and in general economic affairs the period 1950 to 1960 was one of world-wide expansion. West Africa shared in the prosperity, and it was all the more exciting and stimulating because in West Africa the starting point had been so low. A few figures will illustrate the speed and scale of expansion. In Table 11.1 the year 1938 is used as the base year, because

TABLE 11.1 Foreign trade of British West African colonies in millions of US dollars

	1938	1950	1960
Exports	111	473	860
Imports	106	325	946

the figures for 1940 were upset by the war. The figures for the French territories are more difficult to present, because of fluctuations in the value of the currency and changes in the areas for which statistics are available; but they showed the same trend. The major contributor to the growth of exports was agriculture, and since the increase was achieved without any striking improvement of techniques, it must have been due to cultivating more land and applying more labour. Land had been (in most areas) under-used, so the cultivated area could be extended: and the population was increasing rapidly so that more labour was available. As will be seen in Table 11.2, government expenditures increased in Ghana by more than eleven times, and in Nigeria by more than twelve times.

Unfortunately it is not possible to give any figures for gross domestic product nor for changes in personal incomes, because the techniques of working out these figures for African countries had not received any attention at the beginning of the period, and even at the end of it the World Bank, in publishing figures of gross domestic products, gave a warning against placing reliance on them. However, no one who travelled about in West Africa in 1938 and 1960 could have any doubt that the standard of living of people in towns and villages had markedly improved, and since through those years the number of the population

TABLE 11.2   Annual expenditure budgets of governments in millions of US dollars

Nearest available year to	1938	1950	1960	
Gambia	1.18	2.97	4.79	
Ghana	21.4	33.6	241	(1959–60 including development expenditure)
Nigeria	33	196	411	(public expenditure centre and regions)
Sierra Leone	4.1	10.63	36.75	

had greatly increased the total rise in gross domestic product must have been large.

The prosperity of those years was caused by various factors. Perhaps the most important was the advance of technology. The war had greatly accelerated the process of applying science to production and to social welfare, and the leading nations continued the war effort into peacetime by devoting large funds to research and development. Public opinion in North America and Western Europe was determined to have no more unemployment such as there had been in the 1930s, and was prepared to put up with inflation if it was the price that had to be paid for full employment. Governments were resolved that there should be growth, and the teaching of Professor Maynard Keynes about the management of demand guided them in seeking it. The agricultural and mineral products of West Africa were therefore in strong demand, and prices were good.

The terms of trade during this period turned in favour of less developed countries generally, and of West Africa in particular. As shown in Table 11.3, for developing countries the terms of trade were 40 per cent

TABLE 11.3   Terms of trade (Unit value index of exports divided by unit value index of imports: 1950 = 100)

	Developing countries		
Year	Quantity	Value	Terms of trade
1938	94	30	71
1950	100	100	100
1960	142	141	93

SOURCE: World Bank, *Trends in developing countries*, 1973.

better in 1950 than they had been in 1938, and most of the improvement was retained through the decade to 1960, although there was a slight falling-off so that in 1960 the terms of trade were 31 per cent better than in 1938. However in French West Africa farmers and workers did better than the general average for developing countries. The figures in Table 11.4 illustrates this.

TABLE 11.4 Indicators of changes in real incomes, French West Africa, 1949 to 1955 (1949 = 100)

| Year | Terms of trade of farmers | | | | Wage earners unskilled | |
| | Ground-nuts | Cocoa | Coffee | Real wage | Import purchasing power of wages | |
	Senegal	Ivory Coast	Ivory Coast	Dakar	Dakar	Abidjan
1949	100	100	100	100	100	100
1952	105	136	253	106	113	135
1955	144	153	303	127	175	243

SOURCE: Elliot J. Berg, 'Real income trends in West Africa 1939–60' in *Economic transition in Africa*, Melville J. Herskovits and Mitchell Harwitz, eds (Routledge and Kegan Paul, London, 1964) p. 224.

The prices of groundnuts, cocoa, and coffee which form the basis for the figures in the table were higher than world market prices because the French government subsidised the prices which were paid for these crops in Africa. In British colonies on the other hand farmers were receiving prices which were low in relation to the world market, and the next pages will be devoted to explaining how this came about. As a preface to the story, it will be as well to glance back at the events of 1937.

The price of cocoa on the world market is subject to wide fluctuations, and in 1937 it fell to a low level. Producers in Gold Coast were hard hit, and so were the trading companies which bought cocoa in Africa. A group of companies entered into an agreement aimed at imposing some regulation on the trade to meet the adverse conditions. The producers regarded this as a plot to keep prices low, and they organised a hold-up of cocoa, refusing at the same time to buy goods imported by the firms. The government appointed a Commission to examine the situation, and its findings are known as the Nowell Report (1938). It recommended that an organisation should be set up to break the direct link between prices paid to producers and the world market price of cocoa. Soon after, war broke out, and private trading became difficult. There was anxiety lest private companies might be unable to buy the crops, so the

British government (acting through the Ministry of Food) bought all the cocoa, groundnuts, and palm products which were offered for sale (see Chapter 1). After a couple of years, in order to protect the interests of producers, the West African Produce Control Board (WAPCB) was formed, and took the place of the Ministry of Food in buying West African crops and disposing of them. When the war was over, the British government handed over the functions of WAPCB to local boards, namely the Gold Coast Cocoa Marketing Board (1947), the Nigerian Cocoa Marketing Board (1947), the Nigerian Groundnut Marketing Board (1949), the Nigerian Cotton Marketing Board (1949), the Gambia Oilseeds Marketing Board (1949), the Sierra Leone Produce Marketing Board (1949), the Gold Coast Agricultural Produce Marketing Board (1949), and the Nigerian Oil Palm Produce Marketing Board (1950). The Nigerian boards were broken up in 1954 and their functions were handed over to regional boards in the three political divisions into which Nigeria was divided in that year.

The boards had by law the sole right to export produce, and thus they held monopolies. They also held by law the sole right to buy for export the produce under their own control. They exercised this right by granting licences to persons, companies, and co-operative societies to buy on their behalf. As time went on, the licences were progressively restricted to local people or to companies formed by the governments. As a corollary of their monopoly rights, the boards had the power to fix the prices which were paid to producers. They also had extensive powers to control the work of people who set up industries to use raw materials such as cocoa and palm products and groundnuts. In view of all these powers the boards became important organs of government.

The WAPCB fixed the prices which were paid in Africa with a view to curbing inflation. It accumulated the difference between the price which it paid to producers and the price which it received from buyers, and held this sum; it was handed to the local boards when they were formed, and they increased their reserves by continuing to withhold part of the world price from producers. The surpluses of the eight boards had reached the amounts listed in Table 11.5 on the dates shown.

These reserves were sufficient to purchase all the major export crops for a year at the price levels established in recent years. When the local boards were set up, no one foresaw or expected that they would pile up so much money. In setting up the boards, the British government had indicated that it expected them to stabilise prices: 'the intention is that "profit" will be utilized primarily to maintain the maximum possible stability in the price paid to the producer.' To the extent that the boards

TABLE 11.5   Marketing Boards' reserves

	Date	£
Gold Coast Cocoa Marketing Board	30.9.53	77,236,343
Nigerian Cocoa Marketing Board	30.9.53	28,792,458
Nigerian Groundnut Marketing Board	31.10.53	20,153,632
Nigerian Cotton Marketing Board	30.11.53	5,343,710
The Gambia Farmers' Fund	30.9.53	1,822,772
Sierra Leone Produce Marketing Board	31.12.52	3,840,000
Gold Coast Agricultural Produce M.B.	31.12.53	530,055
Nigerian Oil Palm Produce M. Board	31.12.53	24,369,836
		162,088,806

SOURCE: F. J. Pedler, *Economic Geography of West Africa* (Longman, 1955) p. 198.

fulfilled this intention, their action in stabilising prices had the effect of destabilising incomes. For instance, in one year the Nigerian groundnut crop was 130,000 tons and in the next year it was 400,000 tons, due to climatic influences. With the price of groundnuts stabilised by law, the farmers' income varied in these two years by more than 300 per cent. If the board had not interfered with the normal effects of supply and demand, the short supply in the year of 130,000 tons would have raised the price (other things being equal) and the abundant supply in the year of 400,000 tons would have lowered the price (other things being equal). The variation of incomes would then have been less than 300 per cent.

The colonial governments decided that the reserves of the boards should be used not only for stabilising prices, but also for the economic development of the producing industries, and for the benefit of the producers, or at any rate of the people of the producing areas. In 1953 the Gold Coast Cocoa Marketing Board announced that this had become its principal objective; it was spending money on roads, dispensaries, clinics, wells, water-catchment devices, maternity and community centres, and schools. The Nigerian boards in 1956 allocated $22\frac{1}{2}$ per cent of their surpluses to the regional production development boards, and $7\frac{1}{2}$ per cent to research. The boards had great powers to affect the social and economic situation of the country, and by way of illustrating this, the figures of the Gold Coast Cocoa Marketing Board in Table 11.6 may be considered.

A noticeable feature of this table is the limitation of the surplus per

TABLE 11.6　Gold Coast cocoa

	Price per ton paid to seller in Africa	Expenses to fob per ton	Total cost per ton fob	Sales pro-ceeds per ton	Surplus per ton	Total operating surplus for season
		To nearest pound				£'000
1947–8	75	11	86	201	115	24,069
1948–9	121	18	140	137	−3	−134*
1949–50	84	26	110	178	69	18,022
1950–51	131	65	196	268	73	20,109
1951–2	149	86	236	245	10	3,530
1952–3	131	82	213	231	19	6,420

* A loss. The board had to draw on its reserves.

SOURCE: F. J. Pedler, ibid., p. 201.

TABLE 11.7　Gold Coast cocoa: export duty per ton

	£
1947–48	1.799
1948–49	6.129
1949–50	13.836
1950–51	51.074
1951–52	70.010
1952–53	64.750

SOURCE: F. J. Pedler, ibid., p. 202.

ton secured by the board in the 1951–2 season, when the proceeds of sales were remarkably high. The reason was that the export duty on cocoa was increased in that year, so that the government might take a larger part of the surplus. The figures for export duty, which are included in the column for expenses in Table 11.6 are given in Table 11.7.

In 1950–51 there was a change in the method of calculating export duty. The governments of all the British colonies introduced schemes for raising export duty when world prices were high and lowering it when world prices were lower. Cocoa farmers in Ghana lost more than two-fifths of their potential incomes as a result of deductions made by the marketing boards between 1947 and 1961, and Nigerian farmers lost, on the average, more than a quarter of their incomes for the same reason. Thus, the farmers growing the crops received much less than their crops were worth, and paid high taxes. There was a vigorous protest by the Nigerian Farmers' Union in 1953. The withholding of such large sums prevented the standard of living of the farmers from rising as high as it might otherwise have risen. The strength of the local market for consumer goods was thereby diminished, and this may have retarded the development of industry. Producers were subjected to compulsory saving for the benefit of public projects, and were thereby discouraged from making personal savings which might have been invested in improvements of agriculture or in private industry. These factors affected the kind of society which took shape in Africa, restraining the growth of a prosperous peasantry and of a property-owning middle class.

The Nigerian government reversed the policy in 1975, and from that date farmers might hope to receive the full commercial value of their crops (Chapter 26).

There has been much controversy about the boards, but it is certain that both farmers and merchants welcomed the elimination of day-by-day fluctuations in prices. In pre-board times a farmer taking (for example) cotton to market might find that the price had just been reduced from 2 pence per pound to $1\frac{1}{2}$ pence per pound. Away went a quarter of his year's income. He could hardly avoid bitter thoughts, thinking perhaps that the merchants were putting the halfpenny in their pockets. Yet these merchants were middlemen, and had to set their prices in accordance with what they could expect to recover in oversea markets. The removal of one of the principal causes of racial bitterness was a fortunate thing.

Critics of the colonial system are apt to say that the colonial powers promoted the cultivation of crops for export, to the disadvantage of the internal development of the colonies. However, the system of produce control boards, which was a feature of the final phase of British colonial policy, restrained the cultivation of crops for export. Paying low prices reduced the incentive to extend and improve the crops, and gave an advantage to competitors in other countries, where the incentive was greater; while at home it increased the comparative attractiveness of growing crops for the local market. Nevertheless, exports flourished in the decade 1950 to 1960, thanks to the strong demand of a prosperous world; and exports were the leading sector in a process of growth which affected the whole economy. Money received for export crops stimulated demand in the local markets, and the overspill effects benefited growers of food, providers of services, and most of all (as will be shown in the next chapter) local manufacturing enterprises. In West Africa the staple crops for export were all grown by peasant farmers, and therefore the prosperity generated by good prices was widely disseminated; there was no danger that all the gains might be concentrated in small 'islands' of production, as in countries where large plantations had been established.

The technological advances already mentioned were perhaps most apparent in the sphere of communications. Passengers and freight now moved by air; the ships which plied to African ports were larger and faster than before the war; therefore many small ports ceased to have any trade; ships now burned oil instead of coal; motor transport increased enormously, and attracted many African entrepreneurs, who found it very profitable. Four-wheel-drive vehicles (which had not existed before the war) were able to cross country where there were no roads, and made an end of treks on foot and of head porterage. The camels disappeared from the savannah countries and their drivers, the Bussu people, made their living as night-watchmen instead.

While exports were the leading sector in stimulating growth, they were not the only stimulus. The metropolitan countries Britain and France, and the United States in respect of Liberia, adopted new policies of making large sums of money available for investment in Africa. (Details of the British Act of 1940 were given in Chapter 1 and particulars of the French FIDES in Chapter 7.) The effects of international aid are a matter of controversy. It is now widely recognised that what a country does for itself is much more important than any help which it receives from outside. Furthermore much aid has been wasted and some of it has done harm by bolstering governments which were inefficient or corrupt. Aid has probably encouraged some developing countries to adopt unwisely the expensive standards of the more advanced countries. Some critics regard aid as a bond which ties African countries to the wealthy donors and destroys their independence. But these criticisms belong to the phase of disillusion which has set in; they were not heard in 1950, and not much in 1960. The yield of capital input (which is what most aid consists of) is subject to the law of diminishing returns. When a country has received aid of a hundred million dollars, the input of another million passes unnoticed; but when a country had been short of capital for the most urgent requirements for many years, the first million dollars might work marvels; and so they did in Africa, pounds and francs and dollars, in the period when aid first began to flow.

The provision of money under schemes of aid inevitably led to planning. In 1944 the British government, believing that the war would soon end, asked all the colonial governments to prepare plans for development over a period of ten years. Nigeria was among the first colonies to publish its plan; it was drafted on the lines of a military plan of campaign covering intended policy, but which is nevertheless sufficiently flexible to meet changing conditions. The proposed sources of funds are shown in Table 11.8.

TABLE 11.8   Sources of funds for the Nigeria development plan 1946

From the Colonial Development and Welfare Vote	£23,000,000
To be raised by loans, partly internal	8,000,000
From Nigerian revenues	22,000,000
Total	53,000,000

The plan consisted 'largely of extensions to existing departmental activities', but priority was given to supplying water, adequate and pure. The most important provision of the plan was said to be the development of services leading to economic betterment. A board was set up to determine priorities and to allocate resources. This was essentially a policy of creating conditions conducive to development, while leaving the private sector to use the opportunities thus afforded.

The colonial plans of 1946 made no pretence to direct the whole economy. Colonial governments possessed neither the power to restrict the free choice of consumers and producers in the manner that is postulated by plans of that kind, nor the statistical bases for such planning. The earliest studies of national income in tropical Africa became available only in 1948. Furthermore, the colonial governments had neither central banks nor national currencies, so they could not work effectively through the monetary system.

It has been suggested that the plans were blind, in the sense that they did things which were bound to have important consequences, without defining what social objectives were being sought. British colonial governments in 1946 were committed to two policies of considerable social importance: one, that the native authorities should constitute the social framework; and the other, that farmers should receive the full value of their crops. Both these policies, as has been explained, were abandoned during the currency of the plans. The social consequences of using the crop-marketing system to impose forced saving and high taxation on the rural community, and of employing resources thus diverted to subsidise the urban community, were not planned. The native authority policy was abandoned because it became politically impossible to maintain any system that was not consistent with the rapid achievement of independence on the basis of parliamentary democracy. Therefore the ten-year plans were not related to social objectives, but they did provide a frame of action for making government more effective.

In accordance with the terms of the Colonial Development and Welfare Acts Britain spent in West Africa £55,000,000 (approximately $154 million) before the Acts were allowed to lapse in 1970. The Acts were however not the only source of aid from Britain. Considerable sums were invested in West Africa by the Colonial Development Corporation and its successor the Commonwealth Development Corporation, and from 1966 the new aid was given in accordance with the terms of the Overseas Aid Act.

The French Aid programme of 1946 set up a *Fonds d'investissements pour le Développement Economique et Social* (FIDES) which was fed by large contributions from the metropolitan budget and small contributions from African revenues. The original ten-year plan was replaced in 1949 by a series of four-year plans which were frequently revised. Between 1948 and 1952 FIDES distributed the sums to West African countries shown in Table 11.9.

TABLE 11.9   FIDES aid to West African countries 1948–52

Senegal	$140,500,000	
Guinea	78,700,000	
Ivory Coast	109,000,000	Total
Soudan (Mali)	79,400,000	$526,500,000
Upper Volta	44,700,000	
Dahomey	49,000,000	
Niger	25,200,000	

Dollar equivalents are used to avoid the complications of the devaluations of the French and African francs.
SOURCE: L. H. Gann and P. Duignan (eds), *Colonialism in Africa 1870–1960* Volume IV (CUP, 1975): Virginia Thompson and Richard Adloff, 'French Economic Policy in Tropical Africa', p. 132.

About two-thirds of these funds were spent on communications, less than a fifth on increasing production, and the balance on social services. There was much dissatisfaction with the achievements of FIDES, and in 1952 decisions were taken to place its activities on a new footing. It was decided to concentrate on increasing production for African consumers, on projects that promised quick financial returns, and to encourage the investment of more private capital. There was much discussion of social objectives and it revealed a conflict of opinions. Some people wished to concentrate on large enterprises in industry, mines, and hydroelectric dams, while others preferred to foster the growth of the traditional African society by agricultural research and extension work and rural public works. The debate led to a compromise, an attempt to achieve both objects at once. The French government made large sums available to several African countries year by year to enable them to balance their annual budgets. The subsidies for crop prices have already been mentioned.

American aid to oversea countries began with the Marshall Plan (1948–52), a grand design to revive war-stricken Europe. In 1949 President Truman added to that aid programme Point 4, which was to make money available to the poorest countries of the world to save them from 'hunger, misery, and despair'. The quantity and destinations of American aid are indicated by the figures in Table 11.10. In Guinea and Mali the United States came in to 'fill the vacuum' when those countries fell out of agreement with France, in order that they might not feel compelled to rely wholly on the communist countries, Russia and China. West Germany became a substantial donor of aid in 1957.

The year 1958 witnessed the declaration of independence by Guinea, and the USSR, believing that Sekou Touré (president of Guinea) was

TABLE 11.10 American aid in West Africa (1963 as a representative example)

	$m
Dahomey	0.6
Ghana	1.6
Guinea	12.0
Ivory Coast	2.4
Liberia	39.8
Niger	1.2
Mali	3.9
Nigeria	27.4
Senegal	2.1
Sierra Leone	2.5
Togo	0.7
Voltaic Republic	0.5
Total	94.7

SOURCE: T. Geiger and W. Armstrong, *The Development of African Private Enterprise* (National Planning Association, Washington, 1964) p. 110.

completely committed to the communist cause, moved into Guinea energetically with aid and advice. This was the beginning of Russia's commitment to Africa, which subsequently became very important; but Russia's experiment in Guinea turned out differently from what the Russians had expected, and it led to a reappraisal by Russia of her policy in Africa. The facts will be told in a later chapter; here it suffices to say that Sekou Touré resented the interference by the Russians in the affairs of his country, and expelled the Russian ambassador. The result, after a period of reconsideration, was that the Russians decided that their official relations with independent African governments should be separated from the machinery for communist indoctrination and political subversion in Africa, which is directed from communist headquarters in Moscow. Nationalism is suspect to the communists because it engenders exclusive loyalties; nevertheless, the Russians decided to support nationalist movements in Africa, even when these movements rejected the class struggle or when they were classified as 'bourgeois'. The Russians recognised that in Africa it was no good basing their policy on making friends with the proletariat, because the proletariat hardly existed.

The Chinese came to Africa with the Russians at a time when they regarded the Russians as their friends. Yet even then they had a special diplomatic approach to African governments. China first appeared on the African scene when she established diplomatic relations with Egypt after the Bandung conference in 1955. The founding of the Afro-Asian Solidarity Committee in 1957 gave China a channel for conveying the message to Africa that the Chinese and the Africans were essentially people of the same sort, coloured victims of white imperialist aggression. As communist China moved into Africa, establishing diplomatic missions and aid programmes, the Chinese of Formosa came in competition, and a curious chequer-board pattern was established, one African country having the Pekingese and the next the Formosans. Meanwhile the Chinese from Hong Kong established their private enterprises in many African countries. Chinese aid or investment, from whatever part of China, usually involved the employment of large numbers of Chinese; in 1963 there were 4000 Chinese in Guinea, for instance. President Houphouet-Boigny of Ivory Coast became very upset about Chinese penetration, and publicly denounced their methods (1964). By this time delegates to international meetings had grown tired of the Soviet-Chinese quarrel. At the Afro-Asian Peoples' Solidarity Conference in Tanzania, President Nyerere referred to it as a 'second scramble for Africa'. The conflict came into the open at the meeting of the World Peace Council in Stockholm in 1961; and it is of interest to mention that on that occasion the representative of Guinea supported the Chinese against the Russians. The main point on which they quarrelled about Africa was not concerned with doctrine but with America; for Russia was by this time committed to the policy of coexistence, which made it necessary to tolerate the American presence in Africa; while China regarded America as her arch-enemy and wished to exploit every situation in Africa which might embarrass the United States.

In the decade 1960 to 1970 three additional sources of aid became important, namely:

(1) The International Bank for Reconstruction and Development (commonly known as the World Bank) concentrated on loans for transportation and electric power. Its affiliates, the International Finance Corporation (IFC) and International Development Association (IDA), provided funds for infrastructure and industrial development.

(2) The European Development Fund (EDF) was established by the European Economic Community to provide development grants and loans, and it became important for those African countries which entered into association with the European Economic Community.

(3) The United Nations Secretariat Technical Assistance Programme, the United Nations Special Fund, the United Nations Educational, Scientific and Cultural Organisation (UNESCO), the Food and Agriculture Organisation (FAO), the International Labour Organisation (ILO), the United Nations Children's Fund (UNICEF), and the Economic Commission for Africa (ECA) financed and conducted research and surveys, and provided funds, equipment and personnel for technical assistance and training programmes of various kinds.

With all these sources of aid, the governments of West Africa, whether before or after independence, did not find difficulty in financing any projects which could be supported by good arguments on economic or social grounds.

In the decade 1950 to 1960 West Africa, enjoying a decade of peace, had advantage over competitors in south-east Asia, which was troubled by wars and political confusion. In the private sector there was a movement of funds and staffs from south-east Asia to West Africa.

In or near the year 1960 the world's economic climate changed. The inflation which had been accepted as the price of full employment got out of hand. The prices realised by the principal exports of West Africa declined. The World Bank's index figure of the terms of trade for all developing countries which was shown as 93 for 1960 in Table 11.3 fell to 87 in 1962; after which it revived a little and settled at 90 for the years 1968 to 1970. Thus the newly-independent countries had to face difficult conditions.

In this decade 1960 to 1970, five main economic trends may be noted, and they were all interconnected:

(1) Import substitution;
(2) Local consumption of crops previously exported;
(3) Increase in the exploitation of mineral resources;
(4) The development by independent governments of new economic policies;
(5) A general tendency of West African countries to isolate themselves from their neighbours, and to become separate and different.

Import substitution was associated with the increase of manufacturing activity, and may conveniently be left to the next chapter. The local consumption of crops previously exported was most noticeable in respect of palm oil, and this was the result of the increase in the population, of the increased spending power, and of the improvement in internal communications. To a less extent groundnuts, converted into oil and animal feedstuffs, were taken by the local market; and cotton was now spun and woven in local mills. Mining activity revolutionised the economies of Guinea (bauxite) and of Liberia (iron ore) and was important in Senegal and Togo (phosphates) and Niger (uranium): while in Nigeria the production of petroleum opened a tremendous new source of wealth. It is not possible to attribute any of these three trends to the action of the independent governments because they had all commenced before independence, but they were all extremely acceptable to the sovereign governments, and official policies supported and accelerated the trends. In international trade the autonomous governments were much more inclined than the colonial governments had been to adopt a tough line in defence of the prices of their exports. The United Nations Conference on Trade and Development (UNCTAD) set up its secretariat at Geneva in 1965, and this organisation provided a forum in which primary producers joined together in stating their case; but the major successes of primary producers in confronting the international markets (led by OPEC) had to wait for the decade of the seventies.

Some of the independent governments abandoned the open economy policy which had, on the whole, been followed by the colonial governments. They gave protection to local manufacturing industry by means of import duties, import licences, and even (in Nigeria) by banning imports from Japan save for a limited quantity of cloth. It follows that whereas, under colonial regimes, the import and export statistics are an index of the progress of the economy, after independence they are no longer useful for that purpose.

Despite constant declarations in favour of African unity, and/or in favour of economic co-operation between neighbours, in the first decade of independence the countries fell apart in their economic affairs. There were some exceptions, such as the willingness of Ivory Coast to help Mali, and agreements between Togo and Dahomey (Benin). The Economic Commission for Africa, a United Nations organisation with headquarters in Addis Ababa, did its best to bring neighbours together, but during this decade the only result was sweet words. Investors were compelled to treat the area as fourteen separate and isolated markets, and attempts to supply one country from a factory in another usually met with stern refusal. The governments wished to control and direct their economies, and this led them to demand a great deal of information about commercial transactions; and each state had its own special requirements. This caused, in the import and export trades and in manufacturing, an increase in documentation which added appreciably to the cost of goods.

In the 1970s the world economic climate was more favourable for African producers than it had been in the 1960s. Industrial activity in developed countries increased in 1972 and 1973. The effect on the prices of raw materials was dramatic, for in the year between October 1972 and October 1973 average prices of all traded commodities doubled in terms of dollars. In 1973 and 1974 the Organisation of Petroleum Exporting Countries (OPEC) was successful in enforcing a policy which increased the price of petroleum by 400 per cent. The producers of some other primary products attempted to follow the OPEC example, but conditions in other trades were different. Cocoa however rose to more than £2000 a ton: it is interesting to recall that when Nkrumah held his cocoa mountain over the market the price fell below £100 (see p. 134). Even after allowing for devaluation of sterling, it was a good level for producers. The price of coffee also rose high. Vegetable oils and oilseeds were not so buoyant but prices were good.

However, the effect in West African countries varied a good deal. All countries save Nigeria were badly hit by the rise in the cost of petroleum. Their economies depended heavily on this fuel. For several, such as Niger, it was the only source of energy, while even in Ghana, which had electricity from the Volta dam, petroleum was the source of 74 per cent of the energy consumed. Nigeria had the benefit of petroleum, and her cocoa did well, but the groundnut crop suffered from drought and disease, and this traditional leader in the groundnut trade was actually importing groundnuts to provide material for the mills. Other Sahel countries suffered severely from the drought of 1969 to 1973, and short rains in 1977 again caused distress. Ivory Coast had a bonanza with both cocoa and coffee but Ghana failed to take advantage of the high price of cocoa. Crops were small; it was attributed in part to ageing trees and ageing farmers, but enormous quantities were smuggled over the borders to be marketed in Ivory Coast and Togo. This happened because the Ghana currency was officially over valued, and cocoa which in Ghana would fetch only ¢40 for a load of thirty kilograms might be sold beyond the frontiers for prices ranging from ¢200 to ¢400.

The boom was short-lived and in 1975 world economic activity sank to a low level. There was a fragile recovery in the early part of 1976, but before the end of that year the world's level of economic activity turned down again. It was a period of see-saw price movements, for world market prices of the major export crops increased significantly in 1977, and the cocoa price was above £2000 a ton again in 1978. Summing up, it may be said that with the cost of oil and the effects of drought most countries in West Africa had an anxious period: the prosperous exceptions were Nigeria, Ivory Coast, Togo, and the Gambia.

12 Manufacturing Industry

At the beginning of the twentieth century the manufacturers of Britain looked upon the British Empire as part of their 'natural market'. However, in the second and third decades of the century it became impossible to maintain this position, and companies found it necessary to establish factories in Canada, Australia, and South Africa. In the 1930s a similar position arose in India, for although the government of India was at that time still run by British civil servants, it took energetic steps to advance what it conceived as the interests of India, and manufacturers were left in no doubt that, if they wished to retain a share of the Indian market, they should develop industrial activities in India, should train Indian managers, and should enter into partnership with local shareholders. Thus before the beginning of the period with which this book is concerned the principal industrial companies of Britain had become accustomed to dealing with the problems of manufacturing in distant parts of the world.

In 1941 the Colonial Office appointed a committee on post-war planning for the colonies with Lord Hailey as chairman. Among the subjects which he listed for study was the possibility of developing industries in West Africa. He communicated with the United Africa Company, and the board of that company resolved (September 1941) that 'if such development were contemplated, it was obviously in the interests of the company that it should take its full share'. Studies were put in hand by the company and in 1944 conversations were opened with the government of Nigeria with a view to undertaking five projects in that country, namely:

(1) mills for crushing oilseeds, extracting edible oils, and making nutritionally valuable products;
(2) a brewery;
(3) a spinning and weaving mill for cotton cloth;
(4) a plywood factory;
(5) a meat industry.

As soon as peace came the company went ahead in Nigeria with the manufacture of plywood and veneers, and of beer. The 'nutritionally valuable products' and the meat industry came to fruition some years later. The spinning and weaving project on the other hand ran into difficulties, which are worth noting because they illustrate some important points. Although at first sight it looked obvious that spinning and weaving should be undertaken in a country which had both raw cotton and a market for the product, yet a study of the subject revealed that the cloth spun and woven in Africa would cost more than the prices charged for cloth exported to Africa from Asia or from eastern Europe. Furthermore there were complications about the raw material. Grey-cloth for Africa was made out of cheap cotton, but the government in Nigeria had been at great pains to ensure that the farmers grew a high quality with a long staple, in order that they might secure the advantage of a high price in the world market. The government and the company therefore agreed that spinning and weaving were not practical propositions, and the company turned its attention to the idea of printing cotton cloth imported into Nigeria. The plans were well advanced when the company was informed by the government of Nigeria 'that if the company's projected textile factory resulted in any appreciable diminution in the yield of import duties on textiles, the factory's products would be made liable to an equivalent excise duty' (1946). The company felt that it had been badly treated, and the project was cancelled. It was nine years before the United Africa Company was again concerned with manufacturing textiles in Nigeria, and by then other firms were already established and the attitude of the government had changed considerably. The speed with which local industry replaced the imported product is shown by the decline of imports of foreign greycloth into Nigeria from 33,800,000 yards in 1953 to 6,630,000 yards in 1960.

It is easy to suppose that it must be an economic proposition to provide manufacturing processes to treat a raw material near the place where it grows, but that is not always the case. A groundnut for instance provides the manufacturer with oil, glycerine, and cattle cake. If these things are produced in Africa, it is expensive and technically difficult to convey them in prime condition to Europe; whereas the groundnut is an ideal traveller, and moves in perfect condition at low cost. (The investment in groundnut oil mills in Senegal in 1941–42 was due to temporary causes arising from the war, as explained in Chapter 6.) In making chocolate out of cocoa beans there are advantages in working in a cool climate. There are materials however which lend themselves to treatment in Africa. The transport factor provides strong reasons for turning logs into veneers and plywood in Africa on the edge of the forest; consequently the timber industry was a leader in processing raw material in Africa.

The factor that provided the impulse for industrialisation on a large scale was not attributable to Africa's raw materials, but to the growth of its purchasing power. In the previous chapter attention has been called to the prosperity of the decade 1950 to 1960. The value of imports multiplied by three. The growth of the market was such that of many manufactured articles enough could be sold to keep a factory at work. As soon as that position was reached, it became certain, in a free economy, that some enterpriser would start a factory sooner or later. This does not mean, of course, that at the first moment when the economic quantity for local manufacture has been reached, the enterpriser pops up and begins work; but it does mean that large importers turn their thoughts to the question whether they wish to remain in the trade; for if they do, they will be well advised to set up local manufacture before a competitor takes advantage of the situation. From 1954 onwards the leading companies which possessed import businesses in Nigeria, Gold Coast (Ghana), and Ivory Coast were studying the position and deciding what industries they would choose for investment. Other West African countries had to wait longer, for they were too small or too poor to attract interest at that stage.

Thus the commercial companies became pioneers of industrialisation, but soon many others were in the game. Powerful manufacturers who had previously depended on the commercial companies as their intermediaries decided to go to Africa and supply the market direct. Concerns displaced from Indo-China and Algeria arrived with capital and skills. Chinese investors from Hong Kong set up industries. The Lebanese community established in West Africa sought in industrial development the means of rendering their continued presence acceptable. Public works contracting firms started subsidiaries to make furniture, ceramic tiles, or prestressed concrete units. Makers of machinery in Europe entered into various arrangements for setting up new factories, with the primary object of selling the equipment which they made in Europe. Then there were adventurers, men whose experience of manufacturing was sometimes a little sketchy, who believed that they could secure a privileged position in a new industry if they offered a share to a politician. While all these varieties of expatriate enterprise were at work Africans too were starting industrial enterprises – bakeries, laundries, bicycle-assembly, singlets, travel goods, and enamelware, to mention but a few examples. Table 12.1

TABLE 12.1 Nigeria: increase of manufacturing industry in the decade 1950 to 1960 (gross product of manufacturing in constant 1957 prices, £'000)

	1950	1960	% increase
Total	3,129.3	15,650.0	398
Bakeries	19.0	316.0	1,550
Oil milling	363.6	2,610.0	618
Beer and soft drinks	257.9	2,800.0	911
Tobacco	1,395.8	2,190.0	57
Textiles	4.5	613.0	1,350

SOURCE: Federal Office of Statistics, Lagos, *Annual Abstracts*.

shows how quickly manufacturing industry increased in Nigeria in the decade 1950 to 1960.

Thus, by the time that independent governments took control, industrial development for 'import substitution' was beginning. It was immensely welcome to the independent governments. Many of the men who led the independence movements were convinced that manufacturing industry was the basis of the strength of Europe and America, and that its absence was a principal cause of the poverty of Africa. Furthermore, it was widely believed that the absence of industry from Africa was due to the policies of the colonial powers, and if that were true, then of course the end of colonialism ought to be the beginning of industrialisation. There followed a political effort to create manufacturing industries.

Some governments contracted for factories to be built, and created official corporations to manage them. Ghana had several of these, a steel works, a packaging factory, a meat cannery, a printing press, a cocoa processing works, and a number of others. A notable example was the packaging factory at Jebba in Nigeria; while in countries where Soviet influence was strong (principally Guinea and Mali) the governments acquired manufacturing plants from eastern Europe. On the whole it proved difficult to find suitable managers for these places.

Another method, widely followed, was to set up a partnership in which the government held shares, and in which an experienced manufacturer of international standing also invested. Sometimes the government insisted on having 51 per cent but in many cases the government was happy with a minority shareholding. Whatever the size of the shareholding, if a government is determined to direct a company to take certain action, it has the power to do so.

The willingness of independent governments to provide tariff protection for new industries was remarkable. The fact that consumers would have to pay high prices, and that their standard of living must consequently fall, did not seem to be taken into account. The years 1960 to 1970 therefore in most countries of the region witnessed the imposition of import duties on many consumer goods. Systems of import licensing were also used to protect local industry, and these systems sometimes amounted to an embargo on imported supplies.

Most countries enacted laws which conferred special benefits on 'pioneer industries'. The original idea was to encourage an investor to start something new. However, the pioneer industry arrangements led to some curious situations. In some countries more than one firm was granted pioneer status for the same trade. Sometimes it turned out that the pioneer shut up and departed when his period of privilege was over. Discerning investors tended to take the view that if a market was not worth entering on competitive terms, it was not worth entering at all; to these, pioneer status might provide a welcome bonus, but could not be a determining inducement.

The provision of industrial estates with facilities such as roads, drains, water, electricity, and accommodation for workers was a major inducement to manufacturers. Among the most impressive of such estates were the new town of Tema in Ghana, the industrial zone on the seaward side of Abidjan, and Trans-Amadi at Port Harcourt in Nigeria.

Much was heard about guarantees against nationalisation, and understandably these were strongly voiced in countries which proclaimed faith in socialism, while at the same time wishing to encourage free-enterprise investors from abroad.

Some governments asked investors to 'plough back' a percentage of their profits by investing in industry, and encouraged them to do so by tax concessions, and by permitting the repatriation to the investor's home country of the balance of the profits. Especially in Ivory Coast this scheme provided stimulus for further industrial investment.

It seems doubtful whether any West African government, during the period under review, gave serious thought to the question whether to place the weight of its influence in favour of capital-intensive industry or in favour of labour-intensive industry. Some industrial operations have to be capital-intensive anyway, but over a wide range of others it is possible to adjust the proportions in which capital and labour are mixed. Cardboard packages, for instance, can be folded either by men or by machines. There was a tendency for African governments to expect the most advanced technological methods of operation, and to object to labour-intensive methods on the ground that they were old-fashioned, and that Africa was being 'fobbed-off' with second-rate machinery which the industrial west had thrown aside. Yet the problem of urban unemployment became serious as explained in Chapter 11.

Under these conditions the large countries, which provided attractive markets, experienced rapid increase of industrial production. In Nigeria, taking 1963 as the base year, the index of manufacturing production increased from 100 to 250.2 in 1970 – and this in spite of the elimination of industries at Onitsha, Aba, and Trans-Amadi as a consequence of the civil war. Meanwhile in the smallest countries hardly anything had happened. President Hamadi Diori of the Niger Republic complained of this situation, and urged his powerful neighbours to let Niger have her share; but progress along that line would have to wait for another decade.

Concomitant with the growth of the market was the growth of 'marketing'; that is to say, of advertising in all its forms, of sales promotions, and of organisations specialising in the storage and distribution of goods. The beginning of these processes was noticed before there was much import substitution; it happened as soon as the market became important to large foreign manufacturers. As soon as import substitution began, marketing and sales promotion became vital; for the product of a local factory has to be sold for 52 weeks of the year. The import merchant could cease to order supplies if he found that sales were poor, but a local factory simply must sell and go on selling.

High norms of production could be expected from West African workers. There were factors which contributed to this which may have been temporary. When a new factory was started, the managers (if they knew their business) selected the staff by means of aptitude tests and medical examinations. The numerous urban unemployed supplied plenty of applicants. As a result, factory staffs were young, fit, and apt. In a number of factories piece rates were set at norms which were greatly exceeded by many workers. It must not be supposed however that West Africa was a reservoir of cheap labour for industry. The wage rates which were established in the urban centres might look low when compared with the incomes of workers in the United States or in some parts of Europe, but they were high in comparison with some parts of Asia. Furthermore, social costs were comparatively high for the factory in West Africa. Factory clinics with professional attendance were expected, and maternity leave loomed large in the cost accounts.

PART III

THE INDEPENDENT COUNTRIES

13 Liberia

A chapter will be devoted to each independent country, and they will come in chronological order, according to the date on which independence began. The first is therefore Liberia, which was recognised as an independent state in 1847. According to its constitution, the purpose of the state was 'to provide a home for the dispersed and oppressed Children of Africa, and to regenerate and enlighten this benighted Continent'. In area the country is about half as large as Ghana, but more than $1\frac{1}{2}$ times the size of Sierra Leone. In 1940 it was difficult to know how large the population was, because no census had been taken, and in providing estimates or statistical publications the Liberian authorities may have been influenced by considerations of prestige. The true figure was probably rather less than one million people.

The Afro-Americans, descendants of the repatriated slaves who had founded Liberia, lived in the coastal strip. Estimates of their numbers varied from 12,000 to 20,000. They were a zealous Christian community; they spoke English; and they used United States money. By 1940 a number of indigenous Africans had come to live in the coastal towns with the Afro-Americans. If such Africans established a home in a town, or if they could read and write English, they were recognised as 'civilised men'. They were then permitted to vote in the elections, and they became subject to the courts in which Afro-American judges presided, whereas 'uncivilised' Africans were justiciable in the courts of their chiefs.

The inland areas were known as hinterland, and were organised under four Liberian provincial commissioners. The inhabitants of the hinterland, and of some parts of the coast, were indigenous Africans of the Kru, Bassa, Grebo, Mandingo, Gissi, and Kpwesi tribes. Despite the willingness of the Americo-Liberians to accept indigenous Africans if they became 'civilised', up to 1940 they had been more concerned to keep the hinterlanders in order than to take them into partnership. Inevitably the 'civilised' feared the 'uncivilised'. There was much hostile feeling between the two ethnic groups.

Liberia in 1940 was still a poor country, but in the years 1926 to 1940 its economic position had improved, thanks to the activities of the Firestone Company. Firestone leased 100,000 acres for 99 years for the purpose of planting rubber. By 140 their enterprise was already well established, but development was still proceeding. The business grew until it employed 25,000 people. The employer provided living quarters and amenities on a family basis, so that the labour force was stabilised. Firestone distributed planting material to Liberian landowners, encouraging them to make their own plantations, and undertaking to process and market their latex. The rubber produced on these locally owned plantations increased in quantity until in 1960 it exceeded the quantity produced by Firestone. The company introduced an improved type of oil palm, which they cultivated in order to augment the food supply for their workers, and they experimented with fruits and livestock. In the absence of public utilities, the company installed an electric generator and established telephone communication between the estate, the port of Monrovia, and the aerodrome – also built by the company. It operated a bank and built two hospitals and seven schools.

In the nineteen-thirties Liberia had suffered a severe financial crisis. America had come to the rescue, and as part of the rescue operation Liberia accepted an American financial adviser and an American auditor. The financial adviser was associated in the preparation of the estimates of revenue and expenditure and he attended meetings of the cabinet when financial matters were considered. The auditor, with a small staff who were also American, scrutinised every order for payment before any cash was released, and disallowed any order which was not within the terms of the approved estimates. This system was in force in 1940 and continued for some years.

The year 1942 may be regarded as the opening of the modern era in Liberia – an era of rapid economic expansion and of political consolidation. In that year President Franklin D. Roosevelt of the United States visited Liberia, and a treaty was concluded under which Liberia provided miitary facilities for the United States in their war against Germany and Japan. The United States army and navy developed important transit facilities with airfields, and the spin-off in economic stimulus for Liberia was very valuable. Furthermore it shook the Liberians out of encrusted attitudes and enabled them to appreciate that the policy which they had followed towards the hinterland did not seem appropriate in a free world that was at war against racism.

Fortunately the moment produced the man. A new president had to be elected in 1943 and the True Whig Party – the only party that counted – chose William Tubman. He continued as president (being re-elected from time to time) until 1971.

As President Tubman was being installed he looked out upon a scene such as Monrovia had never known; for the Americans were building a deep-water port, to replace the old open roadstead where ships had anchored to communicate with the shore by means of small boats. The American work was carried out by the largest varieties of earth-moving equipment, and the drivers and mechanics expected accommodation and amenities which were lavishly and speedily provided.

Tubman proclaimed two new policies. First, the Open Door Policy: foreign enterprise was welcome. The experience of Firestone had convinced him that it was a good thing. Second, the National Unification Policy: Americo-Liberians and hinterlanders were to become one people. Both these policies were pursued by Tubman through 27 years of rule with outstanding success.

Among the earliest enterprisers who took advantage of the Open Door were the professional philatelists. They persuaded the Liberian post office to allow them to design and print for Liberia attractive postage stamps, which were sold to collectors throughout the world, earning revenue for the Liberian government. Many other countries followed this example in later years.

The operators of convenience flag ships came to Monrovia. Liberia, as a sovereign state, was entitled under international law to provide certificates of registry for merchant ships. The flag operators suggested to the Liberian government that they should provide certificates at lower fees than the leading maritime countries, under conditions acceptable to the shipowners. In a short time Liberia had an enormous mercantile marine, owned by companies of many nations, but all registered at Monrovia (though few of the vessels ever went there). The revenues were most attractive. By 1970 more ships were registered in Liberia than in any other country, and her mercantile marine comprised 14 per cent of the total world tonnage.

During the war the head of the American Lend/Lease Administration was Ed Stettinius, and after the war he devoted himself to developing Liberia. He formed the Liberia Company. The first flush of optimism was followed by disappointments, and unfortunately Stettinius died; but a cocoa plantation survived to commemorate his enterprise.

Between 1944 and 1946 a number of study groups visited Liberia from the United States to identify what help America might give in public health, economics, education, geology, and agriculture. The health mission found that 30 per cent of the population suffered from malaria and that sleeping sickness was prevalent over wide areas. There were only six physicians in the whole country. The only hospital was one which Firestone had completed. Money was raised, partly from government and partly from private sources, and was entrused to a body described as the Americo-Liberian Foundation. It aimed at providing a physician in every administrative district and clinics sufficient to cover the country at distances 30 miles apart. A school was established for nurses, and it was soon expanded to train medical, sanitary, and dental personnel; it became known as the Tubman National Institute for Medical and Applied Arts. With generous financial help from Harvey J. Firestone Junior a Liberian Institute of the American Foundation for Tropical Medicine was opened in 1952. By 1955 there were 57 physicians, 14 hospitals, 58 clinics, eight leprosaria, and a sleeping sickness team. The development of the health service was in line with Tubman's National Unification Policy because it was concerned with all the people, and not only with a 'civilised' few.

In 1948, pursuing his Open Door Policy, Tubman provided a large area adjacent to the port of Monrovia to be a free port. Businessmen could hold goods there without paying Liberian customs duty. There was space for warehouses, workshops, and factories. Taking advantage of the free port a road transport operator established a service between Monrovia and the Macenta area of Guinea, which at that time was still a French possession. It was only 200 miles from Macenta to Monrovia, and the Liberians had built a good road to the border. The route to the sea through Guinea involved 125 miles of bad road to the railway at Kankan, and then 400 miles of slow and expensive rail transport to Conakry, which as a port was inferior to the new quays and cranes of Monrovia.

The building of roads was financed by loans from the Export-Import Bank at Washington, five million dollars in 1951 and $15,000,000 in 1955. In 1950 a General Agreement for Technical Assistance and Co-operation was concluded with the United States. A five-year programme was drawn up, envisaging expenditure of $35½ million. The Liberian government pledged 20 per cent of its annual revenue, and the balance came from American sources. The greater part of the funds were devoted to roads and other communications, but there was a hydroelectric generator on the Saint Paul river to provide current for Monrovia. When the programme was concluded in 1955 the Export-Import Bank provided a loan of $15 million for the construction of more roads. Harbours were built at Cape Palmas, Harper, and Greenville. The effect of all this activity may be judged from the following statistic.

After the financial crisis of the thirties an international committee had expressed the hope that, with good management, the revenue of the country might rise to $650,000 a year. In 1953 revenue exceeded $10,000,000! What is more, all floating debts had been paid off. Under the terms of the agreements with the United States, this entitled the Liberian government to dispense with the American financial adviser and with the American auditor. Those gentlemen therefore departed, with mutual expressions of esteem, for against all probability they had made themselves well liked. In 1959 revenue was $25,000,000 and in 1967 the budget balanced at $50,000,000.

The National Unification Policy began with an amendment of the constitution in 1944. For the first time the indigenous people were given representation in the House of Representatives: six members out of 39: not generous, but a beginning. They did not however receive even one place in the senate, the upper chamber of ten members.

An important new departure in the political life of Liberia came in 1950 when Didwo Tweh organised the Reformation Party to speak for the interests of the Kru people. In a sense it was a challenge to the National Unification Policy, this attempt to enter politics on an ethnic basis; but it might also be regarded as a concomitant of that policy, since it signified the entry of indigenous people into Liberian politics. Tubman replied with a restatement of his views on National Unification. Two years later (1952) indigenous people were able for the first time to exercise the franchise in a presidential election. Didwo Tweh offered himself as a candidate for the presidency and after his defeat he lodged a complaint with the United Nations alleging unfair electoral practices. This attempt to seek outside support in a Liberian quarrel was more than Tubman was prepared to put up with. Tweh was charged with sedition and treason and fled from the country. He lived in exile in Freetown but in 1960 his health was failing and Tubman allowed him to come back home.

Tubman showed foresight with his Unification Policy, for the indigenous people could not fail to be influenced by the upsurge of nationalism, and if the Amerco-Liberians had continued to treat them as a subject race Liberia might have gone the same way as her neighbour Sierra Leone, where the indigenous people took control of the government, compelling the Creoles (who had roots similar to the Americo-Liberians as repatriated Africans) to accept the position of a small minority. However, the Creoles did not have anything like the True Whig Party of Liberia, which managed patronage on behalf of the government. The party decided who should have office, whether in

politics, judiciary, civil service, or army; who should receive scholarships or travel to international conferences; who should 'represent'
foreign companies which invested in Liberia, who should have leases for
land at favourable rents, or legal monopolies over certain commerical
enterprises. Every employed person who was a member of the True
Whig Party (including all civil servants) contributed one month's salary
each year to the party fund. The opportunities for indigenous people to
share in any aspect of public life were therefore controlled by the True
Whig Party, and depended upon the acceptance by the indigene of the
True Whig Party's position. The country was prosperous and the civil
service was expanding so that there were ample opportunities of
extending the net of patronage. However, the creation of a new
relationship between the Americo-Liberians and the indigenes did not
depend simply on jobs and favours. President Tubman frequently
visited the interior and made himself accessible to all. When there were
disputes between chiefdoms or between important persons in the
hinterland, he personally settled the contentious matters, showing
respect for tribal customs. He became immensely popular and rose
above the position of being the head of the Afro-Americans to be a
national leader.

It was the practice of the True Whig Party to try to neutralise
opposition groups by persuading their leaders to come into the
patronage net. Anyone who declined such favours and persisted in
opposition found many difficulties in his way. In spite of everything, an
· opposition party appeared under the title 'Reformation and Independent True Whig Party'; but in 1955 the legislature outlawed it,
alleging that it had engaged in 'dangerous, unpatriotic, unconstitutional, illegal, and conscienceless acts'.

In 1940 the number of children attending school was less than 20,000.
In 1970 however 134,000 children were in school. There were in 1970
1084 schools, of which two-thirds were provided by the government and
the rest belonged to the missions. Liberia college was raised in 1950 to
the status of a university.

There was a great deal of iron ore in Liberia but it had not been mined
because until the mid-twentieth century steelmakers had been able to
buy enough ore near at hand, and the price of ore was not high enough
to stand the long voyage from Liberia to the steelmaking centres. The
mining company of Sierra Leone had been a pioneer of 'inter-
continental ore', and now it was Liberia's turn. By good fortune an
entrepreneur presented himself whose proposals were acceptable to the
Liberian government. He was Colonel Christie, who was well known as

a businessman in connection with New York lighterage. He had the backing of the Republic Steel Corporation, one of the largest firms in the business. He suggested to President Tubman that a new form of mining concession should be negotiated, under which the Liberian government would hold 50 per cent of the shares of the mining company, which became known as the Liberia Mining Company. The government then looked to the dividends on its shares as the main source of the revenue which it derived from the undertaking; so the government's revenue depended on the mine's prosperity. The mine was in the Bomi hills, which were connected by railway with the port of Monrovia, where automatic loading gear was provided to ensure the fastest possible turnround for the ore ships. The success of this business was so great that in 1959 Christie formed a second company, the National Iron Ore Company, to mine ore in a deposit near the Mano river. This time he invited local people to subscribe for shares and made it easy for them to do so by accepting payment in instalments; he secured 1600 local shareholders.

Liberia's foreign policy, during her first hundred years, had simply consisted in cultivating the friendship of America and defending her independence against the colonial powers. There was no African policy because there did not exist in any accessible part of the continent any independent state with which Liberia could establish relations. With the independence of Ghana in 1957 and of Guinea in 1958 a new era dawned, and in 1959 Tubman was host to Nkrumah and Touré at Saniquelli, in the interior of Liberia near the frontier with Guinea. It was typical of Tubman's sensitivity that in his first meeting with the two great indigenous African statesmen he chose a venue where they would see Africa, avoiding the American flavour of Monrovia. Ghana and Guinea had recently declared themselves to be founder-members of a Union of African States which all other African states were invited to join. Tubman presented an alternative proposal, namely that an organisation should be set up under the name 'Associated States of Africa'. It would involve a less binding commitment than Nkrumah envisaged. The Saniquelli conference agreed to convene a meeting of African independent states in 1960 to work out a charter and agree the ultimate goal of unity, and they published 'principles' which were to be presented to the meeting as a basis of discussion. These principles included the following;

The organisation's name would be the Community of Independent African states;

Each state or federation of the Community would maintain its identity and constitutional structure;

Acts of states or federations of the Community would be determined 'in relation to essential objectives which are freedom, independence and unity, the African personality as well as the interest of the African peoples';

The Community would set up an economic, a cultural, and a scientific and research council;

The Community would have a flag and an anthem.

This was a success for Tubman and Touré jointly (since they inclined towards a loose association of states developing functional activities) over Nkrumah, who aimed at close political union. The use of the word 'Community' is interesting, since this was the year in which General De Gaulle was endeavouring to give reality to the 'French Community'. This meeting marked the entry of Liberia into the new African diplomacy. In 1960 Tubman visited Guinea and stayed no less than 11 days as Sekou Touré's guest. He made this the occasion for proposing that three entities should be created to help the independent states of West Africa to work together, namely:

(1) an organisation for economic co-operation:
(2) a council for educational and cultural exchanges;
(3) an organisation for health and nutrition.

This was a practical attempt to follow up the 'principles' which emerged from the Saniquelli conference. It may be assumed that Tubman had Touré's goodwill in making these proposals public, but they ran counter to Nkrumah's ambition of bringing all African states into a political union. Nkrumah would not accept any arrangements for functional co-operation as steps towards his ideal; on the contrary, he regarded them as tiresome diversions. The opposition between the two men was to be accentuated.

This was the year of independence for the Congo (Zaire), and the collapse of the government of that country led to civil wars and to military intervention by the United Nations. This placed a strain on the solidarity of the African countries. Kwame Nkrumah laid the Congo's troubles at the door of 'neo-colonialist' influences from America and Europe, and those who shared his view were described as the Casablanca group. Tubman, considering the advantages which his country was receiving from western governments, companies, and philanthropists, was not inclined to regard them as enemies of Africa.

He emerged as the leader of the 'Monrovia group', African governments who took a less passionate and more objective view of Congolese
quarrelsomeness and foreign intervention, of western 'neo-colonialists'
and communist infiltrators. In 1963 the two groups came together to
form the Organisation for African Unity, of which Tubman was one of
the founding fathers.

In 1960 Liberia was the first African state to become a member of the
Security Council of the United Nations, and this enhanced Tubman's
standing. Liberia, like several other African countries, contributed a
contingent to the United Nations force in the Congo. However, the
Liberian army had not been trained on the lines of the other
participating contingents. It was a militia of the citizens. The expedition
to the Congo revealed some deficiencies, and the United States were
invited to send a military mission to train the army in modern style.
However, the professionalisation of the force led, all too soon, to a
result that was to become familiar in Africa. The commander of the
Liberian army national guard was arrested in 1963, and accused of a
plot to kill the president and seize the government.

In 1961 two problems raised their heads which the Liberian
government had not previously needed to consider. They were in a way
related and they are both typical of very prosperous countries. The first
was shortage of labour. Thousands of acres of mature rubber trees
could not be tapped for lack of workers. About the same time
applications were received from groups of people of African origin in
the United States and the West Indies, who wished to enter Liberia as
immigrants.

In 1961 President Tubman helped to settle a strike involving more
than 1000 workers, and led by his son Shad Tubman, who was president
of Liberia's congress of industrial organisations. The strike halted
building work on a new executive mansion for the president. Strikers,
demanding a wage increase, marched with placards reading 'We are
human workers, not machines'. The police arrived with a brass band
(better, no doubt, than truncheons or rifles) and escorted the strikers in
procession to Mr Tubman's house, where the president promised
immediate action over the claim. In the following month a general strike
occurred in Monrovia. The government arrested the leaders (who on
this occasion did not include the president's son), declared that the
trouble had been fomented by 'foreign influence', and asked Ghanaian
and Egyptian diplomats to leave the country.

In the sixties a third immense iron ore operation began, led by Swedish
businessmen under the name Lamco. A port was built at Buchanan

costing no less than $45,000,000, and it was connected by 170 miles of rail with Mount Nimba, where the iron was found. It was thought possible that Liberia's share of the profits of this enterprise would double the total revenue of the state. Then yet another group, DELIMCO (Deutsch-Liberische Minen) made a similar agreement to mine iron ore in the Bong hills.

In 1964, just twenty years after he had proclaimed his National Unification Policy, Tubman was able to abolish all differences between the coast counties and the hinterland in respect of political and administrative structure. Liberia was making progress towards becoming a united country.

In 1964 Tubman was re-elected to the presidency yet again, and in his inaugural address he spoke in favour of a free trade area, to consist of Liberia and her three neighbours, Sierra Leone, Guinea, and Ivory Coast.

In 1966 the government adopted a four-year development plan. The year was however troubled by strikes in the Firestone Company and in the Lamco iron ore enterprise. The government responded by abolishing the right to strike, expelling foreign trade union organisations, using force against the strikers, and arresting their leader, James Bass. These actions did not pass unchallenged and the Liberian government had to answer charges brought against it at the International Labour Organisation by two trade union federations. However, the government continued to adopt a strong line against any opposition which it considered dangerous, and in 1968 a certain Henry Farnbulleh was sentenced to imprisonment for twenty years because he had written that Liberia belonged 'to the aborigines and not to these strangers from America'.

In 1968 the budget balanced at $55 million, but it was described as an austerity budget because the country was suffering from inflation and it was necessary to check luxury spending. The year 1969 marked the centenary of the first occasion when the True Whig party took office; President Tubman surprisingly took this opportunity for stating that he favoured a two-party system. He invited any group which could muster 300 supporters to form an opposition party to contest elections. However, the form in which opposition manifested itself was rather different, for in 1970 General George Washington was dismissed from the army and arrested for plotting against the government.

In 1971 Tubman was elected for yet another term as president, but he died before the inauguration could be celebrated. His running-mate as vice-president had been William Tolbert, and in accordance with the terms of the constitution William Tolbert was installed in January 1972 as acting president for a term of four years.

The period 1943 to 1971 will undoubtedly be named, in the history of Liberia, the Tubman era. It witnessed tremendous growth in the economy and general prosperity. On the political side President Tubman and his associates worked hard to build a nation; but while greatly widening the base from which they drew their authority, they left no doubt that they were determined to rule.

In 1973 the assistant defence minister and two lieutenant-colonels were arrested and placed on trial, accused of plotting to assassinate President Tolbert and his brother the minister of finance. In 1976 President Tolbert was re-elected for a term of eight years. He appointed a commission on national unity, to carry the task of nation-building a step further; but he took the opportunity of stating what progress had already been made. He was able to say that the cabinet had a majority of people of indigenous origin, and the same could be said of the legislature and of senior civil servants. He added that there had been so much intermarriage between Americo-Liberians and hinterlanders that it had become difficult to maintain those classifications.

14 Nkrumah's Ghana

The story of Ghana from 1957 to 1966 is largely a biography of Kwame Nkrumah, for after he had won independence he put into practice the motto of Louis XIV of France, 'I am the state'. Nkrumah was inspired by the vision of the African continent liberated and united. He was determined to pursue those ends and he regarded any internal opposition in Ghana as something amounting to treason against the cause of African emancipation. In the interests of freedom for the continent he suppressed freedom in his own country.

Although the declaration of independence in 1957 had taken place among scenes of jubilation in Accra, there was much opposition to Nkrumah in the country. In the recent elections (1956) the parties hostile to Nkrumah had polled 299,116 votes, compared with 398,141 votes cast for Nkrumah's Convention People's Party. At independence the people of Southern Togoland refused to celebrate, and the ceremonies which took place in Kumasi were formal. In the weeks following independence the Ga people of Accra became alarmed at the way the CPP was taking charge of everything in their home town, and they formed the Ga Shifimokpee (Ga Standfast Association).

Nkrumah replied by enacting a law banning organisations which were confined to tribal, racial, and religious groups, and under its terms most of the opposition parties became illegal. The Kumasi City Council (which was controlled by the National Liberation Movement) was suspended and an inquiry was held into the activities of its members. The British regional commissioners departed and were replaced with political appointments. The regional councils, which had been set up at the request of the British government to satisfy British liberals that the views of minorities could be heard, were abolished. A deportation act was passed and Nigerians and Lebanese who had befriended the NLM were expelled. The machinery of suppression was completed in 1958 by the Preventive Detention Act under which the government could put any person in prison without trial.

Under these blows the opposition parties came together to form the United Party (UP) under the leadership of Dr K. A. Busia. Dr Busia was a man whom Nkrumah might well fear as an adversary. He was a member of one of the most distinguished families of Ashanti. He had had a successful career at the university of Oxford, and he was among the first Africans to be appointed to the Colonial Administrative Service. Then he entered academic life as a sociologue. He was among the few African leaders of the 'independence generation' who showed a deep concern about the liberty of individuals. His new party appeared to be gaining support. However, at the end of 1958 many opposition leaders were imprisoned in accordance with the terms of the Preventive Detention Act. Those who remained at liberty had to choose between going into exile or joining the next batch of prisoners, unless they went over to the CPP.

When Ghana became independent Nkrumah was at last able to develop a foreign policy, and this was his main interest. 'When I returned to West Africa in 1947', he wrote in *Africa Must Unite* (1963),

> it was with the intention of using the Gold Coast as a starting-off point for African independence and unity. With the mass movement I was able to build up in the Convention People's Party, the Gold Coast secured its freedom and emerged as the sovereign state of Ghana in 1957. I at once made it clear that there would be no meaning to the national independence of Ghana unless it was linked with the total liberation of the African continent. While our independence celebrations were actually taking place, I called for a conference of all the sovereign states of Africa, to discuss plans for the future of our continent. The Accra Conference of Independent African States met in Accra in April 1958. There were then only eight, namely, Egypt, Ghana, Sudan, Libya, Tunisia, Liberia, Morocco, and Ethiopia.

Of the eight, five were Muslim Arab states whose principal interests and commitments were in the Middle East and in the Mediterranean. The Emperor of Ethiopia and President Tubman of Liberia were surprised and disconcerted to find themselves in such company. It was curious that Nkrumah should have wished to involve these states in the problems of Africa south of the Sahara, for it was obvious (perhaps to everyone except himself) that his personal leadership would never be accepted in that society.

In September 1958 Guinea became independent, and Nkrumah immediately made overtures to its leader Sekou Touré. They declared the two countries to be united. The new entity was to be named the Union of African States, and others were to be invited to join. This was a help to Sekou Touré at a moment when he was in a lonely position, bereft of French aid, on which Guinea had been very dependent. Nkrumah handed him £4,500,000; Nkrumah called it a loan but Touré treated it as a gift.

Before the end of 1958 Nkrumah brought together in Accra the All-African People's Conference. It was attended by delegates of 62 nationalist organisations from 28 African countries. At this meeting Nkrumah came into closer association with people who were working for the independence of their countries, either peacefully or violently; and also with several groups which were concerned with overturning the governments of independent African countries.

In the previous chapter attention was given to the conference at Saniquelli in 1959 and to the antagonism which emerged from it between Tubman of Liberia and Nkrumah of Ghana. Tubman favoured a 'Community of Independent African states' with functional activities in economic, educational, cultural, and medical affairs, and Nkrumah advocated a close political union of African countries.

Towards the end of 1959 trade unionists from many parts of Africa were convened to Accra and the meeting gave birth to the All-African Trade Union Federation. It was, in Nkrumah's plan, a political organisation devoted to mobilising wage-earners in support of nationalist movements. Nkrumah had no use for trade unions as independent champions of the workers; in Ghana he placed the unions sternly under the control of his party. Strikes were not allowed.

Nkrumah was anxious that Togo, Ghana's small neighbour in the east, should not become independent, but should unite with Ghana. In February 1960 he made a speech at a place near the Togo frontier in which he appealed for this, pointing out the ethnic bonds which united people on both sides of the border. The Togo leader, Sylvanus Olympio, refused to listen and his country became independent in April. Nkrumah was disappointed but he believed that if he could talk with Olympio in an informal way he would win him over: so in June of that year, without any warning, he went by car to Lomé (capital of Togo) and called on Olympio. It was a most unusual thing for a prime minister to do. Nkrumah trusted the pull of his personal charm, but he could not win Olympio. The rebuff made him so angry that Ghana broke off diplomatic relations with Togo and closed the frontier.

Nkrumah was sincere in wishing to merge the identity of Ghana with that of Guinea in a union which would provide a nucleus for something larger. Sekou Touré was embarrassed because the French African franc was in use in Guinea, and this made Guinea perforce a member of the franc zone. Touré regarded this as a neo-colonial shackle, and he felt no confidence in the goodwill of the authorities who governed the zone. The obvious solution for Guinea appeared to be, to use the facilities available within the Ghana-Guinea union, namely the Ghana currency and the Bank of Ghana (established 1958). Nkrumah was amazed and offended when Touré announced (1960) that he had withdrawn from the franc zone, and that Guinea would have her own central bank and her own currency – printed in Czechoslovakia! Thus Sekou Touré, who made history by saying 'Non' to De Gaulle, made some more by saying 'Non' to Nkrumah. It was some weeks before Touré could find time to discuss the matter, because he was distracted by a plot to overthrow his government, but at last he received Nkrumah's minister of finance, Gbedemah. The visit ended with a communiqué that Touré would visit Accra 'to examine a number of questions relating to the political and economic union of the two states'. They met from time to time, but Touré always talked without stopping in French, which Nkrumah did not understand. The two men were temperamentally poles apart, Touré didactic and prone to quarrel, Nkrumah pragmatic and sweet-mannered to all. Touré was suspicious and contemptuous of Ghana's membership of the British Commonwealth. Nkrumah could hardly avoid appearing to the patronising, for although Guinea was of about the same area as Ghana, its population was less than half Ghana's, and its economic activity was tiny compared with Ghana's; this is illustrated by the figures of wage-earners as a percentage of the economically active population, 19.9 per cent in Ghana and 2.8 per cent in Guinea (ILO, *African Labour Survey 1958*); hence Ghana's ability to hand over the millions.

When Ghana became a republic in 1960 Nkrumah inserted in the constitution a clause empowering the government to enter into arrangements which might reduce Ghana's sovereign independence in the interests of African unity. The inauguration of the republic in Ghana and the independence of the ex-Belgian Congo happened on the same day. The prime minister of the new Congo state, Patrice Lumumba, had visited Nkrumah in Accra and they were friends. Nkrumah set great hopes on Lumumba, and entered into an agreement with him, which was kept secret at the time, under which Congo was to join the Union of African States, which would have its capital at Kinshasa, capital of Congo; and Nkrumah undertook that at the appropriate time Ghana would leave the British Commonwealth. However, these plans were set back because Congo fell into disorder. The United Nations sent a peace-keeping force, consisting mostly of

African contingents. Ghanaians, army and police, were among the first to arrive, and since they were given the job of restoring order in the capital city, they had an opportunity of proving their worth and they earned golden opinions. Nkrumah's international standing rose to its highest point.

Congo unfortunately sucked Nkrumah into a vortex which did him much harm. He never wavered in his friendship for Lumumba, but Lumumba proved to be inadequate, and Nkrumah was therefore committed to a loser. He devoted to the affairs of Congo a great deal of time which could with advantage have been given to Ghana. As each crisis surged up in Congo, Nkrumah demanded that an African joint command should be established; he addressed the heads of other African states and the secretary-general of the United Nations in very impatient language, and upset nearly all of them.

Towards the end of 1960 the former French Soudan became independent under the name Mali, and very soon Sekou Touré at Conakry was host to Kwame Nkrumah and Modibo Keita, leader of Mali. The three met again in Accra, and declared (1961) that the three countries were united in the Union of African States. They adopted a charter for the Union. It was less than a constitution, for though it declared that aggression against one would be aggression against all, and although it promised co-operation in diplomacy, economic and cultural affairs, and in research, it provided no common institutions. It was hard to breathe reality into a union with Guinea and Mali because they were so far away. But what if Upper Volta could be persuaded to join? Then there would be four contiguous states and Nkrumah's dream would look like coming true. Kwame Nkrumah made a great effort to win Yameogo, the president of the Voltaic Republic (see Chapter 21). For a moment it looked like succeeding, but Houphouet-Boigny, and behind him the influence of France, brought Yameogo back into the framework of the Entente, which could not be reconciled with membership of Nkrumah's Union. Nkrumah did not meet Touré and Keita within the framework of the Union after June 1961. The three countries continued to be members of the United Nations as separate entities, and to conduct their own policies, both internal and external. When the Organisation of African Unity was formed in 1963 Touré made it the occasion to announce the dissolution of the Ghana–Guinea–Mali Union.

However, Guinea and Mali did at all events support Nkrumah in his Congo policy, and they were the only states south of the Sahara which did so. The group met at Casablanca in January 1961 in company with

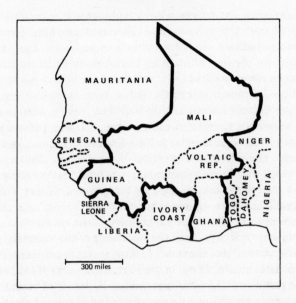

Map 3　Illustrating Kwame Nkrumah's bold bid to create an area of four
contiguous countries for the Union of African States by bringing in
Voltaic Republic

Libya, Egypt, Morocco, and Algeria. Shortly afterwards a different
group of African states assembled at Monrovia (as noted above). No
less than twenty states were there, from which Nkrumah might draw the
melancholy conclusion that the majority of African governments were
more inclined to accept leadership from Tubman than from himself. It
was a humiliation. Unwilling to believe that the cause of failure lay
within himself, he looked for scapegoats and found them in the shape of
'neo-colonialists'. He published (1963) a book in which he wrote that the
USA, Britain, France, West Germany, Israel, Belgium, Netherlands,
and South Africa were neo-colonialist. As his relations with the west
deteriorated his links with Russia and China became closer.

However, the Casablanca and Monrovia groups came together to
form the Organisation of African Unity in 1963, and Nkrumah received
well-deserved acknowledgement as one of the architects of this body.

Nevertheless the African states which adopted views different from
his own continued to be attacked as stooges of the neo-colonialists, and
Nkrumah allowed his dislike to be carried to the length of encouraging
rebel groups in exile. In the case of the Niger Republic he provided

training and arms for people who actually raised a revolt. Nigeria, Togo, Ivory Coast, Upper Volta, and Liberia accused him of interfering in their internal affairs. He spent millions of pounds in East Africa in order to prevent the formation of an East African Federation. In 1965 the summit conference of the OAU was due to be held at Accra, and for its reception Nkrumah commissioned a very expensive conference centre which became known as 'Job 600'; but many governments said that they would not attend a meeting in Accra. It was Tafawa Balewa, prime minister of Nigeria, who helped Kwame Nkrumah out of this predicament. He convened a meeting of the foreign ministers of the OAU, at which the Ghana minister had to submit to proceedings which were like a trial of Ghana, accused by Ivory Coast, Upper Volta, and Niger. Ghana gave an undertaking to cease to harbour dissident movements and to provide special security at the conference: and the foreign minister of Kenya, with the assistance of the secretary-general of the OAU, was to check the state of affairs in Accra before the meeting took place. After all this, 28 out of the 36 members of the OAU attended the meeting, but only 13 were represented by heads of state.

To support an ambitious foreign policy Ghana needed prestige, and Nkrumah therefore invested in expensive projects which were intended to impress foreigners, but which sapped the resources of the country. Examples were the international airline, the airport terminal building, the navy, the expensive diplomatic service with its champagne parties, the stadium, the presidential palace, a steel complex, an atomic reactor, nine bronze statues of himself, and the Kwame Nkrumah tower which was to have had a revolving restaurant on top – but this was still in the planning stage when Nkrumah ceased to rule.

In 1957, when the country became independent, Nkrumah stated that he would construct 'a socialist pattern of society', but at the same time he and his ministers assured investors that they were welcome. Many international companies placed investments in Ghana. Nkrumah frequently attended the opening ceremonies of the new factories. In some of them the government became a partner by subscribing part of the capital. However, in the CPP there were people who were opposed to free enterprise in economic affairs, and they felt that when the republic was declared in 1960 it was time for them to assert their influence. From their point of view the coming of independence in 1957 had made hardly any difference; Ghana had just gone on enjoying prosperity as it had done under the dual regime of 1951 to 1957. In 1960 Nkrumah was absorbed in Congo affairs and for a critical period he was attending the United Nations Assembly in New York. The 'scientific socialists' in the party tried to seize power – not in a violent manner, but operating through the party committees, rallies, schools, and newspapers. A number of senior members of the CPP, who had stood close to Nkrumah since 1949, saw themselves in danger of losing their positions. Ghanaian business people were angry, because it appeared, from a statement made by a minister in parliament, that Ghanaian private businesses were to be suppressed. International investors were frightened, and Nkrumah was made to look foolish in view of all the promises and guarantees which he had held out to them. Returning from New York, he addressed the nation over the radio and tried to satisfy everybody. This experience influenced his future behaviour. On becoming president he had tried to get rid of the detailed work by passing it down to his ministers, but the events of mid-1960 seemed to prove that they could not control the situation. He gave up the effort to decentralise, and submitted to the process by which everything was referred to the top man – an impossible situation in a modern state, and one which has plagued other African countries as well as Ghana. As regards foreign investors, assurances were renewed, and Nkrumah continued to attend their opening ceremonies until shortly before his fall from power. From time to time however he would alarm the free-enterprise sector. For instance on 1 May 1961 he made himself general secretary of the CPP and chairman of its central committee, and this was an occasion for a speech. May Day is of course an emotional day for those who claim to speak for the workers, and Nkrumah informed his audience that they were attending the inauguration of a 'new political revolution'. By the time the world's newspapers and telecasters had treated this statement, it was felt necessary in Accra to summon the press to a conference at which no less than six ministers informed the journalists that Nkrumah had no intention of 'swinging' to Leninism. Even that did not quite steady the boat, and the minister of information, Adamafio, followed up with a statement that the government had no intention of nationalising foreign companies.

In 1963 several of the factories built for Nkrumah were standing idle because no management was available, and he asked a multinational company established in Ghana to take one of them over. When he finally ran out of money, it was to a group of foreign companies that he appealed for help. His relations with the west had therefore become impossible to understand: on the one hand he was attacking the western countries, their governments, companies, even their trade unions, and on the other hand he continued to promote their activities in Ghana and to appeal to them for help.

Nkrumah, in speech and book, constantly declared his belief in the principle of planning; but he was temperamentally unable to keep to any plan. He had immense personal charm and public magnetism, and he had high intelligence fortified by wide reading; but impulse, including an impulsive wish to please his friends, governed his decisions more than reason.

During the period of dual rule from 1951 to 1957, when Nkrumah and his CPP had been in partnership with the British, important advances had been made in education, communications, health, and other spheres; it had been in accordance with a plan which provided public investment at the rate of £G17 million per annum. Early in 1959 Nkrumah launched a second plan, which contemplated public investment of £G68 million per annum: four times as fast. Six hundred factories were to be created, and at the same time vast projects were contemplated in agriculture and the social services. The plan contained little information as to how the resources were to be found. As the years went by, while capital expenditure was running riot, the people were short of food and clothes, and the Bank of Ghana could not provide foreign exchange to pay the import bill. This was obvious by 1964 when the five year plan was supposed to be completed, yet Nkrumah then adopted a third plan which named an even higher rate of investment than the second.

Those parts of the plans which related to education were carried out more consistently and effectively than the others, and in 1961 Ghana became the first country in Africa to introduce compulsory primary education.

For many years one of Nkrumah's closest associates had been Komlo Gbedemah. He had organised the victorious election campaign of 1950/51 when Nkrumah was in prison. Under the 1954 constitution he was minister of finance, and he showed great competence in that position. He gained high international reputation and the great prestige which Ghana and Nkrumah enjoyed were in some measure due to him. In 1961 Nkrumah quarrelled with Gbedemah about practices by which funds were diverted from the public coffers into the hands of the party and even to Nkrumah's personal use. Gbedemah resigned from the ministry of finance and was appointed minister of health. However, the scientific socialist wing of the party did not leave him in peace; he was subjected to outspoken attacks, and felt it wise to leave the country secretly. He continued to live in exile as long as Nkrumah was in power.

Nkrumah must have the credit for the great achievement of the Volta dam. This created the largest man-made lake in the world and generated plentiful electricity. The project had been planned before Nkrumah moved into the seat of power, and it was estimated to cost £231,000,000. It was just the thing for Nkrumah – prestigious, revolutionary, and capable of achievement in a few years. Ghana could provide part of the money, but the balance would have to be raised on loan, and negotiations were opened with the American government, the British government, and the World Bank. The main problem was to find a customer who would buy, at commercial prices, the huge quantity of electric power which the dam would produce. If some great company could be persuaded to make aluminium in Ghana the problem would be solved – for the processes by which bauxite is converted into alumina and then into aluminium consume an enormous amount of electricity. Henry J. Kaiser, head of an American company which produced aluminium, was introduced to Nkrumah as a possible candidate for this role.

In 1958 Kwame Nkrumah visited the United States and talked with President Eisenhower about his hopes for the Volta, and he secured Eisenhower's personal interest. His charm would probably have been sufficient to win the president anyway, but it was necessary for American politicians to take Nkrumah seriously because he had received such an ovation from black Americans. With encouragement from Eisenhower, Kaiser sent a team of engineers who approved the scheme, suggesting several substantial improvements. With this report in his hands Nkrumah decided to set work in motion. He had still to conclude a loan agreement, had still to find a suitable contractor, and had still to agree with someone (who might be Kaiser) to build an alumina smelter; but he was not prepared to suffer the frustration of delay. Without waiting for all those weighty matters to be settled, he declared that if Ghana could not secure loans, she would build the dam with her own resources, and he started preparing approaches to the dam site. He indicated his interest in employing the Italian consortium which was just completing the dam on the Zambesi. Although the method of construction of the Volta dam was to be different from the method by which the Zambesi dam had been made, this Italian group could offer experience of organising a major hydroelectric undertaking in Africa. The loan agreements had not been concluded, but Nkrumah signed a contract with the Italians in February 1961 and asked them to begin. In August the loan agreements with the American and British governments and with the World Bank were completed. The loans covered 50 per cent of the cost, and Ghana was to provide the other half. In September the contractor was at work on the site. In January 1962 there was an impressive ceremony at Akasombo, which was described as the 'official opening of the Volta scheme'. On that same day Nkrumah signed an agreement with Henry Kaiser for the building of an alumina smelter at a cost of £56,000,000. Work on the smelter began about the end of 1964, and Nkrumah himself 'broke the first sod'. His faith and determination had overcome the cautious hesitation and the doubts which had been holding things up.

However, Nkrumah had not secured all that he wanted. He still had no miner to dig Ghana's bauxite. Kaiser's smelter was to treat imported material. It disappointed Nkrumah to find no customer for his ore. It made nonsense of those things which he had written, and would write in future, to the effect that in 'the last stages of capitalism' there was intense competition for all raw materials available in colonial and ex-colonial territories. Still, he accepted Kaiser's offer. As a commercial decision it was undoubtedly the right one. The firm of Kaiser was a first-class company whose word could be relied on. The fact that the bauxite ore would not immediately be developed was disappointing; but if the dam and the smelter could be brought into existence, the likelihood of using Ghana's own bauxite in the long run could be rated high.

All this took place in a political atmosphere which was heated by memories of what had recently happened in Egypt. The Egyptian government had hoped that the American government would finance the construction of the dam on the river Nile at Aswan. When the Americans drew back, the Russians moved in. In the Ghana situation, while conversations about the loan dragged on, people asked whether this would be 'another Aswan'. Would it provide an opportunity for the Russians to move into Ghana? By this time John Kennedy had become the president of the United States – a man whom Nkrumah liked. Kennedy wanted to provide funds to help with the dam, but a group among his advisers, led by his brother Robert Kennedy, was opposed to the whole thing. They believed that Nkrumah was committed to the communists, whether or not America helped with the dam. Nkrumah chose this moment to pay a visit to Peking and that played into their hands. They thought that the money should go to Tubman and Houphouet-Boigny, sound private-enterprise men. President Kennedy urged Nkrumah to make it clear that he was not anti-American in world affairs and sent a personal envoy to convey the message. There can be little doubt that this fortified Nkrumah's belief that the major powers would always compete for his goodwill, and come to his rescue if need arose.

In Accra the 'scientific socialists', led by Adamafio, were urging

Nkrumah to have nothing to do with the western powers in financing the Volta scheme. However, their hostility towards the western powers was brushed aside by Nkrumah for a reason which may seem irrelevant but which nevertheless counted for much. The Queen of England was due to visit Ghana. Nkrumah had been her guest and was devoted to her personally, and apart from that nothing could be more prestigious than to be host to the Queen. Nkrumah's great wish to entertain her in Ghana was one of the reasons why he overruled the left wing of the party, and accepted the American and British offers of financial help for the Volta. It took several years to build, but the opening ceremony took place on 22 January 1966. It was almost the last official act of Kwame Nkrumah. It was a great moment for Ghana, because when the great switch turned over, Ghana's economy ceased to be one-legged, depending on cocoa, and gained electric power as a second leg: enough power to drive as many factories as she would want for a long time, and also to sell to neighbouring countries.

In banking, cocoa buying, the import trades, mining, and constructional work, Nkrumah made arrangements to place local people in control of much larger shares than they had previously enjoyed. The Ghana Commercial Bank was established in 1952 and in 1964 it held 52 per cent of total deposits.

In the cocoa trade Nkrumah inherited from the colonial regime a government export monopoly (Chapter 11), in which the exporting board employed agents to buy the cocoa and deliver it to the ports. Most of these agents were foreign companies, and Nkrumah set up a Cocoa Purchasing Company to take over from them as the board's agent. As with so many other things, he staffed it with party members and it became an instrument of the CCP's patronage and power.

The import trades also were predominantly in the hands of large foreign firms. Nkrumah created the Ghana National Trading Corporation, acquired two middle-sized companies for it to take over, and set it to work in competition with the foreign companies. It had a bad start, because like the CPC it was treated as an instrument of party patronage; but Nkrumah lost patience with it, sacked the directors, and placed the enterprise under the control of an Englishman who had previously been the head of the largest foreign company. He had no reason to regret his action, and it is an illustration of how Nkrumah would find solutions to problems without reference to ideologies. In 1961 he set up a Mining Corporation which took over several mines, and there were also corporations for construction and insurance.

In the cocoa season 1964–65 he decided to exact a high price by withholding supplies of cocoa from the international markets. He had prepared for this by spending a great deal of money on storage for cocoa at the Ghana ports, and he now formed the Cocoa Producers' Alliance which included Nigeria, Ivory Coast, Congo-Brazzaville, Togo, and Cameroon, producing between them 82 per cent of the world's cocoa. World crops of cocoa had been exceptionally high in the two previous years, and estimates of the production expected in the crop-year 1964–5 were even higher. Therefore cocoa was plentiful and prices were rather low. Manufacturers were well stocked. In October 1964 the council of the CPA advised its members to cease sales. Ghana made no offer of sale for 15 weeks. The refusal to sell was accompanied by defiant words and gestures. There was talk about finding new ways of using cocoa, and statements were made that cocoa would be burned if the price did not rise. Sir Tsibu Darku, chairman of the marketing board, applied a ceremonial torch to a pile of 500 tons of cocoa. The market was not impressed. Plenty of cocoa was moving forward. Eighteen per cent of world supplies were outside the CPA. Ivory Coast did not respond to the call to stop sales. Cameroon could not stop because there was no storage, and the government of that country was not prepared to ruin the cocoa by stacking it in the open. Consumers were well content to see Ghana holding stocks. They knew that those stocks would have to be moved before the next crop came forward, for even Ghana, with her storage, could not hold two crops. The market sensed a tremendous weight of cocoa which was bound to be offered for sale in a selling scramble, and in anticipation prices drifted down. The other members of the CPA realised what a predicament they were in, and Ghana stood in danger of being left alone. Cocoa was – or should have been – responsible for two-thirds of Ghana's earnings of foreign currency. It was essential to keep exports moving, because foreign currency was so scarce that the Bank of Ghana was unable to provide money to pay contracted bills. By the end of January 1965 Nkrumah had to make the choice between selling cocoa or suffering a complete collapse of the economy. Ghana began to make sales on 1 February, and for the reasons indicated above the price continued to fall until it was below £100 a ton in March. Towards the end of 1965 the Bank of Ghana had no foreign exchange to meet 'irrevocable' letters of credit as they fell due, so that the country was bankrupt.

In 1965 an election was due to take place, but Nkrumah dispensed with it. He announced over the radio the names of those whom he had chosen to go to parliament. This indicated at home and abroad that he no longer enjoyed the support of his people, and that he dared not submit his fate to their votes. Several attempts were made to assassinate him. More people had been imprisoned under the preventive detention act, and the much-respected Dr J. B. Danquah and Obetsebi Lamptey had died in prison. People were shocked by the sudden and mysterious disappearance of respected citizens, who subsequently turned out to be in jail. The universities were made to understand that academic freedom did not entitle them to criticise the government; and to emphasise the point Professor J. S. de Graft Johnson was sent to join the distinguished company of 'prison graduates'.

In 1957 Nkrumah took over foreign reserves amounting to £200m and a foreign debt of only £20m. By 1965 the reserves had all been spent and foreign debt was about £400m though commitments were so badly controlled that no one knew exactly how much was owed. The people were indignant about the waste and extravagance, humiliated by the disrepute into which Ghana had fallen, and shamed by the corruption which was rife. People were suffering from acute shortages, and the money-inflation was so bad that the prices of local foodstuffs rose to astronomical heights.

In these sad conditions the army turned Nkrumah out of office. The soldiers shared the general distress, but they had also special reasons to be displeased. The army had been organised on British principles and armed with weapons from western countries. Neither the principles nor the weapons suited Nkrumah, because he wanted an army which would train guerrillas to fight in those parts of Africa which were under governments with which he disagreed, and which would act as a supply base, issuing weapons to such people. These ideas fitted in with Russian policy, and with Russian help Nkrumah formed what was, in effect, a second army, described as the President's Own Guard Regiment. It was initiated in 1960, as a battalion of four rifle companies. At first it was ostensibly part of the regular army, but in 1962 an independent commander was appointed. It was expanded, its training was directed by Russian officers, and it was fitted out with Russian material. At the same time the regular army was kept short of arms and uniforms, and its members began to fear that they were being phased out of existence in favour of the Guard Regiment, which seemed to enjoy the best of everything. By 1966 Nkrumah could not fail to be aware that his position was precarious, and the defence of his residence and of key points in the capital was taken out of the hands of the regular army and entrusted to the Russians and the Guard Regiment. The two most senior police officers were arrested and imprisoned, and the two most senior generals of the army were dismissed.

Nkrumah had probably always assumed that his position in Africa was sufficiently important to enable him to claim an economic rescue operation from either America or Russia in case of need, but by 1966 it had become plain that this was not going to happen: and so he went to China, no doubt to beg for help from the third world power. He wrote afterwards, when he was in exile, that the purpose of his journey was to stop the war in Vietnam!

His absence provided an opportunity of which conscientious and patriotic Ghanaians could hardly fail to take advantage. On 24 February 1966 the army, led by Colonel E. K. Kotoka and Major A. A. Afrifa, took over the government. The public expressed approval with spontaneous jubilation.

Kwame Nkrumah found political sanctuary in Guinea with Sekou Touré, who treated him as an honoured guest. He is remembered as the first great political leader in Africa who rallied the mass of the people, farmers and workers, in a demand for independence which was so overwhelming that it was quickly victorious. Thus Ghana became a sovereign state and following Ghana the pace of de-colonisation speeded up. In Ghana his great memorial is the Volta dam.

15 Ghana after Nkrumah

Following the seizure of power by the army a proclamation established the National Liberation Council (NLC) which was to legislate by decree, dispensing with parliamentary forms. The members of the council were General J. A. Ankrah as chairman, J. W. K. Harlley (commissioner of police) as deputy chairman, Colonel, E. K. Kotoka, B. A. Yakubu (deputy commissioner of police), Colonel Ocran, J. E. O. Nunoo (assistant commissioner of police), Major Afrifa, and A. K. Deku (deputy commissioner of police). As instruments of government the NLC set up five committees, each under a civilian chairman; one for economic affairs, one for foreign relations, one for administrative questions, one for publicity, and the fifth's assignment was described as national relief.

The NLC decided to honour all the debts of the Nkrumah regime. This was much criticised because it was believed that some of the debts were owing to individuals and companies who had entered into complicity with Nkrumah in enterprises of doubtful character, under arrangements by which sums were diverted to political and personal ends. However, the NLC took over all Nkrumah's liabilities, and appealed for help to friendly governments. The US, Britain, West Germany, and Canada came to Ghana's aid. Quantities of food were received from US and Canada. The International Monetary Fund and the World Bank gave help. Arrangements were made with western and eastern creditor nations to repay the loans more slowly and at lower rates of interest than Nkrumah's government had arranged. Prestige projects were cancelled and reductions were made in the number of ministries, embassies, and administrative districts. The state corporations were purged of political elements and placed under the best available managers. The two state-owned hotels were entrusted to the management of an American company. Ghana Airways cancelled loss-making routes and the Soviet Ilyushin planes which were idle at Accra were sent back to suppliers. As a result of these measures the trade balance became favourable in 1966 for the first time in many years.

Commissions were appointed to examine the conduct of Nkrumah

137

and of members of the CPP, and they exposed corruption and waste.

To relieve the prevailing distress, import taxes on essential foods were reduced, the lower incomes were exempt from tax, and the price paid to farmers for cocoa was increased. In 1967 the currency was devalued; this was a recognition of the fact that Nkrumah had debased it by pumping so much money into the economy. Devaluation helped to check smuggling and black market currency dealing, but of course it made imports more expensive. In recognition of this wages in the public sector were increased by 5 per cent and the price paid to farmers for cocoa was again increased. The NLC overhauled the educational system, insisting on high standards. To help Ghanaians to understand their rights and responsibilities, a Centre for Civil Education was inaugurated, and Dr K. A. Busia was placed in charge of it. This was seen as a preliminary move towards the restoration of civilian government. Freedom of speech and of the press were guaranteed. Chiefs destooled for their opposition to Nkrumah were reinstated. A goodwill mission visited nearly all African states to repair the strains which Nkrumah had created.

The NLC declared their intention of restoring civilian rule and appointed a commission under the chief justice to draft a constitution. They set up an electoral commission which began registering voters in anticipation of the return to democratic processes of government.

In April 1967 two lieutenants with a platoon of soldiers, stationed at Ho, moved to Accra and attempted to seize power. They were not successful, but General Kotoka was killed. This was a great loss to the NLC, because Kotoka was probably the person who by his qualities held the other members together as a team. The reasons behind the *coup* were never satisfactorily explained and it appears to have been an irresponsible act, but it had considerable effect in strengthening the voices of those of the public and in the NLC itself who believed that civilian rule should be restored as soon as possible.

In July 1967 seventeen commissioners (of whom fourteen were civilians) were appointed to take charge of the seventeen ministries. They sat with the members of the NLC as the executive council. A national advisory committee was appointed, bringing together persons who commanded respect in many walks of life, to consider public policy and to keep the government in touch with public opinion. By 1968 the position had been consolidated sufficiently to enable the NLC to inaugurate a two-year development plan, dealing in practical terms with agriculture, fisheries, mining, roads, water supplies, and sewerage. However, unemployment and high prices persisted and the euphoria with which the NLC had been greeted gave way to disenchantment. In 1969 the regime sustained a cruel blow when its chairman General Ankrah resigned in distasteful circumstances; he had been accepting money from some foreign companies with the idea of financing a political party and thus assuring himself a place in the civilian government which was expected to follow in due course. Brigadier Afrifa succeeded General Ankrah as chairman. He lifted the ban on party-political activities and fixed dates for a general election and for the return to civilian government.

Five parties contested the election, namely:

The Progress Party led by Dr K. A. Busia;
The National Alliance of Liberals led by K. A. Gbedemah;
The All People's Republican Party led by P. K. K. Quaidoo;
The People's Action Party led by Imoru Ayarna; and
The United Nationalist Party led by Dr H. S. Bannerman.

One hundred and forty seats were contested, and of these the Progress Party won 105. The Liberals won 29. On 3 September 1969 Dr Busia, leader of the Progress Party, was sworn in as prime minister of the second republic of Ghana. The constitution provided that for an interim period of three years the functions of head of state should be exercised by a commission consisting of three senior members of the NLC, but in 1970 the commission was dissolved and parliament elected chief justice Akufo Addo as president. He was to hold office for four years.

The brief story of the second republic of Ghana is of great interest, and it was a tragic episode. The prime minister, Dr Kofi Busia, was a man of high international standing and in his books and speeches he had expressed more concern than any other African leader of his time for individual liberty and for democratic processes of government. Speaking at the ceremony in which the NLC handed over power he thanked the soldiers and policemen for what they had done, proudly asserted that not a single person was under detention for political reasons, and said that the new constitution 'seeks to place the exercise of power under restraint'. So it did; the constitution-makers had been very conscious of the abuse of power by the CPP regime; but they went too far and made it difficult for the government to act at all.

Everything seemed to go wrong for the civilian government. Hardly had they come into office than they were carried away on a wave of xenophobia in which the people of Ghana turned upon alien Africans and Lebanese. The agitation had started under the military government, and in 1968 the NLC had made a law under which foreigners could be summarily deported. Action under this law had already begun, but under the new government it became very violent and no less than 500,000 people were driven out of Ghana. Many of them were Nigerians who had lived in Ghana for many years. Under another law, described as the Business Promotions Act, aliens who owned small businesses were compelled to sell them to Ghanaians. The victims included many people who had created private businesses in the distributive and craft trades. They contributed to the wealth of Ghana and their expulsion damaged the economy. They naturally took away all that they could move, both legally and illegally; and this was bad for the balance of payments. The government, in yielding to public clamour and identifying itself with the persecution of the foreigners, damaged its image at home and abroad. This was not what had been expected from liberal democratic idealists.

The second stroke of ill-fortune was a poor cocoa crop and a fall in the international price of cocoa, which came down to £194 a ton. The revenue suffered and the balance of trade went wrong. In order to balance the budget the government had to ask everybody to make sacrifices. The ministers showed a good example by cutting their own salaries by a third, but even the finest examples do not make austerity popular. In asking for sacrifices the government did not exempt the army. This was not a government of sabre-rattlers, and it would have liked to cut down the fighting services and use the money for growth and welfare. However, in the year 1970, with so many examples of soldiers seizing power, it was a risky thing to cut the army vote.

It was impossible to service the foreign debt, even on the reduced scale which the NLC had been able to negotiate; so the Ghana government asked the creditor governments to 'reschedule' the loans on even more lenient terms. The governments of the western world had given much aid to other West African governments, including some which seemed to be less well disposed towards the western way of life than the government of Dr Busia. He was perhaps entitled to hope that the twelve western creditor governments would be willing to make an investment in liberal democracy. However, the negotiations involved hard bargaining, and although it was agreed that half the payments due in 1970–72 should be deferred, it turned out that even this lightened load was too heavy.

The economic troubles produced a number of strikes, and the government came into head-on collision with the trade union congress, which it abolished by Act of parliament; but no Act of parliament could 'abolish' the 200,000 unemployed. Inflation was out of control, and in

December 1971 the Ghana *cedi* was again devalued, this time by the enormous percentage of 48.6 per cent against the dollar.

A further misfortune was the prime minister's poor state of health. In January 1972 he was in London for medical treatment. His deputy was away from Accra, as were most of the other ministers. Hardly anyone was on duty, and no one was on guard. A group of officers, led by Colonel I. K. Acheampong, occupied the government offices without firing a shot and set themselves up as the government. These soldiers were quite different from the 'reluctant heroes' of 1966, who had 'gone back to barracks' as soon as possible. Colonel Acheampong believed that strong military leadership was what Ghana needed, and he intended to stay.

This military government described itself as the National Redemption Council (NRC). It immediately revalued the *cedi* by 42 per cent, thus cancelling most of Busia's recent devaluation. About a third of the oversea debt was repudiated; the dishonoured obligations were mostly owed to contractors who had financed works during Nkrumah's rule; but this act, done without securing the agreement of the creditor nations, provoked the USA and Britain to cancel their aid programmes. 'Operation Feed Yourself' was inaugurated.

Kwame Nkrumah died and the body was brought back to Ghana and accorded a state funeral at his birthplace, Nkroful.

In five years five plots were discovered against the security of the state. Some of the plotters were army officers. There were many trials, in which convicted persons were condemned to death, but all the sentences were commuted to life imprisonment.

In 1973 the price of cocoa rose to £400 and the economic situation improved. A national service scheme was introduced for students. The government acquired a shareholding of 55 per cent in foreign mining and timber companies.

In 1974 Colonel Acheampong instituted a consultative committee, of twelve, in which some civilians participated. The demand for restoration of civilian government was heard, and the agitation led to the closure of all the universities. The price of cocoa rose yet higher, but the economy suffered badly from the sharp rise in the price of petroleum.

In 1975 Britain and the USA renewed their aid. Acheampong appointed a new Supreme Military Council, discarding his three closest associates. He declared that there was no prospect of restoring civilian government. By decree restrictions were placed on the percentage shareholding which foreigners might possess in Ghanaian companies.

In 1976 Acheampong assumed the title of general. Revenue was insufficient to cover expenditure, and the government bridged the gap by borrowing from the banks. The result was an inflation rate of 70 per cent. The international price of cocoa continued to be very good, but the price paid to the farmer in Ghana was at a lower rate, fixed by the government. Large quantities of cocoa were smuggled over the frontiers to be sold in Ivory Coast and Togo (see Chapter 11). Food prices were high and imported goods were acutely scarce. Acheampong modified his unbending attitude towards the restoration of civilian government, and mentioned the possibility of 'a Union government to which everybody will belong'. It was to be a kind of hybrid between military rule and civilian government, and Acheampong named July 1979 as the date at which it might be established.

During 1977 inflation continued. University students made a mass protest against food prices and against the Union government proposal; soldiers and police took vigorous action against them, and again all the universities were closed.

A question was submitted to a national referendum in 1978 as to whether a new constitution should be prepared to give effect to 'Union government'. There was much public criticism of the refusal by the Supreme Military Council to permit any discussion of the basic conception, and about the framing of the question which was put to the electorate. Less than half of the registered voters went to the poll, and when the result was announced the government claimed that the question had been answered in the affirmative, though by a rather narrow majority. The credibility of the result was affected by the fact that the electoral commissioner, Mr Justice Abban, 'disappeared' and was subsequently dismissed. In any case, less than a quarter of the registered voters had accepted the government's proposal, and even though they were a majority of those who had cast their votes, this was not solid support on which the government could go forward in confidence. There was an outburst of strikes and protest meetings and the Supreme Military Council found it necessary to make numerous arrests: however, human rights had now become a tender subject and an assurance was issued that the government was not arresting anybody on account of political views! The economic situation went from bad to worse, and conditions contrasted strangely with the prosperity of the two neighbouring states, Ivory Coast and Togo. On the black market the *cedi* was worth only one tenth of its official value. The government announced that it would adopt a flexible exchange rate which would vary in accordance with circumstances, but in fact what followed was devaluation by 38 per cent.

General Acheampong had linked his reputation to two things – the revaluation of the *cedi* and the Union government scheme. Under both heads he had suffered humiliating experiences. His colleagues in the Supreme Military Council no longer felt able to support him, so he resigned and the chief of defence staff, Lieutenant-General F. W. K. Akuffo, became the head of the government. He released all those who had recently been detained and promised that the soldiers would make way for 'a popularly elected government' by 1 July 1979. The phrase 'Union government' was abandoned, but in its place 'National government' was adopted. It was to be civilian, without army or police participation, but no political parties were to be permitted. The press, and public meetings such as those of the legal profession, continued to enjoy freedom of expression, and they were not noticeably more favourable towards 'National government' than they had been towards 'Union government'. The trade unions joined in the protest, and a state of emergency was declared. However, General Akuffo took 'cognizance of public views freely and frankly expressed'. He changed his mind about the embargo on political parties, and it was lifted on 1 January 1979.

16 Guinea

Guinea has an area of 95,000 square miles. It is three times as large as Sierra Leone, and larger than Ghana or Senegal. Its population at the time when it became independent was believed to be about 2,600,000. The principal tribes were:

Fulani	800,000	N-E, pastoralists
Malinke alias Mandinka, Mandingo	450,000	In Beyla, Kanka, Kouroussa; agriculturists
Susu	250,000	Swampy coastal area; rice etc.
Kpelle or Guerze	115,000	S-E, forested hills
Kissi	140,000	Gekedu; forest
Loma	80,000	Macenta; forest

The majority were Muslim but there were about 45,000 Christians and some of the forest communities clung to the pagan religion.

In the previous chapter attention was drawn to the low level of economic activity in Guinea compared with Ghana. Communications were very poor. The railway from the port of Conakry to Kankan, 415 miles, crossed the river Niger near its source in the Futa-Jallon mountains. Beyond the railhead at Kankan a mountainous road extended for 190 miles more to Nzerekore through beautiful hills clad with forest. The railway was inadequate for bringing to port the produce which might have been exported from the far interior, so in the main Guinea was a country of subsistence agriculture.

After the war of 1939 to 1945 four political groups were active, all based on ethnic sentiment and confined to particular localities. A socialist, Yacine Diallo, secured sufficient support from these groups to be elected deputy. He died in 1954, and by that time Sekou Touré was ready to take the lead.

Sekou Touré, born in 1922, was the great-grandson of Almamy Samory Touré, a king who fought against the French from 1872 until 1898. His father was Malinke, his mother Fula. He attended a Koranic school, and then completed primary school in French, after which he

engaged in secondary studies by correspondence. He became a clerk in
the postal service, and was elected secretary of the postal workers' trade
union. In 1948 he became secretary-general of the Guinea branch of the
Confédération Générale des Travailleurs (CGT), a French trade union
organisation affiliated with the communist party. He became secretary-
general of the CGT for West Africa but in 1956 he broke away from it,
and the reasons for the break were interesting. The French communists
who controlled the CGT wished people to believe that the only hope of
freedom for Africa was a communist victory in France; but Sekou Touré
wanted to secure independence without waiting for that. In 1957 the
UGTAN (*Union Générale des Travailleurs de l'Afrique Noire*) was
formed, separate from the communist party, and Sekou Touré became
its federal director. He improved the occasion with a *bon mot*—UGTAN
rejects the class struggle for the anti-colonial struggle.

Sekou Touré was a founder member of the RDA in 1946. In 1952 he
became the secretary-general (i.e. leader) of the *Parti Démocratique de
Guinée*, which was the Guinean constituent of RDA. He was mayor of
Conakry in 1955, deputy (in Paris) for Guinea in 1956, member of the
grand council at Dakar in 1957, vice-president of the government of
Guinea in 1957 and prime minister of Guinea early in 1958. He was of
impressive stature, known to his people as 'Silly' which means elephant.
He was a powerful orator and chewed kola nuts. His wife Andrée,
daughter of a French doctor and a Fula mother, gave him valuable
support.

Sekou Touré was well acquainted with the theory and practice of
Marxism, but he was not a communist. His attitude was clear in his
speeches:

> We have used certain parts of the Marxist doctrine to organise
> rational foundations for African trade unionism. We have adopted
> from Marxism everything that is true for Africa . . . We formally
> reject the principle of the class struggle . . . In fact, the new African
> society cannot depend on European-inspired doctrines if it is to
> succeed. If we prove that without the class struggle a profound
> transformation of our country is possible, we will have made our
> contribution to political science . . . Communism is not the way for
> Africa. The class struggle here is impossible because there are no
> classes.

Sekou Touré through his PDG organised the village people into
political units. There was a committee in each village and town ward,

7164 in all. These committees were more than mere instruments for winning elections. Each had an executive consisting of ten members; four men, three women, two representatives of youth, and the chief (new style) who was elected by the party members. The committees governed their areas, and enforced their will by social or physical pressures. Support was encouraged by holding rallies and marches, and anybody who stayed away was made to suffer. Sekou Touré set little value on personal liberty. 'Liberty', he said, 'is only a tool, a tool for organising and orienting our activities to conform with the popular will.' The party enrolled the women and children in its branches as well as men, and the enthusiastic support of women was a great source of strength. Young people were organised in the *Jeunesse du Rassemblement Africain*. For children up to the age of fourteen there was a junior section, the Pioneers. In public speeches Sekou Touré encouraged people to denounce anybody who in word or deed deviated from the party line. The branches were used as a means of intense political education, concerned especially to eradicate sentiments which had come down from the past and which divided the people of Guinea – which meant tribal sentiment and non-Islamic religions. The chiefs had been powerful, yet one of Sekou Touré's first acts when he became head of the government was to abolish the office of chief in all town wards and rural cantons. The party committees were thus left in command. A few months later the larger, more traditional, chiefs were also suppressed. Expatriate Christian missionaries were driven from the country, and it was made a criminal offence to practise certain pagan ceremonies.

The people were instructed in the social and economic policies of the government, and were encouraged to promote them by voluntary work both on major national undertakings and on local amenities. Sekou Touré made sure that all wage-earners were drawn into a trade union, and he knew how to use the unions for political purposes.

In 1954, when the deputy Yacine Diallo died, there was a by-election and Sekou Touré stood as a candidate, but he was defeated by a Gaulliste candidate named Diawadou Barry. It was said that the government used its influence in favour of Barry, but no doubt there were many people who for tribal, religious, and social reasons were alarmed by Sekou Touré's radical policies. The declaration of the result provoked a riot in Conakry. Two years later it became necessary for Guinea to elect three representatives to go to Paris, and PDG won two of the places, the Gaullistes gaining the third. Sekou Touré was one of the successful candidates and this took him to Paris. In 1957, when elections were held for the territorial assembly, PDG won 57 places out of 60.

Under the constitution which was adopted in 1958 the president of the country was elected by the members of the party. Thus the party was formally identified with the state. The political bureau of the party was the effective seat of government. Debates in the legislature were purely formal, and the annual budget was adopted in half an hour because everything had been decided in the bureau. Members of the legislature were elected on a single list, and since there was only one list electors had no choice. When the country became independent the bureau renounced its link with RDA, and it took the opportunity of declaring that RDA did not understand 'the personality, dignity, and real aspirations of Africa'.

Everyone was expected to participate and to behave, and there was no place for slackers, still less for miscreants. The death penalty was introduced as a penalty for theft, and the sentence was carried out in certain cases; death was also the doom prescribed by law for killing a person while driving a motor vehicle.

When Sekou Touré decided that he would not accept De Gaulle's proposal that Guinea should become a member of the French community, but would choose independence with all the consequences, he commanded a party machine which could produce an almost unanimous vote in his support. So he pronounced his historic *NON* to De Gaulle. Most categories of French aid ceased immediately, but not quite all. In spite of the anti-French feeling which must have made their lives unpleasant, 150 French teachers stayed through 1959 and 111 remained at their posts through 1960. Diplomatic relations with France were established in 1961, and a cultural agreement was then signed under which a great many more French teachers came in.

However, in 1958 all French officials in the administration and in services other than education were abruptly withdrawn, and subsidies in aid of the budget ceased. This created a financial crisis. Guinea continued, however, to use the African franc as currency, and this made her, willy-nilly, part of the franc zone. So long as Guinea remained part of that zone, and observed its rules, her trade deficits (which were considerable) were financed by the Bank of France. One of Sekou Touré's immediate problems was to extricate himself from this position, because he did not wish to be beholden to the franc zone authorities. Furthermore, he wished to have freedom in his choice of trading partners, and this was not possible for a government which abided by the rules of the franc zone; for foreign currencies were rationed, and the purchases which members could make outside the zone were restricted accordingly. Sekou Touré was not friendless, for he received the most amiable approaches from Kwame Nkrumah of Ghana, and from Russia and her satellite states; but they pulled him in different directions. Nkrumah helped him in his financial crisis by handing over £4,500,000, and he invited Touré to unite with Ghana and to find a solution of his financial problem by sharing Ghana's bank and currency. The Russians however advised him to allow experts from Czechoslovakia to provide a currency for him. It is probable that at first he did not take Nkrumah seriously; he saw a white man sitting in Christiansborg Castle as Nkrumah's governor-general, and he knew that the Queen of England was Queen of Ghana, and this seemed to him to be a colonial situation, the kind of relationship to which he had just said 'No' when it was offered to him by De Gaulle. Sekou Touré adopted the Russian solution, and by March 1960 the Czechs had printed new notes and Sekou Touré announced that he was leaving the franc zone and issuing his own currency. Thus for the second time he pronounced a highly significant *NON* – to Nkrumah's proposal for an effective union of African states.

The new currency had no backing but it was forced on the country with the power of the party machine. Everybody had to exchange his francs for the new notes within a few days, and woe betide the defaulter! The francs thus acquired were used to discharge foreign obligations, which drew a sharp protest from the bank of issue. Unfortunately the Czechs did not manage the new currency well. The notes were not proof against forgery, and before long large quantities with duplicate numbers were in circulation, the spurious notes being indistinguishable from the genuine. Sekou Touré turned to an English firm of security printers and bought from them a new set of notes, which went into circulation just two years after the original Czech issue.

The use of paper money which had no backing (except that it was legal tender in Guinea) raised a problem of frontier control. Much has been written about the frontiers adopted by the colonial powers, but except where main roads or ferries crossed the boundary, there was nothing to tell a wanderer in which country he was. All along Guinea's frontiers with Senegal, Mali, Ivory Coast, Liberia, and Sierra Leone traders moved to and fro, and if they were satisfied with head-loads or donkey-loads they met no customs men on the routes which they followed. Cattlemen from Mauritania and Mali drove their beasts southward to market across the frontiers, and returned northwards to their homes with loads of goods. At the tripartite point where the frontiers of Guinea, Sierra Leone and Liberia meet, a large market was held every Sunday – a day when, by a long-established gentlemen's agreement, the customs officers of the three countries observed the sabbath. This area was an important source of 'illicit' diamonds – that is, diamonds that had either been mined by people who had no licence and paid no tax, or that had been stolen. The illicit diamond traffic was large and highly organised and it paid no regard to the frontier. Guinea's new notes began to be exchanged at or over the frontiers at a heavy discount. Guinea was not prepared to tolerate this, and effective control of the frontiers was established. It involved armed conflicts with cattlemen and diamond-runners, some of whom lost their lives.

So much for the currency; returning to the general question of help from communist countries, the Russians helped to inaugurate a national airline. The East Germans contributed a radio transmitter. The Poles made fishing their sphere. With the help of Russian technicians a three-year plan was set on foot in 1960. The money was to come mainly from Russia, but China contributed a substantial amount, and (strangely) West Germany donated £4,000,000. The plan provided for the improvement of communications, for housing, schools, and a polytechnic for 1500 students, and also for factories for making cement, canning pineapples, tanning hides, and processing fish and rice. Russia, China, and Yugoslavia constructed barrages on rivers, producing electricity, but works of that character take time and those schemes came to fruition in the late sixties.

In April 1960 Sekou Touré announced the discovery of a subversive plot. He complained that 5000 saboteurs were engaged in this intrigue, sponsored by Gaullist organisations, and he accused Senegal and Ivory Coast of aiding his enemies. Nineteen people were condemned to death, twenty-one were sent to prison for fifteen years, and six French nationals were expelled. After this on several occasions Sekou Touré uncovered plots of similar character, and each time a number of people were eliminated, including persons who had been his close collaborators. In August of that same year he announced that another plot had been uncovered; France, he said, had made 'diabolical plans' with the connivance of Senegal. At the end of 1961 there occurred the 'teachers' plot'. Five members of the teachers' trade union were convicted for having intended 'to use trade unionism as a springboard to undermine the foundations of the revolution and to divide the workers'! They were sentenced to terms of penal servitude. Then Sekou Touré announced that they had belonged to 'a Marxist-Leninist group, based in Moscow, Paris, and Dakar, whose Machiavellian plan was to unleash

a Marxist revolution in Guinea'; and he expelled the Soviet am-
bassador. At a conference in Stockholm his envoy supported the
Chinese against the Russians (as noted in Chapter 11) and when the
Cuban crisis occurred Sekou Touré refused landing rights to Russia.
This was the third time that Sekou Touré had pronounced an important
NON. No to De Gaulle, No to Nkrumah, and No to Russia.

The Russians were not accustomed to such treatment, and sent one of
their deputy prime ministers to repair the broken bridge.

Sekou Touré had received a technical assistance team from the
United Nations, but they too failed to please him, and they were
expelled because they were said to have interfered in matters beyond
their competence.

In 1961 Sekou Touré's government declared its intention to abolish
private schools, and as these were mostly Roman Catholic, the threat
produced a vigorous protest from the archbishop. However, that kind
of religious freedom had no place in Touré's scheme of things, and the
archbishop was expelled.

Guinea had mineral wealth in the form of iron ore and bauxite, and in
the last years of French rule plans had been elaborated with international groups to develop these deposits. In 1952 a Canadian firm
began mining bauxite on Kassa island. The same company engaged in a
larger bauxite undertaking near Boké in 1958, and was in the earliest
stage of development when the country became independent. Even
more important bauxite deposits occur at Kimbo, and these also were in
process of development by an international group known as FRIA
(American, French, British, Swiss, and German). It began to produce
and export alumina in 1960. A British company had been extracting
diamonds in Upper Guinea for many years, and recently a Franco-
British group had begun to mine iron ore in the Kaloum penisula. A
concession was granted in 1961 to a consortium of European and
Japanese banks (Consafrique) to develop iron ore in the Nsimba
mountains. Sekou Touré had no intention of becoming so deeply
committed to the Russians that western investors might be scared away.
In 1959 he visited the United States, and his visit resulted in a cultural
agreement and in the shipment of supplies of food to Conakry to relieve
shortages. In the same year Sekou Touré visited London and a
commercial agreement was concluded with Britain. British merchant
houses were surprised that it was the same kind of agreement that the
eastern countries like to make with African states – a statement of
principle that a number of items, listed, were available for mutual
exchange. The British list included textiles and motor vehicles, and

trading houses established in Guinea took advantage of those opportunities.

Relations with the United States continued to improve, and in 1960 an agreement was made for technical assistance and economic co-operation. There followed in 1962 an agreement under which the United States allocated $70 million as aid to Guinea. The aid was to be concerned with telecommunications, and a national school of administration was to be provided. Also the United States sent a team of experts to assist in the improvement of rice cultivation (it was usually the Chinese who sent rice experts to Africa!). The United States opened a 'guarantee programme' for United States firms which placed investments in Guinea.

In 1961 the Aluminium Company of Canada suspended work on the Boké project, saying that it was unable to secure financial support to enable it to continue. The works completed had cost millions of pounds, and were placed on care and maintenance. Touré was very angry, and the company was 'nationalised' and all its people expelled. However, its action may have made some impression, for in the following year a law was enacted to encourage investment; it included an assurance that foreign enterprises would not be nationalised, it gave favourable tax and customs treatment, and it guaranteed the transfer of incomes derived from capital investment 'within reasonable limits'.

An American company (Harvey Aluminium) agreed to take over the property of the expropriated Canadians, and to resume the work on the basis that the government would hold 40 per cent of the equity of the company. Under this arrangement Boké came into production in 1969. The FRIA factory was fully working in 1966 and produced 252,000 tons of alumina. Earlier, iron ore had been brought into production on the Kaloum peninsula, whence it was exported to Britain, West Germany, and Poland. With generous aid from east and west, and with the development of the mines, Guinea's financial difficulties were alleviated.

Since the mining groups included French participants, it was convenient for Guinea to resume diplomatic relations with France, but in 1965 Sekou Touré announced that a plot had been discovered which was to overturn his regime, and that the French government, together with the heads of state of Ivory Coast, Upper Volta, and Niger, had participated in it. Relations with France were broken off again.

It was mainly the United States and West Germany that granted aid to Guinea. In 1962 a trade-and-aid agreement was made with West Germany, and by 1965 the United States were making up the shortfall in

Guinea's annual budget, amounting to 40 per cent of the government's expenditure.

When Guinea became independent banking was conducted by French and British banks, and they were nationalised. The foreign trade was largely carried on by a few companies, of which two were British and the others French. The government did not formally prevent these companies from continuing in business, but state trading *comptoirs* were set up and since it was impossible to engage in any import or export business without a licence, and since most of the licences were reserved for the *comptoirs*, there was little for the companies to do. Since several Europeans had been imprisoned under suspicion of 'spying', apprehensions were felt about the safety of expatriate staff, and nearly all the foreign commercial community left the country. The companies continued to exist under African managers. In 1961 Sekou Touré surprisingly called them together and said that he had felt obliged to create the *comptoirs* 'because the private sector had not carried out its responsibilities', but unfortunately the *comptoirs* had made mistakes; they were corrupt and inefficient, and goods had been allowed to rot, so that they had to be thrown into the sea. He therefore invited the private sector to put forward proposals on how best to revive trade and ensure that supplies were adequate and regular. The response of the firms was mixed; some did their best to co-operate, but others saw no prospect of remunerative trading in Guinea, and withdrew from the country. In spite of his appeal to the private companies, Sekou Touré made it so difficult for them to carry on that later in the year he was compelled to create more state organisations to engage in the import trade. This time he avoided the pattern of the clumsy large *comptoirs* and set up twelve specialist companies to handle classes of imports such as (for instance) textiles and pharmaceuticals. It was announced (1963) that all retail distribution should revert to the private sector. It was in fact carried on by a very large number of small traders, and many of these tried to increase their profits by evading the official controls on currency and prices. To overcome these bad habits, in 1965 the government made it illegal for anyone to engage in retail trade unless he could show that he had a capital of ten million Guinean francs, of which a quarter was to be held on deposit in the national bank. Penalties for breaking the law were severe, and for repeated infractions the punishment was death. Thus small traders were suppressed, apparently in the belief that the larger operators would be more law-abiding.

Local committees of the party were not only instruments of mass education – they could also serve as sounding-boards for local opinion;

and at the end of 1961 Sekou Touré had to deal with a general protest against the pressure that was exerted to make people perform unpaid work. It was officially described as 'human investment' and it was supposed to be voluntary, but Sekou Touré was told that it had become nothing different from forced labour. Differences of opinion about 'voluntary' work continued to embarrass the president, who was prone to angry outbursts about the laziness of the people who complained. The army (with a professional strength of 4800 men) was sometimes employed on development works. In 1967 compulsory military service of two years was introduced for all fit men, and it may be assumed that one of the reasons for creating such a large disciplined force was to reduce the number of calls for 'voluntary' labour.

A seven-year development plan was inaugurated in 1964. It incorporated the investment code, as described above, and defined a larger role for the private sector in order to stimulate production, to expand exports, and to reduce imports. However, Sekou Touré's views and actions regarding the private trading sector went up and down like a see-saw, for later in the same year he withdrew all licences for private traders to engage in the import and export trades, and again entrusted these functions to state organisations, the twelve specialist companies mentioned above.

In 1966 Kwame Nkrumah was overthrown by a military revolt, and Sekou Touré immediately offered him a home in Guinea, saying that he should be regarded as the joint head of state. It was a great gesture to a friend in distress. Although the so-called union of Ghana, Guinea, and Mali had not developed as Nkrumah had hoped, he and Touré had acted in concert in the affairs of the African continent. A number of Ghanaians, faithful to Nkrumah, gathered around him at Conakry. Sekou Touré refused to recognise the new regime in Ghana. The Ghana government, resenting his hostile attitude, arrested nineteen Guineans, including the foreign minister, who were travelling in an American aircraft which came down at Accra airport. The party were held as hostages for the return of students and others alleged by the Ghana government to be 'detained in Guinea'. Touré's first reaction was to accuse the USA of complicity, and to arrest the American ambassador and all the airline officials. This was an astonishing act, for under diplomatic practice, recognised by all nations, ambassadors are never arrested. The US government announced that the episode might compel them to reconsider their aid programme, which may be regarded as a calm retort in the circumstances. Eighty-one Ghanaians were interviewed in Guinea by a neutral agent, and they all said that they wished to stay there; thus it appeared that the specific allegation of the Ghana government was unfounded, and the hostages were released.

In this year several projects came to fruition which had been under construction for some years; for instance, plantations of tea and tobacco, and a factory for matches and cigarettes sponsored by the Peking Chinese; a truck assembly plant in which the management and 49 per cent of the equity were provided by an American firm, while the Guinea government held 51 per cent; and a textile mill of British manufacture.

Sekou Touré had great difficulty in adjusting his relations with the French. He saw deep problems in establishing normal relations with the ex-colonial power; and possibly so long as De Gaulle and his close associates were in power in France the difficulty was mutual. Since Touré's neighbours, Senghor in Senegal and Houphouet-Boigny in Ivory Coast, enjoyed the close friendship of the French government, Touré was apt to direct the venom of his anti-French feelings towards them. In 1967 he suspended participation in the Senegal River Basin Commission (which seemed to have made a good beginning) because he accused Senghor of introducing pro-French considerations into its proceedings, and a few weeks later he seized a fishing trawler belonging to Ivory Coast. Houphouet-Boigny followed the example of the Ghanaians and arrested ten Guinean diplomats, including the foreign minister, when a Dutch aircraft in which they were travelling made stop at Abidjan. Touré's anti-French attitude was particularly strong this year; he announced a 'cultural revolution' which was to involve 'de-westernisation', discontinuing the use of the French language, and substituting a Guinean *lingua franca*. As a beginning a hundred Europeans were deported, mostly priests, nuns, and other missionaries. By the end of the year the quarrels with Senegal and Ivory Coast were formally healed, though in both cases relations continued to be bad for a decade.

In 1969 Sekou Touré announced the discovery of a plot hatched by senior army officers and others, with the support of France and Ivory Coast; thirteen persons were sentenced to death.

Sekou Touré furnished every possible help to Amilcar Cabral (Chapter 9) in his war against the Portuguese in Guinea-Bissau, another neighbour of Guinea. Towards the end of 1970 the Portuguese endeavoured to retaliate by providing facilities for a seaborne expedition which was intended to capture Conakry and instal a government of Guineans hostile to Sekou Touré. The forces under Touré's command repulsed the attack and made a number of prisoners. It was alleged that 300 'mercenaries' had landed, both Africans and Europeans. Touré reported the situation to the security council of the United Nations, and that body sent a mission to inquire into the facts; for news of attempted coups had been so frequent that there was some scepticism about how genuine they were. On this occasion there was no doubt about the reality of the incident, and the investigators reported that there had been Portuguese participation. They were however unable to see any of the Europeans whom the Guineans claimed to have captured. Among the first to say that they accepted Sekou Touré's charge of foreign participation were the French government (wishing no doubt to make it clear that on this occasion they could not be accused) and the Americans, who sent a message of support followed by 'extraordinary aid' to the tune of $4,700,000. Thus far, Sekou Touré seemed to have enhanced his prestige by repulsing an attack from outside and enjoying sympathy and support in the comity of nations. Then the atmosphere changed. Touré used the occasion to set going a reign of terror. Sixteen of his twenty-four ministers were arrested, which made the affair look like an internal movement of which the invasion had been an adjunct. Ninety-two people were sentenced to death and seventy-four to life imprisonment; but these were not the waterborne attackers. The death sentence was passed on several men who held high positions in the government, and those condemned to life imprisonment included Monseigneur Tchidimbo, archbishop of Conakry. The sentences were passed by the legislature sitting as the 'supreme revolutionary court'; the accused were given no opportunity of offering a defence, and there was no appeal. Fifty-eight people were publicly hanged and the official radio described it as a carnival. Party committees throughout the land were told to root out traitors, and to demand the death sentence. Ordinary men and women who were not identified with the party were in fear of their lives, and many of them fled over the borders into neighbouring states.

The imprisonment of the archbishop naturally provoked a vigorous protest from all the other archbishops of West Africa. Senegal, embarrassed by the flood of refugees and horrified by the stories they told, broke off diplomatic relations. It was alleged that the invading force had received some support from West German sources, and more than a hundred West German aid technicians were expelled. Two however were not so fortunate, but received sentences of life imprisonment, and one of these died in prison; the government announced that he had committed suicide. The West German ambassador was arrested, which a serious breach of diplomatic practice. Guinea had received

$35,000,000 in aid from West Germany, including a water system for Conakry! It was generally supposed that the attack on the West Germans had nothing to do with the waterborne expedition, but was due to the influence of East Germans who had recently arrived in Guinea, following the recognition by Guinea of the East German government. Thus Guinea was made to appear like a shuttlecock in the cold war – a humiliating position for a leader who had on several occasions taken a strong line with foreign powers from both sides of the iron curtain.

In 1975, ten years after the break of diplomatic relations, Guinea and France again exchanged ambassadors. Guinean exiles in France were attacking Sekou Touré for despotic practices and denial of human rights, but in the interests of restoring friendly relations the French government banned a Guinean exile publication entitled *Guinée – Perspetives Nouvelles* and seized all copies of a book by Jean-Paul Alata entitled *Prison d'Afrique*. About the same time diplomatic relations were restored with West Germany, and Guinea, overcoming her angry feelings towards her neighbours, joined the Lomé convention and the Economic Community of West African States (ECOWAS). However, Touré's career continued to be stormy. In 1976 another serious plot was alleged. This one was said to have been led by Diallo Telli, who was minister of justice, and by Alioune Drame, also a minister. Diallo Telli had for some years been the secretary-general of OAU, in which position he had won an international reputation. He was arrested and his fate remained a secret.

The International League for Human Rights made serious accusations against the Guinean government, which in 1977 were laid before the secretary-general of the United Nations. It was alleged that two million exiles had fled from the country, to Senegal, Ivory Coast, Sierra Leone, Liberia, Mali, and France. If it were true, it would mean that about half the population had left the country. In the following year, 1978, Amnesty International, publishing a pamphlet on the violation of human rights in Guinea, alleged that one million people had left the country. Figures like these can be no more than guesses, for no one had counted two million people, nor one million. It was not necessary to assume that all the exiles had fled for political reasons, for Guinea's economic state was bad, and Ivory Coast and Liberia had much better attractions for ordinary people in the remuneration of work and a choice of goods to buy. However, whatever the motives of the emigrants, they proved that Touré's government was hard to live under. There had been so-called land reforms which were supposed to ensure that the cultivator had the land he needed; but that had been a feature of African village life before the political theorists set to work. Peasants had been organised in co-operatives and much agricultural machinery had been imported. Yet the country did not grow enough food to feed the towns and the mining settlements, and their hunger was only assuaged by consignments of food from America, sent over as aid.

By decree, farmers were now obliged to deliver all their crops to the co-operative stores, and consequently the traditional markets were abolished. These measures were enforced by special police, whose methods gave rise to complaints of roughness. The suppression of the markets was very unpopular with women, for many of them had made their living as market traders, and the markets were the women's social centres. The co-operative stores were run by party officials, and they did not succeed in alleviating the food shortages. The situation provoked a tremendous protest by thousands of women, who demonstrated by marching through Conakry in August 1977. The militia opened fire on them and there were fatal casualties. This, at last, was opposition which could not be described as a plot nor blamed on foreigners. Sekou Touré was emotionally upset, and there were indications that he would adopt a more practical, less doctrinaire, attitude both in internal policy and in his foreign relations.

Aid was received from a new source, Saudi Arabia, in the form of a loan of a hundred million dollars. At the eleventh Congress of the *Parti Démocratique de Guinée* Sekou Touré announced the desire for 'broad co-operation without exclusivity with capitalist as well as socialist states', and paid homage to the 'grandeur' of the USA. In the last days of 1978 President Giscard d'Estaing of France paid an official visit to Conakry, and received a very cordial welcome. It was just over twenty years since Charles De Gaulle's dramatic visit, and it appeared to mean that the problem of establishing a new relationship between the ex-colonial power and the newly independent state, which had proved more difficult in Guinea than anywhere else, had at last been overcome.

17 Togo

At the celebration of independence in April 1960 Sylvanus Olympio delivered an impressive speech, as was to be expected from him. He generously acknowledged the beneficent role which France had played in the development of Togo, but the most important part of his address was that in which he expressed his plans for co-operation between African states. He waved aside all thought of beginning with political union, and proposed that West Africa should form an organisation for economic co-operation.

In 1961 a count of the population yielded the figure of 1,440,000, from which it may be concluded that the total had nearly doubled in twenty years. Christians numbered 260,000 (17 per cent) and there was a small Muslim element of 30,000. The majority of the population was still attached to traditional beliefs. The sophisticated Christians of the south, Olympio, Grunitzky, and their friends, had little contact with this majority, and the story of the next ten years made it plain that the 80 per cent who adhered to traditional beliefs were the dominating element.

A few weeks after the declaration of independence Olympio received the spontaneous visit of Nkrumah, as told in Chapter 14, but he refused to accede to Nkrumah's plea for political union, and made a statement that 'African unity, so much to be desired, must not be used by any African state as an excuse for an expansionist policy'. He followed speedily with an agreement with France covering defence and monetary affairs. Olympio secured the right to withdraw from the franc monetary zone if he should wish to do so, but he made it known that he had no such intention. The Entente of Ivory Coast, Dahomey, Voltaic Republic, and Niger had recently been formed (Chapter 7) and Olympio formed close ties with the group, seeking within that orbit friends to stand by him against the aggressive intentions of Ghana.

Germany had a historical interest in Togo, which Olympio was in a position to encourage since he spoke the German language. He concluded an agreement for economic and technical co-operation with the German Federal Republic, and Togo received generous aid from that source.

Togo had entered on independence as a parliamentary democracy, in which political parties competed for the votes of the electors. However, after no more than a year Olympio and his party changed the constitution and set up what was, in effect, a one-party state. The intention of the law, it was said, was to prevent small splinter groups from getting into parliament; but Togo had not suffered from a multiplicity of small parties and it was hard to see why such a drastic remedy was needed. The law passed by 25 votes to 12 and an election was held on a party-list system: the whole country would vote as one constituency, expressing its choice between lists of candidates presented to it by competing parties. However, the lists put forward by the two opposition parties, PTP (now known as UDTP – *Union démocratique togolaise du progrès*) and Juvento, were declared by the electoral authorities to be 'out of the time prescribed by law': so people had only one list to vote for (a similar situation arose in Ivory Coast in 1959, see Chapter 20). In the same year the prerogatives of the president were strengthened at the expense of the power of the legislature. Olympio offered himself for election as president and was elected for a seven-year term. It was alleged that leading members of UDTP were plotting against the security of the state and that they possessed arms; several were arrested and others, including Grunitzky, went into exile. The bitter feelings between the parties in Togo reflected the bitter feelings between Togo and Ghana, for it was alleged that the plotters received training in camps in Ghana, and were supplied with arms from that source. Olympio declared (July 1961) that the 'former territory of British Togoland belongs incontestably to the Togo republic'. The legislative assembly endorsed his declaration and called for the unification of the Togolese nation.

With Dahomey (later renamed Benin), his neighbour on the other side, Olympio pursued his design for an economic grouping. A customs and economic union was arranged, produce prices were harmonised, and the dates for opening and closing the produce buying seasons were aligned; a hydroelectric project on the Mono river was joinly set on foot.

In 1961 UDTP had been eliminated, and in 1962 it was the turn of Juvento. The leader, Anani Santos, was an admirer of Nkrumah. He organised Juvento on the lines of the CPP and expressed views inclining towards federal union with Ghana. He and some of his friends were arrested, and others fled to Ghana, where, with a follower of Grunitzky named Méatchi, they formed an organisation to work against Olympio. The party was dissolved by presidential decree. About the same time several numbers of *Présence Chrétienne*, newspaper of the Roman

Catholic church, were confiscated; so it appeared that Olympio and his government were not willing to tolerate criticism from any quarter.

Why did Olympio, with his liberal views and democratic attitude, engage on a policy of suppressing all opposition? Some elements may have had treasonable contacts with Ghana, but that is not a sufficient explanation. Olympio was a man full of kindness, of sparkling humour, and not at all like a tyrant. He told his friends that he was 'fed up with politics'. He was impatient with intrigues and would not tolerate dishonesty when it was a question of money; yet the trick by which the opposition parties were prevented from taking part in the election was dishonesty of another kind. He did not like the opposition, but his opinion of his own supporters was hardly more favourable. He seems to have believed that if he swept away the politicians he could rely upon the good sense of ordinary honest people. He was sure that with his experience of business he could conduct the government more efficiently without the politicians. However, he should have known that power must rest on a base, and that a price has to be paid for the base. The result of Olympio's measures was that although he had a great many devoted friends in other countries, he had few in Togo. He added to the number of his enemies by a policy of financial austerity. Togo had meagre resources, and Olympio with his business background was determined to balance the budget. A new tax on cocoa roused hostility among the farmers, and civil servants complained that their salaries were lagging behind those in neighbouring countries. In cutting his coat according to his cloth, Olympio kept the army very small – only 250 men – and this was to lead to a result which he did not foresee.

In the north of Togo there dwelt a small tribe, the Kabre, whose young men were accustomed to cross the frontier into Dahomey and enlist as volunteers in the French army. They crossed the border because under the trust territory rules recruitment was not permitted in Togo. In 1962 the French demobilised many African troops, and over 300 Kabre ex-soldiers arrived in Lomé. Among them was Sergeant Etienne Eyadema. Born in 1937, he had enlisted at the age of sixteen, and had seen service in Indo-China and in Algeria. He and others now applied for employment as soldiers in Togo. Olympio refused to do anything for them, and early in 1963 he was assassinated by a group of these men who broke into his house at night.

The insurgents did not set up a military government, but put Grunitzky into the presidential office. He submitted himself to the people in an election and received almost unanimous support. A new constitution somewhat reduced the prerogatives of the president.

About a thousand men demobilised from the French army were added to the Togo army.

This was the first military *coup d'état* which occurred in West Africa and it set an example which was widely followed.

Grunitzky continued the policy of close relations with Dahomey, and the two countries set up a joint university, the *Institut d'Enseignement Supérieur du Benin*. It had a faculty of law in Lomé and faculties of science and medicine in Porto Novo. He also continued the association with the francophone countries; in 1964 Togo joined the *Union Africaine et Malgache* (UAM) and the economic group connected with it (OAMCE), and in 1966 Togo became a member of the Entente.

However, in November 1966 the Olympio party raised a revolt, which was suppressed by the army. A few weeks later (1967) the army commander, Colonel Eyadema, persuaded Grunitzky to resign, suspended the constitution, and proclaimed himself as head of state. The persons whom he appointed to run the government departments included four officers and eight civilians. There was a majority of northern men, and this was the first time that the composition of the government reflected the ethnic make-up of the population. Eyadema appointed a National Reconciliation Committee, and asked it to arrange for elections to be held within three months; but the members of the Reconciliation Committee refused to be reconciled with one another, so Eyadema changed course, giving as his reason the 'enervating struggle' between politicians. It sounded as though he entertained the same view as Olympio about the party men, but it is easier for a colonel to override contentious factions than for a civilian. Eyadema escaped an attempt to assassinate him, and after ruling for two years he announced that the time had come to return to civilian government and made it legal for political parties to resume activity.

During these two years Eyadema had the good fortune to see welcome developments. The deep water port at Lomé, built with aid from West Germany, was completed. Revenue began to come in from the exploitation of phosphate deposits by the *Compagnie Togolaise des Mines du Bénin*. This company was founded in 1954 by French investors who were joined, first, by American partners, and then by the government of Togo, which became a shareholder. The deposits were fifteen miles from the sea and a specialised port was built at Kpeme, east of Lomé. The mineral underwent processing there, and a town was created, as well as a training centre where Togolese acquired skills which enabled them to enter the employment of the mining company. Tonnage exported passed the million in the year of

Eyadema's takeover. After 1966 electricity was bought from Ghana (the Volta dam) at favourable prices.

Despite the improvement of the economy, in every year from 1960 to 1973 inclusive the official figures showed an adverse balance of trade. However, it may be doubted whether official figures conveyed a true picture of Togo's foreign trade, because smuggling over the Ghana border accounted for much of it. Especially in the decade 1968 to 1978, when Ghana was struggling with inflation, imported goods were very scarce in Ghana and contraband imports from Togo were very large. The goods paid customs duty on entering Togo, and the trade provided handsome profits for the market women of Lomé, who conducted the traffic with every encouragement from the government, to whom they gave grateful and enthusiastic support.

Responding to Eyadema's invitation, the three old parties resumed their activities (PUT, formerly CUT; UDTP; and Juvento) but the reaction of the public was not very favourable. Eyadema was popular, and petitions and delegations implored him to continue to govern the land. He acceded to these requests and reimposed the ban on political parties. Some of the politicians tried to upset him by means of a coup, but it was not successful, and Eyadema rallied his supporters in a new party, the *Rassemblement du Peuple Togolais*. In 1972 he took steps to legitimise his rule by seeking the people's support in a referendum. More than 99 per cent of the voters expressed approval, and following that success the regime claimed to be a civilian government in which the army fulfilled duties extending beyond the normal military sphere.

In 1977 the president, now enjoying the title of General Gnassingbe Eyadema, celebrated ten years of successful rule. He was still only 40 years of age. He claimed that there was not one single political detainee. He might also have claimed credit for the discipline in the army, for, unlike most military regimes, Togo had not suffered from mutinies or intrigues among the officers. The budget, which in the year of Eyadema's takeover had balanced at about 3500 million CFA francs, was now 55,000 million! Allowance had to be made for inflation, but it was still an impressive increase. The phosphate company had been nationalised. Improvements and diversification had taken place in agriculture, helped by state marketing agencies such as Togo-fruit and Togo-grain. The country was prosperous and the peasant cultivators paid no direct tax.

18 Mali

When Guinea gave the sensational answer '*Non*' to De Gaulle's plebiscite of 1958 all the other colonies of West Africa voted to remain within the French Community. As explained in Chapter 7, they were free after that to decide whether they would be members of the Community as individual units, or as one unit (i.e., a federation of West Africa) or in some intermediate grouping. The governments of Senegal, Soudan, Upper Volta, and Dahomey entered into discussions with a view to forming an intermediate group, and this led to the adoption in January 1959 of a constitution creating a federation of the four countries under the name Mali. The federation would have combined four contiguous areas, a zone stretching from the Atlantic at Dakar to the Bight of Benin at Cotonou, and the population would have exceeded eleven millions. Ivory Coast was not of the party, for Houphouet-Boigny was resolved not to subscribe to anything which looked like a continuation of the federation of French West Africa, with its capital at Dakar. His influence in Dahomey and Upper Volta was exerted against the acceptance of the Mali constitution, and the legislatures of those two places refused to ratify the agreement: so what remained was Senegal and Soudan, which now became the federation of Mali. A federal assembly was elected, Senghor of Senegal was installed as president, and Modibou Keita of Soudan became prime minister.

The outstanding qualities of Senghor have been noted in Chapter 6. Modibou Keita was also an impressive personality, but of a different kind. He was tall while Senghor was short. In flowing robes he looked like a man of the Sahel, while Senghor never failed to look like a professor of the Sorbonne. Senghor was Christian and Keita was Mohammedan. Keita was born in 1910 and he qualified as a schoolteacher after studying at the Ecole William Ponthy. He joined RDA in 1946 and served a term of imprisonment after conviction for offences committed in the cause of RDA's agitation against the government. In 1948 he was elected to Soudan's first territorial assembly but his contribution to debate proved displeasing to the government and he was posted (as teacher, 1950) to a remote school in the Sahara desert.

This is an example of two features of the political life of the period in the French area: some of the politicians were at the same time public employees, and this provided opportunities for the government to exercise pressure upon them. However, it also illustrates the fact that pressure was not always effective, for Modibo Keita came back from the desert and in 1953 secured election both as mayor of Bamako (the capital town) and also as representative of Soudan in the assembly of the French Union. In 1956 he won the coveted post of deputy for Soudan in the Paris Chamber. Here he teamed up with Houphouet-Boigny, with whose help he was appointed to junior cabinet posts in successive French governments. He differed from Houphouet-Boigny over the question of forming the Mali federation, yet the two (although poles apart in political views) remained on friendly terms, and Houphouet-Boigny was to be a true friend to Keita in his hour of need.

Senghor frequently described himself as a socialist, but his socialism was of a gentle quality, with room for all, including the private sector. Keita's socialism was doctrinaire and aggressive. He admired Sekou Touré and tried to organise his party, *Union Soudanaise*, on the lines which Touré had adopted in Guinea. As in Guinea, chiefs were replaced by village councils under the control of the party. His aggressiveness may have been encouraged, in the new Mali federation, by the fact that Soudan had a larger population than Senegal – 3.7 million against 2.7 million. It was therefore not surprising that when De Gaulle visited Dakar in December 1959 he faced a situation in which he felt it wise to recognise that Mali had the right to declare itself fully independent: and he promised to give aid and support if that step were taken. It was taken, and Mali declared its independence on 20 June 1960. Two days later agreements were concluded with France envisaging co-operation in matters of defence, currency, and aid.

In the following month a quarrel developed between the Senegalese and Soudanese ministers about the choice of a chief of staff for the army; should this important post be occupied by a Soudanese or by a Senegalese? The quarrel went much deeper. There was disagreement on political and social objectives. The Soudanese leaders wished to follow communist methods and to establish a unitary state in which they would have dominated the Senegalese by their numbers and discipline. Senegal wanted a very loose federation. The Senegal members of the government complained that Keita acted without consulting them and furthermore, that he considered law as a formalistic anachronism, unworthy of a revolutionary. Modibo Keita as prime minister proclaimed a state of emergency and ordered the army to 'protect' all federal public buildings. However, Senghor as president could rely on the police, who were commanded by a French colonel. The police arrested Modibo Keita and other Soudanese ministers, and the Soudanese candidate for the chief of staff's post. They were all put in a train which in due course puffed over the frontier into Soudan. If they had been sent to Bamako by air, the quarrel might have cooled: but the railway journey from Dakar to the frontier in August is long, slow, dusty, and very hot. It was an insufferable indignity and when Modibo Keita stepped out of the train on his own soil, he ordered the railway line behind the train to be torn up and said that it should never be restored.

The Senegal assembly declared Senegal to be independent of the federation of Mali, so that Modibo Keita's country was left as the only surviving portion, and it has continued to bear the name of the ill-fated federation. It was declared to be the republic of Mali, 'free from all agreements and political ties with France'. It was further declared that the republic would be based on 'true socialism, solely in the interests of the most under-privileged classes of the population'. This indicated a full Marxist position, the acceptance of the class struggle as a basis for revolution – a conception which Sekou Touré had repudiated. Keita publicly blamed the French for the events which had led to his expulsion from Dakar. The country suffered from a chronic deficit in its balance of payments, equivalent to £13,000,000 a year, and France had been covering this. In defying the French, Keita turned to Russia and China for help, and both of those states sent numerous technicians. However, the French, in spite of the obloquy to which they had been publicly exposed, did not discontinue their aid. Five hundred French civil servants continued to be paid by France; the same source covered the salaries of the army and of the gendarmerie, and the cost of three air bases. A French military force remained in garrison near Bamako. Furthermore, in September 1960 that well-known friend of France, Houphouet-Boigny, visited Bamako. He received a great welcome, and stated that he came 'not as a politician nor as a head of state but as a brother, to talk about the essential problems which affect the well-being of our two countries'. The friendship of Houphouet-Boigny enabled Modibo Keita to establish a road route to the port of Abidjan, which was his lifeline during the years when communications with Dakar were impossible.

Ideologically, however, Keita felt more at home with Touré and Nkrumah. These three declared that their countries would unite as the Union of African States. However, no action was taken to make this union a reality.

In the first weeks of 1961 Modibo Keita made arrangements with the Soviet Union much closer than any African state had hitherto entered into. A military aid agreement was concluded with Russia, and that country granted credits of forty million roubles, worth about £16 million at that time. Upon the conclusion of the military agreement with Russia, France was requested to withdraw her troops, and the withdrawal was completed on 1 July 1961.

Mali appeared to have become a critical point in the rivalry between the western and the eastern powers. Diplomats from many countries poured into Bamako, and since there were no houses for them they all lived in the Grand Hotel. Trade agreements were negotiated with the United States and West Germany, and an agreement for economic co-operation with Yugoslavia. The British made a present of three civilian aircraft, whereupon the Russians doubled the bid with six. The French, although their help in defence had been spurned in favour of the Russians, did not give up; their minister of state, André Malraux, visited Bamako and negotiated a new basis of relationship.

A development plan was announced; it expressed hopeful objectives such as doubling the export of groundnuts and raising the exportable tonnage of cotton (grown in the area of the Niger dam) from 9000 tons to 50,000 tons. So long as the railway to Dakar remained closed, this was mere fantasy. The plan contained provisions for exporting meat by air to Ivory Coast, Liberia, and Guinea; and for setting up factories to produce cement, textiles, edible oil, and shoes.

The leading commercial companies, French and British, were called into consultation, and with the participation of the government they set up a consortium called SOMIEX, to which the government granted the monopoly for the importation of the ten basic articles of trade.

In 1962 agreements for economic and technical aid were concluded with the People's Republic of China and with Bulgaria. Modibo Keita visited Russia and it appeared from a communiqué which was issued at the conclusion of his conversations with President Khruschev that these two statesmen were in full agreement on international affairs.

Keita, like Touré, felt unhappy about using the French African franc as currency. He announced that Mali would set up an issuing house and have her own currency, and these things were done on 1 July 1962. As in Guinea, the use of CFA francs was prohibited by law, and as in Guinea serious disorders were provoked. Merchants, transport contractors, and shopkeepers protested, and riots occurred. Keita alleged that they formed part of a plot to overturn the government, and he said that the French embassy had helped the plotters. There were numerous arrests and 91 persons were placed on trial, including two politicians who had held ministerial posts in Paris in the days of the French Union. The two former ministers and one other person were sentenced to death, but Modibo, more merciful than Sekou, commuted these sentences to life imprisonment. Again Houphouet-Boigny held out the hand of friendship in a moment of crisis, signifying his goodwill by concluding a trade treaty, by which the cattle of Mali were to be exchanged for the kola nuts and manufactured products of Ivory Coast. Keita visited his friend Houphouet-Boigny in Ivory Coast and their meeting took place under conditions of great cordiality.

In September 1962 there took place in Bamako the sixth congress of the *Union Soudanaise RDA*, the ruling party, which was the only one permitted to exist. Many foreign guests were invited to attend, including representatives of the Russian communist party and of the Yugoslav socialist alliance. The political secretary of the party, Idrissa Diarra, declared that Mali would pass from the colonial stage to the socialist stage without passing through the capitalist stage. The policy of the party was defined as the collectivisation of agriculture, the enlargement of the industrial sector, the creation of consumer co-operatives in towns, the regulation of imports according to plan, and the imposition of government monopolies on exports.

In 1963 relations with Senegal were restored. It was high time, for the economy really could not do without the railway. Despite the optimistic language of the plan, and even though aid flowed in from east and west, the economic health of the country was bad. It was difficult for Mali even to pay for the use of the railway and the port of Dakar, but this problem was solved by the Americans, who provided dollars by way of aid. The government was embarrassed by a revolt of the Tuaregs, arabs of the desert, but military action was successful in bringing them under control in 1964.

An election was held in 1964 to choose a new legislative body. Only one party list was presented to the electors and it was announced that 99.89 per cent of the votes cast were favourable. Following this, Modibo Keita stated that the deficit on the balance of payments must be eliminated, and this involved a regime of austerity. Imports were drastically limited; all salaries were reduced by 10 per cent and some civil servants were discharged. The adoption of these painful measures enabled the government to receive a credit from the International Monetary Fund of $9,900,000.

Modibo Keita visited China and the Chinese undertook to build a textile complex at Segou. The Russians (who now were unfriendly rivals of the Chinese) undertook to construct a cement works. Both textiles and cement had formed part of the plan of 1960, but five years later they were still awaiting attention.

However, the only way to overcome the difficulty of the balance of payments was to rejoin the franc zone, for there were great advantages in membership. The bank of France in effect guaranteed the international exchange value of the currency. So in 1967 Mali made an agreement with the *Union Monétaire de l'Ouest Africain* to re-enter the franc zone. As a first step, the Malian franc was devalued by 50 per cent. Beyond that, Mali was to set her financial house in order before her currency could be made convertible with *Union Monétaire* francs, and the representatives of the *Union* were particularly concerned about 27 state corporations which were trading at a loss. The employees of these institutions were a pressure group whom Keita could not afford to offend. He argued with the financiers about the conditions which they wished to impose, and on 1 April 1968 he announced that the Mali franc was convertible 'within the framework of the financial arrangements of the franc zone' – and nobody knew what he meant.

Keita seemed to wish to demonstrate that his discussions with the French did not involve any change in his Marxist philosophy nor in his leanings towards the communist states. He governed with the advice of Marxist theoreticians, entrenched in the *Comité National de défense de la révolution*. The marketing boards, co-operatives, and other organisations in the agricultural sector were inefficient, partly because of the weakness of the staff, but also because the village people were hostile. In consequence private operators took over (without lawful sanction), paying prices which the state could not match and offering personal service in which the official bodies were not interested. The damaging phrase *ko-tid-ri* was passed round, meaning 'grow your harvest so that we can share it', an allusion to the co-operative system which obliged peasants (who had been accustomed to subsistence agriculture) to stand in queues to draw food which they themselves had grown.

Three hundred young men were sent to China to be trained as officers of the people's militia, and it was rumoured that on the completion of their training they would replace the regular army. In November 1968 the soldiers forestalled that possibility by arresting Modibo Keita and setting up the Military Committee for National Liberation, with Lieutenant Moussa Traoré as head of state. There was no bloodshed. Modibo Keita remained in custody without trial until his death in 1977. The army officers proclaimed that their takeover meant 'the end of dictatorship, demagogy, oligarchy, and all the malpractices of which the

Mali people have been the victims since independence'.

The new government reduced the powers of the agricultural co-operatives and allowed the peasants to carry on with less interference. The Military Committee was not a happy band. Personal struggles led to a purge in August 1969, and that left Lieutenant Traoré, head of state and slightly inclined towards socialism, confronting Captain Diakité, who held various ministries and was inclined more towards free enterprise. The uneasy partnership broke down in 1971 when Diakité and his friends were arrested, tried on a charge of plotting against the security of the state, and sentenced to imprisonment. Diakité died in jail in 1973.

Traoré continued the argument with the *Union Monétaire*. He discharged a third of the twenty thousand people employed in the state corporations and appointed new managers. However, in most respects there was strangely little change from the policies of Modibo Keita.

In 1970 a group of trade unionists began to agitate for a return to civilian rule, but in 1971 the union was dissolved by decree and its leaders were arrested. However, in 1972 on the fourth anniversary of the coup Traoré declared his intention of preparing a constitution which would be submitted to the people for approval as a preliminary to restoring civilian government.

Although he maintained Keita's contacts with the communist countries, Traoré was successful in concluding an agreement with France in 1973 under which Mali received substantial financial support.

The military National Liberation Committee sought popular support by holding a referendum in 1974, and the constitution which it placed before the electorate received approval by 99 per cent of the votes cast. All political activity was banned for a further period of five years; but constitutional rule was to be restored in 1979. There was tension with both Niger and Upper Volta, and the army was placed on the alert. Mali suffered severely from the drought of 1969 to 1973, and again in 1977.

In 1976 Moussa Traoré, now promoted to colonel, formed a party, which was to be the only permitted party: the *Union Démocratique du Peuple Malien*. Persons who had held any post of political responsibility in the years 1966 to 1968 were excluded from membership. In 1977 the French president, Giscard d'Estaing, paid a state visit to Mali. Modibo Keita, still under detention, died, and his funeral provided the occasion for demonstrations against the government. There was strong criticism from abroad about the treatment which Modibo Keita had received, and, perhaps because of this, many political prisoners were released. This seemed to set things moving in a new direction. In 1978 President

Traoré arrested two ministers and the chief of internal security, and an impressive demonstration in support of his action indicated that he had the public on his side. The arrested persons had represented Marxist and pro-Russian tendencies. After their departure, political discussion became freer and a new government was appointed in which nine of the fifteen ministers were civilians. These developments suggested that Traoré was taking a firm grasp of the situation with the hope of honouring the provision of the 1974 constitution regarding the restoration of constitutional government in 1979. President Traoré pointed out, in a public statement, that what he was committed to establish in 1979 was not 'civilian' rule but 'constitutional' government; and he indicated that this would take the form of a military regime ruling with the assistance of civilians. He appointed a Constituent Commission of 27 people – some soldiers, some civil servants, and some trade unionists – to work out the details.

The negotiations for re-entering the *Union Monétaire de l'Ouest Africain*, which had been languishing since 1967, were resumed.

19 Senegal

In March 1957 Senegal, still a member of the French union, elected an assembly using universal suffrage for the first time. Senghor's party won 47 seats and a party describing itself as socialist (though Senghor also professed socialism) gained thirteen. Senghor's younger lieutenant, Mamadou Dia, became the first prime minister.

Léopold Sédar Senghor, as stated in Chapter 6, was a Roman Catholic and a professor at the Sorbonne university in Paris. In prose and poetry he expounded the philosophy of negritude, affirming it spiritually against white domination. He had studied Marx and liked his humanism but could not accept his thinking as it would lead to a denial of individual liberty; furthermore, it was biased in favour of the urban minority against the rural majority. He discovered philosophic inspiration in the work of Pierre Teilhard de Chardin, believing that 'men of good will are arising in greater numbers', constructing a 'planetary civilisation through socialisation and totalisation'. He saw nothing neo-colonial in continuing in close association with France.

In Senegal Muslim religious leaders had fulfilled political and social roles. The French authorities had paid deference to them and their support of the French was loyal and constant. Two important Muslim brotherhoods in Senegal were the Mouride and the Tijjani, and the peace and ease of movement during the colonial period had assisted the extension of their influence not only through French colonies but also in Nigeria. They were more than doubtful about the advantages of exchanging French rule for the rule of nationalists and social reformers, and in 1958 some of them opposed the government on this issue. However, they received little public support. The decline of their influence was connected with the spread of lay education. In 1958 136,000 pupils (of whom 40,000 were girls) were in primary schools, which was about 30 per cent of the child population of that age. The secondary schools were attended by 8536 pupils, and employed 253 teachers, of whom (surprising though it may seem) only seventeen were African. The university of Dakar had come into existence in 1957, growing out of the *Institut des Hautes Etudes* which had existed for many years.

The Senegalese were very anxious that the federation of West Africa should continue, and negotiations to that end culminated in a conference at Dakar in 1958. The RDA, under the influence of Houphouet-Boigny, declined to subscribe to a federalist programme, but all other parties attending the conference united to form the *Parti du Regroupement Africain*. The two Senegalese parties, finding their views were close, merged to become the *Union Progressiste Sénégalaise*.

This was the Senegal which voted 'Yes' in De Gaulle's plebiscite for the French community in 1958, and which with Soudan formed the federation of Mali in 1959.

In the early part of 1960 Mamadou Dia's government carried out a revision of the administrative structure. Traditional chiefdoms were eliminated, and 139 cantons were replaced by 85 arrondissements, each administered by a civil servant called a *chef d'arrondissement*. *Arrondissements* were grouped in twenty-seven *cercles*, and each of these had a commandant. The powers of this person were like those of the prefect in a French department, but Senegal preferred the old colonial titles. *Cercles* were grouped into seven regions, each with a governor and elected assembly, and each with its own budget and self-imposed taxes. It was a democratic conception, decentralising authority so that it might be close to the people.

The break-up of the Mali federation has been described; it ended, for Senegal, with the declaration of 25 August 1960, by which the country became sovereign and independent. Senghor was unanimously elected as president. The electing body was a congress consisting of all the members of the legislature and of one delegate from each regional assembly and from each regional council. Under the terms of the constitution the president had the right to preside at cabinet meetings, and to appoint senior civil servants and army officers subject to approval of the cabinet. He could communicate with the assembly in writing only, but had the right to address the people. It was necessary for all his acts to be countersigned by the prime minister. The prime minister was designated by the president, but invested by the assembly after presenting his programme. Mamadou Dia, as prime minister, described his policy as the construction of a new Senegal following the requirements of African socialism. After the declaration of independence an agreement was made with France by which France made available 1633 million CFA (= £24m) for development and put 1700 civilian personnel at the disposal of Senegal.

A survey had just been completed by Père Lebret, who found that there were about 2,700,000 people, living at an average density of 36 to the square mile. Forty per cent of the population was under 15 years of age. Nine towns had populations exceeding ten thousand. Eighty-seven per cent of the exports in value consisted of groundnuts or groundnut products, and half of this value was exported in the form of manufactured oil. The budget was balanced without any direct subsidy from France.

Senghor and Mamadou Dia sought to get close to the people by organising the party in depth. Two-and-a-half thousand party committees were formed in villages and town wards, and in addition there were committees for professional and technical bodies. The council of the party, consisting of several hundred members, elected the bureau of the party, consisting of 41 members including Senghor and Mamadou Dia. The bureau met every week, and if it did not give orders to ministers it certainly supervised their activities. The political activity of opposition parties was not prohibited, but it met with severe discouragement. Thus the PRA-Senegal party, a leftist group formed in 1958 to vote 'No' in the plebiscite, was not allowed to publish a paper, and found it difficult to hold meetings. The *Bloc des Masses Sénégalaises* was subject to similar limitations, and the *Parti Africain de l'Indépendance*, which had communist affiliation, was proscribed and went underground.

The breach with Mali was a blow, for Senegal had important manufacturing industries, and 30 per cent of the goods manufactured or processed in Senegal had been exported to Soudan. In 1961 a five-year development plan was adopted, and its designer was that same Père Lebret who had carried out the survey. Its main objective was to improve the standard of living, and it expected to see this rise by $3\frac{1}{2}$ per cent per annum. It had five basic objectives –

(1) to increase the sense of responsibility and make each citizen or group responsible for development in proportion to their capacity or position;
(2) to place Africans in control of all sectors;
(3) to mobilise all forces;
(4) to attract private capital in 'free and trusting co-operation' with a guarantee that there would be no nationalisation;
(5) to structure the economy by integrating regional activities and growth factors more fully.

One of the principal instruments of the plan was a programme of 'rural animation' which had organisations at the centre and at regional and *arrondissement* levels. It was intended to place seven thousand rural 'promoters' in position within four years. They would be young villagers who would begin with a course lasting three weeks. Their work would be supervised by trained personnel and they would return to training centres from time to time for more courses. The government counted on them to extend the co-operative system and to transform the villages into modern societies.

The plan proposed a reform of the commercial sector. The sale of certain essential commodities would progressively be undertaken by state organisations. It was suggested that this would do away with 'middlemen and moneylenders'. The lumping together of middlemen and moneylenders suggests that private traders had been accustomed to grant credit, and that this service was regarded as an evil which ought to stop. It is remarkable how often African governments, whether colonial or independent, express disapproval of distributive traders – middlemen! It was evidently the belief of Senegal planners that civil servants with a monopoly would provide better service than private enterprisers in conditions of competition.

The economy seemed to be in good shape, for in the season 1961–2 870,000 tons of groundnuts (in shell) came to market, a record, and in following years the figure exceeded a million tons. Yet the objectives of the plan were not achieved. To quote Senghor's words, 'The plan ground to a halt'. Yet it might have been truer to say that the plan had galloped too fast. The injection of large capital expenditures into the economy had induced inflation, a deterioration in the balance of payments and a deficit in the internal budget. The budget of 1965–6 courageously attempted to set these things right. Receipts and expenditure were balanced at 40,000 millions CFA compared with 45,000 millions in the previous year. Development expenditure was cut from 12,000 millions to 6000 millions, and this reduced sum was financed by grants and loans from the USA and by a loan from West Germany.

Although the original plan should still have had one year to run, a second plan (this time to cover four years) was adopted. The main emphasis of this plan was to grow 30,000 acres of rice in the Senegal delta, and to improve the quantity of groundnuts and the efficiency of their treatment; but investment in infrastructure was to be discontinued since it was held to be overtaxing the economy.

This was a critical year for Senegal because it became necessary to change the arrangement, dating from the time of the French Union, under which France subsidised the price of groundnuts. Under the rules of the European Common Market, of which France was a member and

Senegal an associate member, the groundnut price in Senegal had to be aligned with the world price, and also import duties on goods from the ECM had to be reduced. These changes were implemented by stages and became complete in 1968. While they were coming into force serious drought occurred (1966) and it became necessary to introduce an austerity budget (1968). Although unskilled workers received an increase of pay of 15 per cent to maintain their standard of living, ministers and members of the legislature had their salaries reduced.

Mamadou Dia, the prime minister, showed himself to be more theoretical as a socialist than Senghor, and wishful to proceed much farther in extending the functions of the government in economic affairs. In December 1962 he was censured by the assembly, and a few weeks later he tried to seize power by means of a *coup d'état*, but it was unsuccessful and he was arrested and imprisoned. Following these events a new constitution was adopted, under which the president received greater powers. Senghor was again elected to the presidency, and he reaffirmed his policy of socialism:

Only socialism can resolve our development problems. It is not a question of a particular brand of socialism, nor even of Marxist socialism. For us, socialism is merely the rational organisation of human society, considered as a whole, according to the most scientific modern and effective means. That is to say that, from the start, socialism demands equality of opportunity and liberty for peoples and individuals . . . This is the proof that our socialism cannot be exactly that of Marx and Engels.

The opposition groups gathered together in the *Front National Sén-égalais*, but in 1964 this was suppressed by law. In 1966 the PRA – the only opposition party permitted – dissolved itself and joined the government party. In the following year there was a grim reminder that opposition cannot be eliminated by pretending that it does not exist, when Senghor narrowly escaped from an attempt to kill him while he was attending a ceremony in the great mosque in Dakar. In 1968 Doudou Thiam, who had been foreign minister since 1960, was dismissed on the ground that he showed 'disrespect' to the president. In the same year very serious opposition broke out among students and organised workers. Student troubles were a feature of nearly all western and African countries in the sixties and seventies. The Senegalese students of 1968 were in close touch with students of Paris where very serious disorders occurred, and their movement continued for years and spread to teenage schoolchildren. The government employed the army to keep the students under control.

In 1970 an important constitutional reform was adopted, which went some way to restore the position which had existed before the establishment of 'presidential government' in 1963. The office of prime minister was revived; the holder of that position was to relieve the president of executive duty, but would be responsible to the president. The choice fell on Abdou Diouf, not a politician but a technocrat. At the same time a new opposition party was registered under the name SUNUGAL. Senegal had never been officially a one-party state, though for the last four years no opposition party had been permitted to exist.

Senghor went to Kayes in Mali to make his peace with Modibo Keita in 1964, and persuaded him to join in a declaration in favour of setting up an inter-state committee for the river Senegal. This idea took a long time to come to fruition, but it was the seed of an important development which later became known as the *Organisation de la Mise en Valeur du Fleuve Sénégal*.

Diplomatic relations with Portugal were broken off as a gesture of support for the Guinea-Bissau nationalists, and every help was given to them short of actually allowing fighting units to use Senegalese territory as a base for incursions across the border.

The British took the view that Gambia was too small and vulnerable to be viable as an independent state, and that it should therefore seek to emerge from the colonial position into closer relationship with Senegal. However, Senegal showed little interest in promoting union (see Chapter 5). Senghor became indignant about the smuggling trade across the border with Gambia, and in 1969 he described this as 'economic aggression' and tightened control of the frontier.

In 1970 it was believed that the population had increased to 3,900,000. Dakar had a population exceeding 500,000. Islam claimed 86 per cent of the population, and 200,000 were Roman Catholics. The percentage of children in school had risen to 50. The oil crushing industry could now treat 700,000 tons of groundnuts in a year. An important phosphate mine had been opened up, and the production of dried fish had made progress. Exports and imports balanced in value.

In 1971 the student unrest continued. The groundnut crop was the lowest since the early fifties, but aid from the European Development Fund enabled the government to cancel the peasants' debts and to increase the groundnut price, so that distress was avoided. The groundnut crop in 1972 exceeded 800,000 tons, but in 1973 it fell to half that figure by reason of drought. Student disorders were again serious.

Senghor was re-elected, unopposed, as president. As a producer of phosphates the country benefited in 1974 when the world price of that commodity trebled. A number of political prisoners were released, and a new party, *Parti démocratique Sénégalais*, was formed. In 1976 three parties were officially permitted to exist. The government party called itself socialist. There was a second socialist party which claimed to be to the left of the government, and the third party was Marxist-Leninist. Elections were held, in which Senghor's *Parti socialiste* won 82 seats, the *Parti démocratique* (left-wing socialist) won 18 seats, and the Marxist-Leninist party had no success. Constitutional rules laid it down that no party might form a parliamentary group unless it had at least twenty seats, but this rule was changed in order that PDS might act as the official opposition.

In 1977 and 1978 President Senghor spoke out in favour of a pan-African defence force, to protect non-aligned states against what he regarded as communist expansionism, supported by Russia and Cuba. He sent six hundred Senegalese paratroopers to help President Mobutu in Shaba. He still valued the garrison of 1300 men which the French had maintained in Senegal under the defence agreement, concluded in 1960.

20 Ivory Coast

In ten years before independence and in the dozen years after independence Ivory Coast was the most successful of West African countries in economic growth. This was the result of a pragmatic policy of welcoming capitalist undertakings and adding effective state enterprises, and of the wise use of French aid funds, mainly for infrastructure.

Ivory Coast had started from a low level, for until the 1930s it was very poor. Its coastline was inhospitable to merchant vessels, presenting a series of lagoon bars on which the Atlantic waves pounded with frightening power. The principal ports, Grand Bassam and Port Bouet, depended on lighters which were tugged out to the ship's side at a distance from the shore. In the 1930s a new capital city, Abidjan, was built; the railway was constructed as far as Bobo-Dioulasso; a commencement was made with the vast enterprise of cutting the Vridi canal through the lagoon bar, to admit ocean vessels to deep-water quays, which were to be built at Abidjan; and the cultivation of coffee by the African population was encouraged. These beginnings began to yield their harvest after 1950, the year in which the Vridi canal was completed. The railway was extended to Wagadugu, over a thousand miles from Abidjan. Exports of coffee rose from 37,000 tons in 1945 to 114,500 tons in 1958, assisted by a subsidy from the French government which enabled producers to receive a price above the international market level. A certain amount of cocoa was grown; to this and coffee were now added bananas, pineapples, rubber, and cotton; while for local consumption there was impressive development of yams, cassava, sweet potatoes, grain, rice, cattle, pigs, and ocean fish. By 1960 the country had fifty industrial enterprises, and in that year power became available from a dam on the Bia river. French investors committed large funds, and other western nations shared in the development, but the communist countries were not welcomed; Houphouet-Boigny had been associated with the French communist party at one time but as president of Ivory Coast he was opposed to Marxism. He described his system as 'state capitalism'.

The low state of the country's development in the thirties had, as a result, an almost complete lack of literate Africans, so the staffs of the government and of private companies were provided by immigrants from Dahomey, Togo and Gold Coast, where education had been more widely available. As part of its general development Ivory Coast provided schools, and by the 1950s there were plenty of local literates. They envied the immigrants, who were mostly still in the prime of life. The *Ligue des Originaires de la Côte d'Ivoire* was formed to act on behalf of the educated local young men. There was a violent outbreak in 1958, when the young men drove out the immigrants, threatening them with the destruction of their houses and with death, and providing enough examples of this treatment to convince the immigrant communities that they must go back home. The victims of the violence crowded into warehouses near the port, where they lived in great discomfort until they could embark in ships. The government appeared to be taken by surprise and was embarrassed, but yielded to the demands of its riotous subjects, helping the immigrants to depart, rather than attempting to provide them with protection.

When Houphouet-Boigny accepted a ministerial post in Paris in 1956 he left his friend Auguste Denise in charge of party affairs in Ivory Coast. In the elections of 1957 the party, *Parti Démocratique de la Côte d'Ivoire* (PDCI) won all the seats in the legislature but in so doing it secured support from only 35 per cent of the registered voters. Opposition parties polled 22 per cent, and there were 43 per cent abstentions. The situation disturbed Houphouet-Boigny, and the events of 1958 (related above) further illustrated the need for the master's touch in Ivory Coast. In 1959 Houphouet-Boigny returned to Africa and became prime minister. He set to work to win over opposing elements to PDCI, by meeting their wishes and by appointments to lucrative positions. Some irreconcilables were imprisoned or went into exile.

The trade unions presented some difficulty, being influenced by UGTAN under the direction of Sekou Touré, whose social philosophy was by no means that of Houphouet-Boigny. Under government sponsorship the *Union Nationale des Syndicats de la Côte d'Ivoire* (UNSCI) was formed. The leader of the local UGTAN (a Guinean) was expelled, and the trade union movement was brought within the party fold. Measures were taken to eliminate a left-wing student movement, and these included the appointment of several of its leaders to responsible positions.

Houphouet-Boigny, a chief himself, did not favour the elimination of customary chiefs, and he enjoyed their support – except the chief of Sanwi, who quoted a treaty made with King Louis-Philippe of France (1830–48) in support of his independence. The Sanwi chief sought help from Ghana, but Houphouet-Boigny was able to win over the Sanwi people by his suave methods.

In the 1959 election voting took place in four large districts, so that opposition based on local support was unlikely to be successful. PDCI was in negotiation with most of the moderate independents with a view to including them in its list of candidates: and since it did not publish its list until a few minutes before closing time, those who were not included had no opportunity to take other action. The result was total victory for PDCI.

Until December 1959 Houphouet-Boigny continued to advocate a French community of which Ivory Coast and other African countries would be members. However, in that month De Gaulle, during a visit to Saint Louis, agreed that the federation of Mali might become fully independent. Houphouet-Boigny decided that if Mali was to be independent Ivory Coast must be so too. He organised a loose association of Ivory Coast with Upper Volta, Niger, and Dahomey, which became known as the Entente. These four republics made agreements with France in 1960 under which they would all become fully independent. Their independence would be 'unconditional' in the sense that they would make no agreements with France regarding defence, aid, or any other kind of co-operation until after full sovereignty had been recognised by their admission to the United Nations.

Ivory Coast became independent in August 1960.

In May 1961 certain agreements were signed with France. They were not concluded without hard bargaining. France agreed to allot funds to each of the Entente states for five years, and they were to be free to decide how the money should be used; but French officials were to have the right of inspection to verify that it was used in accordance with the declaration of intent. France undertook to pay for a university at Abidjan, and to provide the education services of all countries of the Entente with a large number of teachers. Favourable terms in the French market were accorded to certain exports, and it was agreed that each of the Entente countries might issue its own bank notes.

One of the agreements concerned defence. This raised issues which were of concern to several African governments, with which it is convenient to deal here. France offered military guarantees to ex-members of the French community when they became independent, and in return the African partner would furnish facilities in ports and airfields, and accommodation for a garrison. These arrangements were the subject of criticism on the ground that they perpetuated a colonial relationship and rendered independence illusory. Powers which wished to get rid of the French in order to insert their own influence naturally supported the criticisms. The French government was sensitive about the situation. The military agreement was not made a condition of French aid, and Upper Volta, which did not make any military agreement, concluded arrangements relating to aid which were similar to those enjoyed by countries which made defence pacts. The garrisons were withdrawn on request from Mali (1961) and from Niger (1974); and it appears that the garrison in Dahomey was withdrawn in 1965 on French initiative. This implemented a policy of reducing garrisons overseas and relying on an airborne intervention force stationed in France. For Houphouet-Boigny however there was no question of asking the French to withdraw their garrison. He said: 'We have no complexes about this, NATO countries accept American military protection, and eastern European countries rely on the Soviet Union. There is, therefore, no reason why France cannot fulfil its traditional commitment.' The defence agreement was not regarded as a disagreeable imposition but was welcomed as providing good protection without the expense of sophisticated arms, thus liberating resources for investment in growth and welfare. The agreements provided in guarded terms that in certain circumstances, at the request of the African partner, French troops might be employed to maintain public order.

Relying on the protection provided by the defence agreement, Ivory Coast proceeded slowly in forming its own army, which was gradually built up to 4000 men. In the early years the senior officers were French, but in 1964 two Ivorean colonels were appointed and in 1966 Ouattara Thomas d'Aquin assumed command. Houphouet-Boigny had, before this, created another armed service and therefore in Ivory Coast the professional army was not the only disciplined force with weapons. In 1961 a law was enacted by which every male citizen became liable for conscript service, and a call-up was introduced under which those summoned for service spent six months in the militia and six months on civilian works.

The agreements of May 1961 between France and the Entente states were supplemented, in the case of Ivory Coast, by a further agreement with France later in the same year. Large additional aid funds were allocated to Ivory Coast, and France paid for a palace for the president. A trade agreement accorded very favourable treatment for five years to

Ivory Coast coffee, cocoa, timber, and bananas. Ivory Coast was to have complete control of its foreign currency earnings (thus breaching the franc zone monolith). It was recognised that Ivory Coast might impose duties or quotas on French manufactures which competed with goods produced in the country, but in return Ivory Coast undertook to import from France manufactured products to a stated value.

Concentrating on economic growth, the government did not invite its people to devote themselves to any ideology, and in consequence the question of the function of the party and of the legitimacy of opposition was difficult to resolve. Houphouet-Boigny in 1959 said that there was room for an opposition, but that critics must accept the framework which had been established. However, Houphouet-Boigny really could not put up with an opposition party. He had been distressed by the bad effects of the faction-fights in the French Fourth Republic, and he did not want to have that kind of political chaos in Ivory Coast. He constantly tried to win opponents over to his side. His idea of a political party was like Queen Elizabeth I's idea of the Church of England – room for all. In 1962 a party seminar was held at Abidjan and frank speaking took place about the purpose of the party. It was accepted that a single party was a temporary necessity for emerging nations. The party was seen as the link between the government and the people. Its function was to explain government policy and to mobilise voluntary effort. In that year, 1962, Houphouet-Boigny expressed pride that no citizen had been deprived of liberty on account of political belief; but he spoke too soon, for later in that year a 'subversive plot' was discovered, in which it was alleged that three ministers of the government and several members of the legislature had participated, in consultation with a foreign power (unnamed), to seize power. The plotters were placed on trial; thirteen persons were sentenced to death and 51 were condemned to imprisonment with hard labour; but the death sentences were not carried out. Unrest in the party and government continued, and in August 1963 six ministers and four members of parliament were arrested. President Houphouet-Boigny reacted by concentrating power in his own hands, taking over the portfolios of defence, interior, and agriculture. Before long he chose new ministers but they were young technocrats and not politicians.

Shortly before the end of 1963 new elections took place, and since PDCI was the only party which presented a list to the electorate, it was of course successful. However, after the plots a considerable effort was made to widen the scope for public participation both in the government and in the party. A consultative body which had existed under the name National Council was expanded and activated; ministers attended its meetings, together with the heads of public services, prefects, members of the legislature, party leaders, representatives of trade unions, student organisations and women's groups, chiefs, and religious leaders. Recruiting for party membership was vigorously carried out, and the pressures applied were such that by 1965 everybody had to belong. Annual dues were levied on a scale related to income. The peasant's fee was low, but salary-earners had to hand over a substantial proportion of their pay; so that the situation began to look like that of the True Whig party in Liberia. The payment of fees was controlled by methods such as erecting barricades on roads and asking everyone to show the party ticket. The party hierarchy was remunerated, and it was composed essentially of those elements who had been in positions of social leadership before the days of the party. The party devoted itself to educating the public in understanding the government's policies, and to performing good works. From 1963 these included the building of churches, which was remarkable in a country where only 14 per cent were Christian, with 23 per cent Mohammedan and 63 per cent adhering to customary beliefs.

In 1966, still seeking to persuade opponents to change their attitude, Houphouet-Boigny met a number of imprisoned persons to talk about the possibility of reconciliation, and 96 people who responded favourably were amnestied. In 1969 a 'great dialogue between people and rulers' took place within the single party. The president and ministers met civil servants, trade unions, private employers, students, and other groups. In November 1970 another election took place and Houphouet-Boigny was re-elected for five years; 99.19 per cent of those eligible went to the poll, and the president received 99.7 per cent of the votes cast.

Among all the groups with whom he had to deal, Houphouet-Boigny found it most difficult to reach agreement with the students. University people who criticised the government's policies were organised in a body known as UGECI, while those who preferred to support PDCI joined a union known as UNECI. In 1964 UGECI was banned by decree, and membership of UNECI became a condition for receiving financial assistance from the government, as also for enjoying the benefits of the employment agency. At length in January 1965, after intense discussions, the ex-UGECI students agreed to adhere to UNECI, and their leaders were then released from prison. The president himself reasoned with the leaders, telling them that they might hold any ideas they wished so long as they did not engage in action hostile to the policy of the government; he added that they would be wise to attend to their studies and to qualify for good positions in the professions. However, it is hard to make lasting agreements with undergraduates, because a new class of young people come up each year, and students have no corporate memory. In 1969 serious disorders broke out in the university and troops occupied the campus. The rector (a Frenchman) objected to their presence and was sacked.

The university was the apex of an educational structure which was growing quickly, as shown in Table 20.1. However, Ivory Coast did not set a high priority on getting all the children into school. According to plan, half the children were to be in school by 1970. The schools adhered generally to the French type of education. This was what the public in Ivory Coast wanted, but it involved a recognition of the fact that school was not a preparation for agricultural work in the villages. The deliberately slow extension of schools was associated with the view that primary education might produce too many young people who would create a problem of urban unemployment.

TABLE 20.1   Enrolments in schools etc.

	1950	1960	1965
Primary	30,000	239,000	354,000
Secondary	1,000	11,500	28,000
Technical	–	2,000	3,800
Higher education	–	–	1,800
Percentage of children in school	29	44	

However, the schools were not the only educational activity of the government. A service of 'rural animators' taught adults in the villages, dealing with literacy, farm methods and housebuilding, and for the women, child care and sewing. Then there was the *service civique*. It brought young people from the villages to training centres where they were taught improved farming methods together with so-called civic education, which was directed towards liberating them from the dead hand of custom. When they completed the course they were settled on farms near their homes, but not on land which was subject to the customary control of the elders.

This was part of a general policy aimed at doing away with tribal customs and building a modern state. The planning office of the government promoted social and ethnological studies, both in preparation for development projects, and as part of its evaluation of projects completed. The party, as a means of moulding opinion, was employed in imparting modern attitudes in matters such as marriage and the treatment of children, and when the government judged that the public was ready for change, a law was made. The first major enactment suppressed the payment of bride-price in marriage, on the ground that it drove young men to towns to work for money and thus removed them from the farms: a pragmatic reason for an action of far-reaching social effect. Another law forbade the placing of tattoos or ritual scars on children, or the filing of their teeth; the law made such practices an assault on the person under the penal code.

In 1964 the national assembly adopted a new code of civil law. It contained provisions for the registration of family surnames and of births, marriages, and deaths. Polygamous marriages were prohibited. The law provided procedures for marriage, divorce, and separation. It prescribed rules for making wills, and governing succession to property. In this connection the custom of matrilineal inheritance, which was traditional in some tribes, was suppressed. The law eliminated the claims which the extended family might make upon the property of a deceased person, and established the principle that property should pass to direct descendants.

Economic annual growth rates between 1950 and 1965 averaged 7 per cent in agriculture and 18 per cent in industry. Houphouet-Boigny told his people, *'Enrichissez-vous'* – 'make yourselves rich'. On another occasion he said, 'Some choose African socialism; we prefer a policy of realistic peasants.' The success of the economic policy owed much to Raphael Saller, a West Indian who was minister of finance from 1958 to 1963. He began with a four-year plan covering 1958 to 1961, during which $109 million of public money was spent on development. While that plan was maturing, Saller with a highly qualified staff worked out the *Perspectives décenniales de développement économique 1960–69 et projections 1970–75*. It was a description of the way ahead, never formally adopted as a plan, but much more effective than the adopted plans of some other countries. It set targets of 7.3 per cent per annum for the rate of growth, and of $138 million as annual average investment. Between 1960 and 1965 the GNP rose from $616 million to $910 million at constant prices. The production of industry doubled, and per caput income rose 4.8 per cent per annum. The production of food increased just about enough to keep pace with the rise in population.

In 1962 the traditional head tax was abolished and a system of progressive personal tax was introduced. An interesting law was passed in 1963, under which business companies had to pay a tax surcharge of 10 per cent on their profits, but the accumulated surcharges were repaid when the company invested new capital amounting to twice the sum accumulated.

However, Houphouet-Boigny was by no means disposed to leave the direction of development to the uncoordinated thrusts of private enterprise. His advisers worked out a gigantic project of agricultural expansion, and it was inaugurated in 1965. The main part of the enterprise consisted in the development of oil palm estates. It had the financial and technical assistance of the European Common Market, which provided $32,000,000. The clearing and planting of 32,000 hectares (79,000 acres) was undertaken. In addition to oil palms other crops were planted, including pineapples, which proved extremely successful as a crop for export. Management of this government-owned enterprise was provided by a French private company with experience in Asia; under the managers' direction cultivation was undertaken by 8000 families (50,000 people) who enjoyed hereditary usufruct of the land.

An area in the south-west had hitherto been neglected, and in 1965 the government with help from the Special Fund of the United Nations initiated measures to build a port at San Pedro and to connect it with the interior by constructing a railway and roads.

By 1970 Ivory Coast was the most rapidly developing territory in Africa. The urban development of Abidjan was remarkable, and it was matched by agricultural expansion. Coffee, cocoa, timber, bananas, and pineapples were already important, and the palm oil project was immense. The emancipation of women, the improvement of health, and the progress of education, were all impressive. The university of Abidjan was increasing its student numbers, aiming at 10,000. The population had increased from three million in 1958 to about 4,900,000 in 1970. The latter figure included about a million aliens, attracted by opportunities of employment, and no less than 32,000 of these were Europeans. There appeared to be no racial tension, and Europeans intermingled freely with Africans.

Houphouet-Boigny was already a statesman of world standing before he became prime minister of Ivory Coast, for he had represented France at the United Nations. His support through the critical years of the crisis in Algeria was invaluable to the French government. After independence he kept close contact with the French foreign office and his influence with them in forming their policy in Africa was considerable.

Having defeated the efforts of Senghor and others to revive the West

Africans federation, Houphouet-Boigny formed the Entente, an association of Ivory Coast with the Upper Volta, Niger, and Dahomey, to which later Togo was added. The Entente set up a 'solidarity fund' which was fed by contributions amounting to 10 per cent of the customs duties collected in each of the four countries; which meant that the Ivory Coast put in most of the money. The fund was distributed 'according to need'.

Houphouet-Boigny opposed the federalists because he was resolved that Ivory Coast should not play second fiddle to a superior government in Dakar, but his leaning towards France and French culture led him to invite representatives of twelve francophone states of Africa south of the Sahara to assemble in Abidjan in October 1960. They agreed to meet periodically, and out of these consultations there emerged in 1961 OAMCE (Organisation of Africa and Madagascar for Economic Co-operation). However, joint action in economic affairs was not felt to be enough, so the UAM (Union of Africa and Madagascar) was formed, to promote joint political action. All the members of the UAM had been associated with the European Economic Community since 1957, but at that date France had conducted their foreign relations, and now they had to negotiate as sovereign states. This was achieved in the Convention of Yaoundé (capital of Cameroon), which came into force in 1964. Under these arrangements nearly all the agricultural exports of the African associates entered the European Common Market without paying duty, and for coffee, cocoa, pineapples, and palm oil protective duties were levied against competitive products from other sources. The African associates reduced customs duties and other hindrances which affected imports from the Common Market, but they retained the right to protect their infant industries against competition from the Common Market, and to establish customs unions among themselves. The European signatories established a development fund of $730 million a year.

While these links had been formed between the French-speaking countries of Africa, continental politics had taken the shape of rivalry between the Casablanca group and the Monrovia group (Chapters 12–14). Houphouet-Boigny adhered to the last-named. When the two groups joined to form the OAU in 1963, Houphouet-Boigny was present at Addis Ababa as one of the founding fathers. Complying with the resolution that other political associations should be dissolved, UAM ceased to exist. However, Nkrumah offended all his French-speaking neighbours by supporting dissident elements, and Sekou Touré annoyed Houphouet-Boigny and others by vitriolic attacks on the Conakry radio. Largely as a reaction to these experiences, Houphouet-Boigny took a leading part in re-establishing a political union of French-speaking states. This one was known as OCAM (1965) and it included Congo (Zaire).

Among Ivory Coast's numerous immigrants many came from the Voltaic republic, while Dahomey was still smarting from the wound inflicted by the expulsion of Dahomeans from Ivory Coast. Houphouet-Boigny came forward with a proposal that all citizens of Entente states should enjoy dual nationality, being citizens of their own country and at the same time citizens of the Entente. Citizens of the Entente would be equal before the law in all countries of the group. However, the proposal provoked clamorous opposition in Ivory Coast, where alien workers though numerous were not popular, and Houphouet-Boigny had to yield to public pressure and abandon his idea – a humiliating experience.

On the outbreak of civil war in Nigeria in 1967 Houphouet-Boigny committed himself wholeheartedly to the Biafran cause. He accorded full diplomatic recognition to Biafra and persuaded the government of Gabon to do likewise; but no other state of West Africa accorded recognition, and OAU after lengthy consideration supported the federal government. Houphouet-Boigny's commitment went far beyond diplomatic recognition. He created an organisation to help the Biafrans by arranging the transit of persons and arms through the airport of Abidjan, and beleaguered Biafra could not have lasted so long without his aid. This behaviour seemed to be uncharacteristic of Houphouet-Boigny. Nobody had been more outspoken against the practice of interfering in the affairs of other countries, and he had always been identified with policies of moderation. He had made known his opposition to the extension of Russian and Chinese influence in Africa, and also his nervousness at the aggressiveness of Islam; and he professed to see in the Nigerian situation an attack on a Christian minority by a Mohammedan majority in close alliance with the Russians. In addition to all that, the interests of *francophonie* would be served by a break-up of the Nigerian federation. If Biafra seceded there could be no doubt that other parts would also hive off, and Houphouet-Boigny, who had defeated the federalists in French-speaking Africa, would have defeated the federalists in English-speaking Nigeria. Then *francophonie* would be saved from the danger of seeing West Africa led by Nigeria, which by virtue of its large population, more than equal to all the other countries of the area combined, and thanks to its rich resources now fortified by petroleum, was bound to be a magnet attracting smaller countries. The surrender of Biafra was a bitter blow for Houphouet-Boigny.

In 1971 there was a reconciliation with the plotters of 1963, and one of them was appointed to a government post. The year 1972 witnessed the completion of a dam on the Bandama river, creating a lake of 680 square miles; and of the port of San Pedro. In the following year eleven military officers were placed on trial, accused of plotting to overthrow the government. Seven of them were condemned to death, but the sentences were not carried out.

In 1977 Ivory Coast diversified its economy further by becoming one of the world's leading producers of tuna fish, and its tourist industry welcomed no less than 180,000 visitors!

In 1975 Houphouet-Boigny celebrated his seventieth birthday. The constitution was amended in order to make the president of the national assembly (Philippe Yacé) the successor in the event of the death of a president; but Houphouet-Boigny stood for another term and was re-elected. Jean-Baptiste Mockey had been spoken of as a possible successor to Houphouet-Boigny in the early sixties, but he was involved in the plot of 1963 and was jailed; in 1976 he was reinstated in the government. Houphouet-Boigny presented his personal estates (which were considerable) to the nation.

21 Upper Volta or Voltaic Republic

This is the eighth independent state in these chapters; and it is a reminder of how different every country is from any other. The Voltaic Republic was among the most populous of West African countries, coming third after Nigeria and Ghana, with about 3,320,000 people in 1960 rising to 5,400,000 in 1970. By African standards population was dense, although there were differences between areas. Wagadugu and its surroundings had over sixty to the square mile, but in the south-west density was low, for the area was depopulated at the time of the slave trade and had been slow to recover because of the presence of tsetse flies, carrying sleeping sickness for humans and trypanosomiasis for cattle. In the monetary value of incomes, the Voltaics were among the poorest. The majority grew millet, but Tuareg and Fula wandered with livestock, living mainly off milk and curds. The landscape was undulating plain, expecting heavy rain from May to September, but dry for seven months. Water ran very short. Yet it could hardly be said to occupy the margin of the Sahara desert, for Mali, through which flowed the Niger, separated the Voltaic Republic from the Sahara. Its rivers included the three Voltas, the White, the Red, and the Black, seasonal flood-streams providing few advantages. The contours of the country through which they flowed offered no facility for damming for the generation of electricity. The region was always short of food, and many people emigrated to Ivory Coast or Ghana. In 1970 about one-tenth of the Voltaics were in those countries, selling their labour in plantations, on cocoa farms, or as domestic servants. However, if these people were financially the poorest, it was difficult to believe that, on any rational apportionment of values, they were the unhappiest. More than half of them belonged to the Mossi tribe. They acknowledged the Moro Naba as their chief, and had a history of power and stability. There was pride and satisfaction in belonging to the Mossi. The Islamic religion made progress, increasing its adherents from perhaps a quarter of the people in 1960 to about a third in 1970. The number of Christians was about

200,000. The majority of the people still adhered to pagan beliefs. Before 1960 the number of children in school was tiny, but by 1970 about 10 per cent of the children of school age were attending classes. Education was adjusted to the agricultural milieu; three-year school life was provided for children between the ages of 12 and 14, and the emphasis was on rural skills, although the three Rs and French were taught. The development of manufacturing industry (to quote an official source) was embryonic, and mining activity was limited to one small goldmine. Financially, revenue was never sufficient to cover expenditure, and the gap was covered by the Entente solidarity fund (Chapter 20) and by subventions from France.

Maurice Yameogo took the country through the abortive attempt to form a Mali federation, into the Entente, and then to independence in 1960. He did not receive universal support. The majority commanded by his party (*Parti Démocratique Unifie* – PDU) was slender, no more than 37 places in the legislature of 70. As in the other seven countries which have been described in preceding chapters, it proved impossible for the governing party and the opposition parties to live together, so in July 1960, a few days before the declaration of independence with its attendant celebrations, the leaders of the opposition parties were arrested. They were held in jail until November of that year, when they were released just prior to the date of a referendum in which the electorate was invited to approve a new constitution. It does not appear that the jailed men had engaged in any subversive activity. All that was alleged against them was that they had addressed a letter to the government which had shown that they were agitators whose only weapon was intrigue. There was no dispute about basic social or economic policy, nor were the parties sharply divided by ethnic differences. It must be concluded that the conflict was a personal struggle for the perquisities of independence within a small group of educated and sophisticated people, who meant little to the peasants.

The constitution took the form of a 'presidential' democracy. The president was directly elected by the people for five years, and he was answerable only to the people, not to the national assembly. He chose the ministers and could dismiss them. The constitution contained provisions integrating the chiefs into the administrative system.

Following the acquisition of independence by the states of the Entente the other states of the group concluded defence agreements with France, but the Voltaic Republic declined to do so. French military bases were therefore closed and French troops were withdrawn. It was

of interest that when UAM (see Chapter 20) set up a defence secretariat
they placed it in Wagadugu, capital of the Voltaic Republic, where the
French military presence was not close at hand.

Although the country was traditionally associated with Ivory Coast,
and though its railway ran to the port of Abidjan, its shortest link with
the coast would run through Ghana. Geographically it relates to Ghana
in the same way as northern Nigeria relates to southern Nigeria (see
Map 3). In 1961 Kwame Nkrumah, ever thrustful in bidding for the
extension of his 'African union', made an effort to turn this geographical
situation to political account. He visited Yameogo and captivated him
by his charm. They caused a small wall to be erected on the frontier at a
village named Paga, and they knocked it down with axes, a symbolic
gesture to abolish the frontier. As in his approaches to Guinea,
Nkrumah backed this gesture with cash. He gave two million pounds to
the Voltaic Republic, and he also made a loan of two million pounds.
Nkrumah thought that he had won a victory, and publicised it
accordingly; but Yameogo's colleagues in the Entente were angry, and
Yameogo assured them that the arrangement with Nkrumah was for six
months only and that it concerned only a limited list of goods for
consumption in the Voltaic Republic. Yameogo was made to look small
over this incident.

A government organisation was set up to engage in import/export
trade, and a European released by the largest French trading company
was appointed to run it in association with the established trading
companies.

Despite the fact that his statement had alleged that the arrangement
with Ghana was for six months only, in February 1962 Yameogo sent
his minister of finance to Accra and agreed to the establishment of a
committee combining Voltaic and Ghanaian representatives, which was
to meet every three months for the purpose of implementing the
decisions of the previous June to eliminate all customs barriers between
the two countries. However, nothing effective was done and in
September 1963 it was announced in the Voltaic Republic that 'experts'
would draft measures 'to end the shortcomings in the Ghana–Volta
customs agreement'.

A development plan was adopted in 1962 to cover a period of five
years. The European development fund contributed £3m, the French
aid programme earmarked £1.4m, and the USA and West Germany
supplied equipment. Measures concentrated on soil conservation and
on the erection of small catchment dams to provide water for men and
beasts and for local irrigation. The government showed a sense of

realism in concentrating on practical work and avoiding the temptations of showy prestige schemes. In 1963 the government took power to requisition 'for tasks of national interest' any person over eighteen years of age; strangely reminiscent of the *indigénat* of colonial days.

In 1964 the flirtation with Ghana terminated, with a complaint that the Ghana educationists had violated the frontier by constructing a school on the Voltaic side. It may have been difficult for Nkrumah to understand how his men could violate something which had been declared not to exist. At the same moment, Yameogo was engaged in a violent quarrel with Modibo Keita of Mali, alleging that there were incidents on the frontier and that Voltaic subjects resident in Mali were being badly treated. The adverse pattern of international trade, noted in Chapter 11, did not spare even the Voltaic Republic, although its economy was comparatively insulated from international trends. Therefore the budget of 1964 adopted a tone of austerity, and this made it difficult for the government, with its slender majority, to maintain support. Although the International Monetary Fund granted a credit and arranged a rephasing of the country's debts, the financial position grew worse; and in December 1965 the national assembly was asked to agree to a reduction of the salaries of all employees of the government. The capital city consisted mostly of such people, and they demonstrated in the streets against the proposal. In order to restore calm and maintain order, on the fourth day of the year 1966 the army moved in, and Lieutenant-Colonel Lamizana assumed control. This was the third successful military coup in West Africa.

The soldiers had a hard year, for the harvest of 1966 was poor and everyone was hungry, but food supplies were furnished by France, USA, and West Germany. In 1967 steps were taken to increase the production of food under the slogan 'Full stomachs programme'. In 1969 Lamizana announced his intention of re-establishing civilian government. The ban on political parties was lifted. A constitution was drawn up and presented to the people in a referendum. Elections were held for the new parliament in December 1970, and a majority was secured by a party bearing the name *Union Démocratique Voltaique,* which won 37 seats out of 57. The victorious party had enjoyed the support of the chiefs. Following the election of the parliament, Lamizana (now bearing the rank of general) took the oath as president. His prime minister was Gerard Kango Ouedraogo; but the military retained the key posts of finance and interior. Thus the government was half civilian, half soldierly; and their united forces were needed to face the year's disaster, a formidable drought. Drought struck again in 1971 and 1972 but in 1973 the country's experience was less severe than that of other parts of the Sahel. Refugees from Mali poured over the frontier. General Sangoule Lamizana was spokesman for the Sahel states in arranging relief measures at the United Nations and at the European Economic Community. There was discussion of returning to civilian government in 1974, but the prospect provoked a bitter struggle between the prime minister and the president of the legislature for the leadership of the UDV party. Lamizana lost patience with them, suspended the constitution, abolished the post of prime minister, suppressed all parties, and increased the number of military officers in the government. In 1975 and 1976 strikes occurred. Lamizana dropped some military ministers who were unpopular, and appointed trade union organisers to positions in the government. He laid down a schedule of action for returning to civilian rule in 1977. In November of that year a referendum was held, in which the electorate was invited to approve a new constitution. Seven political parties were active in the referendum, and the constitution was approved. In April 1978 voting took place for members of a national assembly, and two weeks later a presidential election was held. The number of active parties had now increased to nine. The elections were quiet, but only about 30 per cent of the adult population turned out to vote. The great chief of the Mossi, the Moro Naba, played no part in this election. The UDV was the most successful party, gaining 28 seats, but the second runner was a party led by Hermann Yameogo, the son of ex-president Maurice Yameogo, who was unable to be personally active because he had been deprived of civil rights. Following the election for the national assembly the vote for the presidency took place. Among the candidates was General Lamizana, who had been military dictator for twelve years. The military ruler invited the people to validate his rule. The result was not all that General Lamizana might have wished, for he obtained 425,000 votes out of 1,050,000 which were cast. In this election the Moro Naba supported General Lamizana, which made it surprising that the General did not secure a majority: but he was not himself a Mossi and did not speak the Mossi language. He belonged to a small ethnic group, the Samo. The runner-up was a candidate who stood in the interest of the disqualified Yameogo. Under the rules of the constitution (which were scrupulously observed) there was a second ballot, in which the public had to choose between the two candidates who led in the first round. This time the General won with 56 per cent of the votes cast.

22 Republic of Niger

The Republic of Niger is remote and probably most readers of the English language do not know where it is; and its problems are so closely related to its geographical position that it seems appropriate to begin this chapter with a map. Its area is one-third larger than Nigeria but a great part of it is occupied by the Sahara desert. The population, about four million in 1970, is concentrated along the southern fringe. It has no railways but at two points a short journey by road reaches the Nigerian railway which provides communication with the sea at Lagos. The capital city, Niamey, is however in the south-west corner of the country and its seaward communications involve road haulage of three hundred miles to the Benin railhead at Parakou, which the railway links with the port of Cotonou. The length of these communications imposed crippling transport costs on imports and exports.

More than half the population were Hausa peasants, concentrated around Maradi and Zinder. They grew millet for food and groundnuts for cash. They were not much concerned with politics provided that no one interfered with them. The region of Niamey however was the home of the Djerma-Songhay people, who had different characteristics. Traditionally warriors, they fought the French at first but subsequently proved very receptive to French culture. They included a literate élite who were interested in politics, and who occupied almost all positions of importance. Other important tribes were Fula (or Peul) and Tuareg, nomadic herdsmen. At the date of independence it was unlikely that any of the tribes felt any sense of common nationhood with the others; but they had a common bond in the religion of Islam.

At the time of self-government in 1957 the most prominent politican was Djibo Bakari. In 1958 he became a founder-member of the *Parti du Regroupement Africain*. This was a movement directed towards the preservation of a federal structure in West Africa; and when news came of the constitutional referendum which was to take place the party congress at Cotonou in July 1958 resolved to vote for immediate independence. However, between July and September (when the referendum took place) the other members changed their minds, and

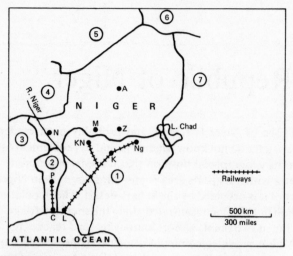

Map 4   Republic of Niger

Neighbouring states		Towns	
1	Nigeria	N	Niamey
2	Benin Republic	M	Maradi
3	Voltaic Republic	Z	Zinder
4	Mali	A	Agades
5	Algeria	K	Kano
6	Libya	KN	Kaura Namoda
7	Chad	Ng	Nguru
		P	Parakou
		L	Lagos
		C	Cotonou

Djibo Bakari was the only PRA prime minister who went into the referendum with the intention of voting 'No' – which would mean taking immediate independence. Sekou Touré in Guinea followed that course, but he was not a member of PRA.

There was an opposition party in Niger led by El Hadj Hamani Diori, who used the old label RDA. He recommended his followers to vote 'Yes', and the French *chef de territoire*, supported by the Songhay 'establishment' and by the chiefs throughout the country, gave him every help. Djibo Bakari had no party organisation such as those which enabled Nkrumah and Touré to rally the people, and only 22 per cent of the votes were cast as he wished. He ceased to be prime minister and was replaced by Hamani Diori, who therefore presided over the independence celebrations in 1960 and became president of the republic, a post which he occupied for fourteen years.

El Hadj Hamani Diori was born in 1916 near Niamey and qualified as a schoolteacher at the Ecole William Ponthy at Dakar. He had represented Niger as deputy in Paris, and became well known in international circles where his contributions gained him a reputation as a liberal and progressive person. Together with president Boumédienne of Tunis and with president Senghor of Senegal he spoke for *francophonie* – the cultural and educational background of states associated with France. At home however the *politburo* of his party left him no freedom of action. It consisted entirely of members of the Songhay or closely allied tribes and its attitude was conservative and self-interested. Hamani Diori's government included three Hausamen and a Tuareg as ministers, but the other members belonged to the Songhay group, and in any case the government was no more than the executive agent of the *politburo*. The constitution of course contained provisions under which elections were held from time to time, but these were perfunctory and no serious effort was made to enlist popular support. A situation was thus created in which opposition could only express itself in illegal and violent ways. In 1963 two ministers attempted to seize power with the support of a captain with a company of troops, but they were all arrested and brought to trial. The court awarded five death sentences and sixty penalties of imprisonment. In the following year Djibo Bakari, who was living in exile, made a bid to seize power. He had arranged for some of his supporters to be trained as commandos in China and in Ghana, and they invaded Niger from a base in Ghana, across Togo and Dahomey territory; but they were defeated and the leaders were executed. In 1965 an attempt was made on Hamani Diori's life.

Niger made a defence agreement with France and a garrison of French troops was maintained in the country. The annual deficit in the budget was made good by financial aid from France, and the annual shortfall in the balance of payments was financed by the Monetary Union of West Africa. Many Frenchmen continued to be employed in senior positions. In 1963, for the first time, the budget balanced without foreign aid; in order to achieve this civil service salaries were reduced, but it was done without fatal results to the government, such as happened in the Voltaic Republic.

In 1965 most of the French Troops were withdrawn, in compliance with the policy of reducing garrisons in Africa (Chapter 20). A squadron of armoured cars, 225 men, remained at Niamey.

Development plans were carried out in the periods 1961–4 and 1965–8. They included the usual range of projects. Rice culture was developed in marshy areas near the river Niger. The Formosan Chinese were invited to help. Attention was paid to the tourist industry because it was believed that visitors could be attracted to a national park in the south-west of the country, or to the 'blue men of Air'. Considerable effort was devoted to the encouragement of industry, and this was not without some result. By 1970 it was reported that 6 per cent of GNP was derived from manufacture. The largest unit was a cement factory, and other activities included a brewery, and works producing plastic articles, tiles, prefabricated concrete, furniture, bricks, soap and perfumery, leather and shoes, matches, and confectionery. A proportion of the groundnuts were locally processed. The enormous transport costs were a natural protective tariff encouraging local manufacture, but on the other hand the purchasing power of the market was small.

Hamani Diori tried to secure an agreement between the states of West Africa to end what he described as 'industrial chaos'. He wanted to 'harmonise development plans' by sharing out the opportunities for building new factories, allocating one industry to this country, and another to that. At his invitation Nigeria, Ghana, Chad, Mali, and the Voltaic Republic sent representatives to a conference, but Ivory Coast and Togo were noticeable by their absence; and nothing came of it.

In 1963 there was a dispute between Niger and Dahomey, and the Niger government expelled about 16,000 Dahomeans. Although, on the surface, the quarrel was over the sovereignty of a small island in the river Niger, the real reason was that (as had happened in Ivory Coast) Dahomey people tended to colonise a territory less educationally developed than their own, taking most of the jobs in the public and private sectors, while their women became successful traders. The departure of the Dahomeans provided the *politburo* of the ruling party with an opportunity of patronage, and the vacant posts were distributed to party supporters.

In 1967 an agreement was concluded for the mining and processing of uranium at Arlit in the mountains of Air. The shares of the company were held as to 50 per cent by private interests, 40 per cent by the French government, and 10 per cent by the Niger government. The latter had no money to subscribe, but the French government lent a sufficient sum to Niger on easy terms. It was agreed that 50 per cent of any profits should be paid to Niger. The enterprise came into production in 1971.

A centre for advanced studies was inaugurated in Niamey in 1971 and it secured recognition as a university in 1973.

The principal export crop was groundnuts. A British company had been the largest buyer and it was therefore natural that the government should invite it (1962) into co-operation for setting up a 'mixed company' for the purchase and marketing of the country's groundnuts. This became known as SONARA (*Société Nigérienne de commercialisation de l'arachide*). Fifty per cent of the equity was taken by the public sector through rural co-operatives and the state development bank. The other half was taken by the private sector, each trading company contributing its share. Groundnuts were bought from producers by individual traders, from whom SONARA took them over at main collecting points. SONARA then moved the nuts to port, and sold them through an office in Paris.

In a remote country where the mass is inarticulate and power is exercised by a small group it is difficult to form an opinion as to the happiness of the people. Perhaps the best indicator of the general state of affairs during the first years of Diori's rule is provided by figures of the export of groundnuts and groundnut products (Table 22.1), which showed gratifying increases. The cultivated area was extended from 2,490,000 hectares in 1960 to 3,150,000 hectares in 1968. This could not have happened without good rains, but the nuts were grown by peasants, and peasants do not increase hoeing and sowing and deliveries to market unless they have confidence in public security and unless they find the price attractive. From 1960 to 1968 groundnut growers did well, and this reflects credit both on the government and on SONARA. Unfortunately a period of dry years then set in, and the crops were small.

TABLE 22.1   Exports in tons

Representative years	1957	1962	1967	1968
Decorticated groundnuts	57,374	72,140	176,000	162,447
Crude groundnut oil	nil	1,911	7,481	3,792
Groundnut cake	nil	5,528	7,484	5,506

The northern parts of Niger never receive sufficient rain to support vegetation. The most southerly parts expect rain from April till September. The border between these zones is determined by the movement of two air masses, the tropical maritime and the tropical continental. Through most of the sixties this dividing line was (at the height of the rains) comparatively far to the north, so that pasture for the nomad herds was found in country which had been desert, and the limit of cultivation for millet and groundnuts was a hundred miles farther north than it had been. In 1969 these favourable conditions were reversed, and for five years the rains were short in quantity, badly distributed in timing, and the northern limit of useful rain moved many miles south. These conditions affected all the countries of the Sahel, from Senegal to Nigeria; but Niger suffered most.

The years 1971 and 1972 were very dry and there was great distress. The country was therefore not in a happy mood in 1972 when the president of the French republic, Pompidou, paid a state visit to Niamey. It should have been a great occasion for Diori, but there were hostile demonstrations and agitators expressed the view that the French should go home. They drew attention to the fact that more than ninety Frenchmen still held high positions in the government. Responding to this pressure, Diori asked the French government to renegotiate the agreements which existed between France and Niger, and he specially requested that Niger should derive more revenue from uranium.

In 1973 the drought became even worse and conditions of utter disaster set in for Niger and for her neighbour Mali. Half a million starving refugees swept over the border from Mali into Niger, and a similar number fled from Niger into Nigeria. Some nomads lost all their beasts, and among the agricultural population some villages were abandoned because there was no water to drink. The displaced people made for the towns and camped around them, presenting terrible spectacles of thirsty, hungry hordes with no shelter, no sanitation, and no means of support. The revenue receipts of the government fell by nearly half.

The government was completely unable to deal with this situation. Since the replacement of the Dahomean professionals by political nominees, efficiency was more than suspect. The stricken countryside was scarcely capable of protest, but groups who were capable of action, students, teachers and civil servants, protested against the government's inertia. The government reacted by using the army – a force of 1200 men – against the demonstrators. There were arrests and a number of people were sentenced to imprisonment for ten years.

Though the Niger government did little or nothing to relieve distress, the world had become aware of the tragedy and supplies of food, medicines and vehicles were arriving from many quarters. The government's inefficiency resulted in much of the aid remaining in warehouses, and some of the food and vehicles even found their way into private hands. Word passed round that the Mali refugees were receiving help while native Niger people got nothing.

The army was unwilling to continue to use force in support of a government which no longer commanded confidence in any quarter. In

April 1974 the army commander, Lieutenant-Colonel Seyni Kountche, arrested the members of the government and the *politburo* and assumed power. The president's personal bodyguard resisted, a force of Tuareg warriors who were urged to fight to the finish by the president's wife, a lady who had been very successful in the real property business. Several soldiers were killed, as also were Madame Diori and her guards.

The army was very successful in administering the relief supplies. Seyni Kountche as head of the government addressed the people in a series of speeches. Referring to the government which had been overthrown, he said:

> Concern for national development gave way gradually to unbridled self-interest, leading in all departments to shocking opportunism and to the meanest calculations. The very party which was supposed to generate creative will was led astray, its militants frustrated and reduced to a mass of bitter and angry hangers-on . . . The administrative machine, encumbered with civil servants who were untouchable because they had been recruited for reasons which had nothing to do with their ability or qualifications, has long since lost all sense of discipline, all dignity of rank, all professional conscience. The only idea of everyone was to get rich quick, even if it meant making improper use of public funds.

The party was dissolved.

Seyni Kountche declined to adopt any particular political theory, opted for the 'liberal economy', and spoke in terms of pragmatism, honesty and hard work. He quoted Boileau and Cervantes. He showed great concern with nation-building, and had much to say about Niger as a united country, combining and transcending tribal divisions. In conformity with this attitude, he wished to do away with things which were left over from the colonial regime – 'anachronisms embarrassing for France as much as for us'. He requested that the French armoured car squadron should be withdrawn, and the French immediately complied. He considered that Niger's diplomatic links with foreign countries were unbalanced, being too much confined to the western world, so he opened diplomatic relations with the People's republic of China, with North Korea, Vietnam, and East Germany.

A reform of land tenure was carried out by declaring that every field cultivated should continue to be at the permanent disposition of the farmer, whatever his legal title to the land might be. By decree various professions and trades were reserved to Niger citizens, and in most of the 'companies of mixed economy' in which the government was a shareholder, the government's proportion was increased to 80 per cent. SONARA was ordered to raise the price paid for groundnuts, and logically (since from that moment commercial people could not be expected to accept responsibility) the government took control of SONARA. As for uranium, the government brusquely doubled the price at which the produce might be sold for export, increased its holding in the mining company to 33 per cent, and brought in a second company to develop another mine, involving Japanese interests. It set up a school of mines at Agades, and in the same year a school of medicine was inaugurated in the university of Niamey.

The rains of 1974 brought the drought to an end. It appears that there was practically no loss of life attributable directly to the drought, and that through the drought years the population continued to increase at an annual rate exceeding 2 per cent. Yet in earlier droughts, and in 1931 when locusts ravaged the crops, tens of thousands of people died. Conditions had changed. With the development of the economy, many nomad and rural families had a relative who earned wages in a town, and he was expected to keep the family alive in circumstances of great distress. Improved communications enabled private traders to import food from the coastal belt. High prices were charged, but it enabled people to live. The splendid new roads of Nigeria, built with the money of the petroleum bonanza, helped in this. Finally, in 1973 international help came on a massive scale, from Nigeria, from Dahomey, from the United Nations and from the Food and Agriculture Organisation.

In 1975 President Kountche attended a meeting of the Organisation of African Unity in Kampala, and during his absence it was alleged that there was an attempt to overturn the government. Its two leaders were said to be the vice-president, Major Sani Souna Sido, and the former prime minister Djibo Bakari. It caused surprise that they should have found it possible to enter into partnership, for the major's affinities were with the conservative elements, whereas Djibo Bakari was a declared marxist. After the coup of 1974 he had been permitted to return from exile on condition that he abstained from political activity. A number of people were placed in jail but they were not brought to trial. In the following year, 1976, an attempt was made to overturn Kountche by Major Moussa Bayere, who had been the minister for rural development. His supporters were partisans of Hamadi Diori, who was still under detention. Eight leaders of this insurrection were brought to trial and were executed.

By 1978, the revenue from uranium was rising impressively. It was used to finance a three-year plan, concentrating on digging wells for the rural people.

23 Dahomey (Republic of Benin)

Dahomey was an accident of the colonial carve-up, a north-south strip 425 miles long but only 75 miles wide at the southern end. In the north, the width was 200 miles. A railway extended from the port of Cotonou to Parakou, 275 miles. The population of about 1,700,000 people in 1960 consisted of three groups who had little in common. On the coast the tribe was Fon, but there was also an important element described as Brazilians, who had been there since the days of the slave trade. The coastal population was dense by African standards, and they had a high degree of literacy. In 1952, according to a UNESCO survey, 41,000 children were in school. It was 2.7 per cent of the population, a higher percentage than any other part of French West Africa, but it was still less than a tenth of the children of school age, and the schoolchildren belonged almost entirely to the Brazilians and Fons.

North of the Fon country was Abomey, which had been the capital of an African kingdom, conquered by the French in 1893. North again was a scattered population of many tribes, mostly devoted to traditional religions, though the more sophisticated had embraced Islam. Few children attended school, but there was a small élite of civil servants and school teachers.

The Brazilians were of the Roman Catholic persuasion and had a tradition of literacy. Ambitious and successful Africans assimilated with this community. Though its numbers probably exceeded 100,000 it had but slight contact with the rest of the population. No doubt the French system had encouraged them to be separate. This reservoir of clerks and accountants was an asset to the French government and to the banks and commercial houses. Dahomey men took jobs in Ivory Coast, Niger, Gabon, and Congo. In the 1950s numbers found employment in France. The circumstances in which 12,000 Dahomeans were expelled from Ivory Coast have been told in Chapter 20. At the moment of independence in 1960 the problem of what to do with these people was acute; and soon thousands more came back from Gabon (600 in 1962),

Niger (16,000 in 1963) and Congo. Pressure on politicians to secure places for relatives of their supporters was intense.

Dahomey exported palm oil and palm kernels, gathered from wild palms in forests near the sea, and small quantities of groundnuts, shea nuts, copra, coffee, and cotton; but in the main its farmers were concerned with growing their own food in a system of subsistence agriculture. Subsistence farming does not generate money, and Dahomey was always short of that commodity. At each annual budget session the situation would be described as 'catastrophic' and each year the French government made good the deficiency.

It might have been thought that in a country where the politically active people were well disposed towards western ways, investors would find it congenial to engage in manufacturing, but unfortunately the country was too small and poor. The trading companies were the same ones as took the lead in industrial development in Nigeria, Ghana, and Ivory Coast, and they came under pressure from the government to do the same in Dahomey. It seemed impossible to identify any activity which offered hope of success. The companies were accused of preserving a colonialist monopoly, though the loss-making competition which existed in Dahomey was a curious situation to describe as 'monopoly'. It was the government which formed a real monopoly by inviting the three principal merchant houses (1962) to join with it in setting up a 'mined company' (that is, in French parlance, a partnership between the government and the private sector) for the purpose of handling the imports of certain staple commodities. It was known as SODACI, in which the government had two-thirds of the equity, and the commercial partners shared the other third.

In a general election the three ethnic groups could reckon to be about equal. Parties formed on ethnic lines, with no discernible difference between their programmes. The leaders were: (1) Hubert Maga in the north, who had been at the William Ponthy training college and was a schoolmaster; (2) Ahomadegbe, ex-mayor of Abomey, for the middle region – he also enjoyed the support of the trade unions; (3) Apithy for the Fon, an accountant by profession and in the French constituent assembly as long ago as 1945: he had an able helper, Zinsou. In its first twelve years of independence Dahomey had five civilian presidents and six military takeovers.

Dahomey was borne on the current of nationalism which swirled around it, but in the late 1950s there was really no demand for an independent state, and many people feared that if independence came it would deprive them of the advantages of the French connection, in terms of subsidies, educational opportunities, and employment. In particular, a deep-water port at Cotonou was an urgent necessity, and at a time when membership of the French community, and/or of the Mali federation, or of the Entente, were options under discussion, politicians in Cotonou were prone to make speeches claiming that the solution which they favoured was acceptable to the French, and that the port would be built if it was adopted. In fact the port was financed by the French and was completed in 1965, but it is difficult to suppose that France was influenced by any feeling of satisfaction about what had been going on in Dahomey.

In April 1960 the country was committed to becoming a sovereign state, not because of any deep feeling about it, but because the other members of the Entente (Ivory Coast, Niger, and Volta) had decided that way. An election was held to prepare for independence, and it was lively. So long as the franchise was restricted to those people who could show certain qualifications, the educated people kept politics for themelves; but in 1957 universal suffrage came in, and the educated few had to take account of the uneducated many. It was then discovered that the village people would vote as they were bidden by their traditional chiefs. This was a surprise, because for many years nearly all the traditional chiefs had ceased to enjoy recognition by the government. They had been replaced for administrative purposes by nominees who were drawn from the military and clerical ranks, and were on the fringe of the educated élite. The process of getting the people to vote, given the nature of the parties and the absence of any principle to fight over, involved nothing but xenophobia against the other regions and their inhabitants; and where there were mixed populations there was danger of violence. In the election of April 1960 the three parties registered approximately equal votes, and the three leaders continued the game of 'two-against-one' which had been going on for some years already.

Independence was celebrated in August 1960, with Maga and Ahomadegbe forming a government. Generally speaking, whenever a new government was formed in Dahomey, a new constitution was adopted, but the provisions of those constitutions were too ephemeral to entitle them to notice. The Maga-Ahomadegbe government did not last long. After three months Ahomadegbe withdrew from it and organised workers went on strike and demonstrated in his favour. It must not be supposed that the organised workers were a social proletariat. They were, no doubt, the lower fringe of the urban élite, workers in railway, postal, and clerical appointments, but they still formed part of the small section whose *monthly* wage was more than the *annual* income of the farmer. Their attachment to Ahomadegbe was a factor in Dahomean politics for many years. To protect himself against the strikers Maga brought archers from the north to Cotonou. He entered into an agreement with Apithy; they made themselves president and vice-president, and held an election. Three people were killed in riots, and the government secured 468,000 votes against Ahomadegbe's 213,000. A little later Ahomadegbe and his closest supporters were accused of plotting to overthrow the government, and were arrested.

This government made aid agreements with the USA and with the Formosan Chinese, so that the country was no longer entirely dependent on France to relieve its poverty. It also concluded the agreement with Togo for customs union, for harmonising rules regarding the trade in produce, and for a hydroelectric project (see Chapter 17). However, the budget of 1961 had to devote 80 per cent of the expenditure to civil servants' salaries. This situation had arisen because the government had 'absorbed' so many civil servants who had been obliged to return home from other francophone countries.

Since the year 1680 the Portuguese had possessed the fort of São Joao de Ajuda, in the coastal town of Ouidah. This enclave had never formed part of the French colony, but in 1961 the government asked the Portuguese to leave. The Portuguese governor defiantly burned the place to the ground rather than allow it to fly another flag.

In 1962 the government felt obliged to cut the salaries of ministers, members of parliament, and civil servants, and in the budget speech the fault was placed upon 'monopolies inherited from colonialism'. Still, the government had been in power for two years and felt sufficiently confident to release Ahomadegbe and his friends. It was over-confident, for in the following year Ahomadegbe, supported again by the trade unions, produced a state of disorder. They complained that while they were being asked to accept lower wages, money was being spent on a palace for the president. The army, led by Colonel Soglo, took charge of the situation. It was a force of 1800 soldiers and 1200 gendarmes. This might be described as the second successful military coup in West Africa; yet the army had no intention of holding power. Soglo's aim was to restore order and to install a viable civilian government. After a brief period during which the three leaders were brought into a committee under Soglo as president, the game of two-against-one was played again, and Ahomadegbe with Apithy formed a government. They accused Maga of trying to murder them and placed him in detention. The north revolted, but the army suppressed the disorders with a number of casualties. While these events were taking place the republic of Niger expelled the Dahomey clerks.

The new government introduced a budget imposing further austerities, and appealed to foreign investors to help with development, promising inducements and guarantees. The merchant companies consulted together, and they felt obliged to do something; they formed a consortium, which at last in 1968 committed itself to manufacture textiles and bicycles.

The followers of Ahomadegbe and Apithy met in a conference, and they asked their leaders to define 'the doctrine of the party' – a confession of the emptiness of Dahomean politics. One reform stands to the credit of this government; an agricultural programme was introduced into the primary schools, and in a few places arrangements were made for the further education of school-leavers in agriculture and crafts. In 1965 the French military force was withdrawn; gratifying to those who were sensitive about neo-colonialism, but a further blow to the country's economy. In the same year the National Company of Oil Mills came into operation as processor of palm kernels.

The government had been in office for two years but there had been riots and plots, and judges had been dismissed, and the budget had as usual imposed new sacrifices, and the begging of aid from France had again been humiliating. Things headed towards another crisis, and perhaps for that reason Maga was released from prison. It was time for another round of two-against-one. Ahomadegbe appeared in Porto Novo wearing uniform at the head of an armed force, and the Porto Novans replied by demonstrating in favour of Apithy. However, Colonel Soglo would not have it. He declared himself to be the head of the state. The three regional bosses, Apithy, Ahomadegbe and Maga, went into 'exile' in Paris, where they appeared to live in amity and comfort. Soglo raised a man named Congacou, president of the national assembly, to be in charge of a government of technicians, three army officers and ten civilians. Recognising that the national assembly, with its regional divisions and its preoccupation with patronage, was of no service to the country, Soglo provided for Congacou the advice of a National Renovation Committee consisting of 35 senior citizens, including some army officers. The Congacou government imposed even more painful economies, but they could not heal the economy, and they were not helped by the three bosses, who continued to command their parties from Paris, united at last in the aim of embarrassing the technocrats.

It was reported that only 10 per cent of children leaving schools could hope to find employment, and that nearly a thousand Dahomeans were pursuing courses abroad in professional disciplines, who would nearly all have to seek employment outside Dahomey – which for practical purposes meant in France. It was a tragic situation.

While the technocrats were contending with their problems, the army was not happy in barracks. In 1967 a Military Vigilance Committee was formed. It consisted of fifteen middle and junior officers and of some NCOs, and from this date the army ceased to be a disciplined force and fell victim to factions, regional or self-interested.

The technocrat government, like its predecessors, lasted about two years, and was overturned by young officers who had been brought into the capital city to deal with labour unrest. The leader was Major Kouandete, a northern man of the Somba tribe, and a graduate of Saint-Cyr. However, there was much hostility towards Kouandete, both at home among the military cliques, and in France where De Gaulle, who had recently been host to Soglo, resented the treatment which Soglo had received from Kouandete. The patience of France was exhausted, and French money ceased to flow. Kouandete, bowing to these difficulties, made way for Lieutenant-Colonel Alley, who was installed as head of state; but he was monitored by a Military Revolutionary Committee of three captains, eight lieutenants, and three NCOs. Investigations were conducted into the behaviour of people who had recently held office, both military and civilian, and serious corruption was revealed. After several months of confusion and two elections (at which politicians who had held office were banned) the presidency was awarded to Zinsou, who had been associated with Apithy. Dahomey now became officially a one-party state (*Parti national unique*). French aid was partially resumed.

The soldiers went back to barracks but not to discipline. They set up an assembly of ninety members, officers, NCOs, and private soldiers; but it did not speak with one voice, for it was riven by faction.

Zinsou established a reputation for probity, but he was no more successful than his predecessors and in 1969 the country seemed to be falling to pieces. The north spoke of secession, and an Assembly of Northern People met, as though to carry out the threat. Apithy (still in Paris) talked of making the Fon country a thirteenth state of the Nigerian federation. Kouandete, now ranked as lieutenant-colonel, again took over the government, and he was assisted in his efforts to restore order by the energetic intervention of French diplomats. France, at that period, could be expected to react strongly against any suggestion that a francophone land might move within the Nigerian orbit. The result, surprising though it may seem, was a presidential committee of three men: Apithy, Maga, and Ahomadegbe. They came back from Paris and carefully divided the patronage between them. Each was to act as the chairman of the commission for two years, and the roster began with Maga. To support the regime's prestige France made a generous contribution so that the half-university, shared with Togo (see Chapter 17), could become a full university.

However, the regime had an old-fashioned look. It took no account of the fact that earnest people had been seeking a national and radical solution – the party members who had asked for a policy; Soglo, who had tried the technocrats; and the young officers who had sought a new start with Zinsou. The triumvirate of old-stagers was a provocation to reformers, and there were plots and arrests. Maga got through his two years and was just handing over to Ahomadegbe when a young officer named Kerekou seized power (1972). He described his regime as the 'Revolutionary Military Government' and announced radical reforms, including for instance the introduction of vernacular languages into the schools, which hitherto had taught only in French. Relations were established with the People's Republic of China (whereat the Formosan Chinese withdrew their aid) and with other leftist governments, and a commission was appointed to revise the agreements with France. Like all its predecessors, this government soon announced the discovery of a subversive plot, and this was made the occasion for public demonstrations against France, which resulted in damage to the French embassy.

Kerekou's financial position was eased by a loan of a million pounds from the government of Nigeria, free of interest for 25 years. However, even with that help, the financial situation simply did not permit any brusque rupture of arrangements with France. Since 1960 Dahomey had received in aid 57.9 billion CFA francs, of which small amounts had come from Nigeria, Canada, the World Bank, the Entente Solidarity fund, 5 per cent from the USA, 29 per cent from the European Common Market, and 64 per cent from France. French help was worth even more by reason of the support given to the currency by the West African Monetary union. Nevertheless, when the francophone states of West Africa set up the *Communauté Economique de l'Afrique de l'Ouest* Dahomey, having signed the agreement (1972), called for the formation of a different economic block, to comprise Nigeria, Togo, and Dahomey under the title 'Benin union', and withdrew from CEAO (1973).

For two years the Kerekou regime maintained its equivocal position, seeking a new basis of international relations and domestic policy.

When petrol prices rocketed in 1974, Dahomey was hit very badly. Its poverty became worse than ever, and the reaction took the form of a complete commitment to communism. Kerekou declared that the country would become Marxist-Leninist, practising scientific socialism. The French-style prefects were replaced by commissars. Trade unions, students' clubs, and women's societies were reorganised on centralised lines. Banks and commercial concerns were nationalised, though the private enterprise partners in certain mixed companies were retained, and notably those in Ibetex, the textile mill.

These measures were not accepted without attempts at opposition, which were denounced as plots, and followed by trials and death sentences. One of the ministers was shot dead when caught in an embarrassing situation with the president's wife; he was however popular with the trade unions and they turned out in force to protest against the treatment which he had received. Their demonstration was ruthlessly suppressed, with several deaths, and it became clear that Dahomey now had a ruler of a very different temper from those who had gone before.

The year 1975 was lively. The name of the country was changed to Benin. Three plots were discovered, and the frontier with Togo was closed because it was alleged that political exiles were gathering in Lomé. The military government brought into being a party under the name Benin People's Revolutionary Party.

In 1977 a curious incident occurred. An aircraft landed at Cotonou and armed men emerged from it. They attacked various objectives but after some hours they climbed into their aircraft and went away. The government protested to UN and OAU and both those bodies sent teams of investigators, but no explanation was provided. It was generally assumed that the armed men intended to displace the Kerekou regime, and that they had expected to be welcomed by a fifth column, which failed to appear. The government reacted by forming a people's militia, and a Marxist-Leninist constitution was promulgated.

24 Nigeria, 1960–67

Under the constitution which became operative at independence, the parliament of the federation consisted of the Queen, a senate, and a house of representatives. The Queen appointed a governor-general to exercise on her behalf the functions of head of state, acting on the advice of the prime minister. The senate consisted of (a) twelve senators from each region, selected at a joint sitting of the legislative houses of the region; (b) four senators from the federal territory of Lagos, including the Oba of Lagos and a chief selected by the white-cap chiefs and the war chiefs of Lagos; and (c) four senators selected by the governor-general on the advice of the prime minister.

The federal house of representatives consisted of 312 members, of whom 174 came from northern Nigeria, 73 from eastern Nigeria, 62 from western Nigeria, and three from the federal territory of Lagos. They were elected by adult suffrage except in the north, where the suffrage was confined to adult males.

In each region there was a governor, a premier, an executive council, a house of chiefs, and a house of assembly. Eastern Nigeria (surprisingly, in view of the earlier decision to have no senior chamber) now had a house of chiefs.

The division of authority between federal and regional governments was in the constitution. Defence, external affairs, communications, customs, and banking belonged to the federal government. There was a concurrent list of subjects on which laws might be made either by the federal legislature or by a regional legislature, but if any law made by a region was inconsistent with an enactment of the federal parliament, the federal law prevailed. Subjects which were not exclusively federal, nor on the concurrent list, were for the regions.

The principal political parties at the time of independence were (a) the Northern People's Congress (NPC), mainly Fulani and Hausa, which had an overwhelming majority in the northern region: it had 142 members of the federal house of representatives; (b) The National Council of Nigeria and Cameroons (NCNC), mainly Ibo, which had a large majority in the eastern house of assembly: it had 89 members in the

211

federal house; (c) the Action group, which had a majority in the western region; with certain allies, it had 72 members in the federal house. No party commanded a majority in the federal house. The NPC and the NCNC entered into a coalition and formed a government, and the Action group became the official opposition.

A few days after independence Sir James Robertson, the last British governor and first governor-general, left Nigeria and was succeeded as governor-general, representing the Queen, by Dr Nnamdi Azikiwe. Two years later Nigeria became a republic and Dr Azikiwe became its first president; the change of title made no difference in practice, but in form the head of state was now a Nigerian, and this was felt to be more dignified for an African country than having the Queen of England as the titular head of state.

In operating the constitution, the leaders had to devote their whole time to the centre unless they preferred to give their time mainly to the region. Azikiwe, in becoming the head of state, gave up his post as premier of the eastern region, where he was succeeded by Dr Michael Okpara. The Sardauna of Sokoto, Sir Ahmadu Bello, preferred to be premier of the northern region; perhaps it was a condition of the coalition that he should remain there, thus making it possible for the vice-president of the NPC to become the federal prime minister – Abubakar Tafawa Balewa.

The constitution was a parliamentary democracy, but politics degenerated into a struggle for regional advantages. The basis of power was patronage; the successful politician secured support by providing his followers and their friends with jobs or contracts or scholarships or local amenities. Conversely, constituencies which supported opposition members of parliament were neglected. Some of the federal ministers, and some ministers in regional governments, engaged in corrupt practices. These became so flagrant that there was really no attempt to hide what was going on. Some people were making themselves rich, but the compulsive reason for corruption was the need felt by politicians to create political funds with which to buy electoral support.

Awolowo made the decision to hand over the premiership of the western region to his lieutenant, Chief Akintola, and to spend his time in Lagos as the leader of the opposition. Awolowo had always been a man of principle and a deep thinker, as his great book, *The path of Nigerian freedom*, had proved as long ago as 1946. He gave up his comfortable position at Ibadan and exchanged it for the difficult role of opposition leader because he believed that it was his duty to create a basic issue of principle between the sides of the house, and to form an opposition which could appeal to people in all regions of the federation. He moved close to the 'democratic socialists'. He made an electoral alliance with Tarka of the United Middle Belt Congress, and their joint manifesto for the elections which were held in northern Nigeria in 1961 included (1) minimum daily wage to be the same as in western Nigeria; (2) nationalisation of the tin mines; (3) a separate Middle Belt state; (4) mechanisation of agriculture; (5) peasant farms to be converted into socialist co-operatives. The methods employed by Tarka to promote the Middle Belt state exposed him to a criminal prosecution and he landed in jail. The Zaria native authority banned political activity because of disturbances. Awolowo visited Accra and after conversations with Nkrumah he expressed the view that Nigeria should join the union of African states. Nigeria, he said, was mistrusted by other African countries because of her military alignment with Britain. For nation-wide appeal he went in for electioneering gimmicks such as helicopters, which could fly everywhere and impress people with Awolowo's ubiquity. However, there was not much support for democratic socialism and it tended to identify Awolowo with persons such as Tarka, whose actions were regarded as treasonable. The helicopters and other ballyhoo tricks infuriated the other parties and provoked exaggerated reprisals. Among those who were most hostile to Awolowo in these matters was his lieutenant, Akintola. As head of the Action group government in the western region Akintola wanted to move in the opposite direction; to make friends with one or both of the parties which constituted the federal government, in order that he and his helpers might do better in patronage.

In 1962 the Action group split into two factions, supporting Awolowo and Akintola. This led to chaos in the western region government. The detail of events can be passed over; the federal government suspended the constitution of the region and appointed an administrator. Awolowo and twenty-four others were arrested and placed on trial for treason, and Awolowo was convicted and sentenced to imprisonment. The removal of the opposition in this manner was the end of the effort to conduct the affairs of the federal parliament on the Westminster model.

Important events occurred in the sphere of higher education. The university of Nigeria at Nsukka was founded, and it enjoyed the support of Michigan State University, USA, whence the vice-chancellor was drawn. Thus Nigeria's second university started with an affiliation which was intended to be different from the Oxford-and-Cambridge background of Ibadan. It was hoped that the new university might be more integrated with the surrounding community. About the same time a report had been received from the Ashby Commission, a body of distinguished academics drawn from Nigeria, Britain, and the USA. Their assessment of the manpower needs of the federation led to the conclusion that the number of university students ought to be multiplied by four, reaching the figure of 7500 by 1970. Following the Ashby report, universities came into existence at Zaria (Ahmadu Bello), Ife, and Lagos. The first vice-chancellor at Lagos was an Ibo, but in 1965 he was replaced by a Yoruba in circumstances which were not accepted without controversy. The new vice-chancellor was stabbed, and serious disturbances on the campus led to the closure of the university.

While independence was being celebrated at Lagos with impressive dignity, in the Tiv division of the northern region serious disorders broke out, because some people wanted to have a separate state within the federation. Armed police were despatched to the scenes of trouble. It simmered for four years and broke out again in violence in 1964, when the army had to be employed.

In 1960 two battalions of troops and a detachment of police went to Congo to join the United Nations force.

There was controversy over the defence agreement with Britain. It provided that Britain should assist in expanding the Nigerian forces, and in return Nigeria granted over-flying rights for British military units. The opposition alleged that the agreement tied Nigeria to British policies, and a good deal of heat was worked up, especially by young people who marched in demonstrations through Lagos. The parties to the agreement, the British and Nigerian governments, came to the conclusion that it was causing more trouble than it was worth, and it was rescinded in 1962.

Important discoveries of petroleum were made just at the time of independence. It has been established as a principle by the colonial government, in the Petroleum Tax Profits ordinance of 1959, that profits derived from petroleum should be shared between the government and the oil company in equal proportions. In 1960 880,000 tons were produced, and the figure rose to five million tons in 1965. In that year a refinery was opened near Port Harcourt. This important new source of revenue helped to finance a six-year development plan, adopted in 1962. It was partly paid for by a loan from Britain, and its most impressive enterprise was the Niger dam.

In 1961 the people of the northern part of Cameroon voted in a plebiscite, held under the auspices of the United Nations, to join Nigeria. The Southern Cameroons, on the other hand, voted to leave Nigeria and form a federation with that part of the old German

Cameroon which had since been a French trust territory.

The NPC-NCNC coalition government divided the western region into two parts by creating the mid-west state, thus hiving off those parts of the western region where the people were not Yorubas.

Akintola left the Action group and founded the Nigerian National Democratic party. He resumed, or was placed back into, the premiership, relying for support in the regional house on members of the NCNC, and receiving financial aid from the NPC. He liked to speak of his friendship with Sir Ahmadu Bello, Sardauna of Sokoto, premier of the northern region and leader of the NPC. He was in the pocket of that remarkable man. Ahmadu Bello was related to the ruler of Sokoto, the Sarkin Musulmi, and he acquired the title of Sardauna when he was the treasurer at Sokoto. He was tall and spoke beautiful English. He saw more clearly than any other member of the Fulani-Hausa establishment how essential it was for the north to accept the inevitability of change and to organise itself politically in order to associate with southern Nigerians on (at least) equal terms. Up to the year of independence and for some years after he appeared to be a moderniser, and showed himself able and willing to co-operate with the NCNC. However, about 1963 he yielded to other inclinations. He devoted more time to religion, and preached in mosques on Fridays, urging people to lead austere lives. He established relations with the heads of certain Muslim states, which could not fail to embarrass the Federal minister of foreign affairs. He maintained a court, and encouraged people to show him exaggerated deference. Perhaps he was at his best in his devoted support of the university, named after him at Zaria. He quarrelled with the Sarki of Kano. There had been rivalry between the Sokoto and Kano families, and there were sectarian differences; Kano adhered to the Tijjania, followers of Sheikh Sidi ben Omar Tijjani, who lived at Ain Mahdi in the Sahara and was linked with Sheikh Ibrahim Niasse of Kaolack in Senegal; whereas Sokoto was the headquarters of the traditional Kadiria. So Kano received no favours from the regional government. It was therefore hardly surprising that many people, not only in the south but in the north, felt uneasy about the Sardauna. It was most regrettable that he made a public reference to the federal prime minister, Sir Abubakar Tafawa Balewa, as 'my lieutenant'. In the hierarchy of the NPC the Sardauna was president and Balewa was vice-president, but the prime minister of the most populous country in Africa cannot be any man's lieutenant.

A general election was due in 1964, and a new party line-up formed to contest it. The coalition, although still forming the government – or at any rate sharing out the ministerial portfolios – did not present itself to the country as a united force. Parties were grouped as follows:

(*a*) Nigerian National Alliance. The largest constituent was NPC. Akintola's Nigerian National Democratic party belonged to it. The Mid-west democratic front and the Niger Delta congress joined. To achieve an all-Nigeria appearance, there was a small but vociferous Ibo group known as the Dynamic party, under Dr Chike Obi.

(*b*) United Progressive Grand Alliance. NCNC was the largest element, supported by Action group (now much reduced), by Aminu Kano's Northern Elements Progressive union, and by the United Middle Belt congress.

In preparation for the election a census was held in 1962 and as soon as the results were announced each party accused its rival of falsifying the figures, for the purpose of securing more parliamentary seats for those parts of the country where its support was strongest, and for establishing a high base for the allocation of the federal revenues. The north scrapped the figure of $22\frac{1}{2}$ million which was reported by the census team, and claimed 31 million. The federal prime minister asserted his authority by cancelling the census, and another was held in 1963. This time all parties had ample time to prepare tricks to inflate their figures. The results were 'reduced' following tests by professional demographers, and a total of 55,600,000 was declared. It was divided between the regions in proportions which were close to those which had resulted from the last colonial census in 1952.

Intense bitterness had entered into Nigerian politics and the conventions of tolerance on which parliamentary constitutions depend were no longer observed. During the election campaign it became obvious to the leaders of UPGA that they stood no chance of gaining a majority, and they boycotted the election. The boycott was effective in the east because polling booths were not opened, but in other parts of the country it was only partly effective. In refusing to participate in the election the UPGA intended to provoke a crisis, and they were successful. The president, Azikiwe, may have had hopes of setting up a non-parliamentary government; the federal prime minister regarded himself as still in office and would have been prepared to treat the situation as an 'emergency', and to govern with the assistance of the armed forces; but the attitude of the leaders of those forces was decisive, for they were not prepared to take orders either from the president or from the prime minister. So Azikiwe and Balewa saw that the only option open to them was to seek a solution in terms of compromise. The chief justices of the federation and of the eastern region lent their good offices, and UPGA finally agreed to allow elections to be held in those constituencies where the boycott had been effective and to recognise a broadly based government which Balewa had formed. In the election NNA secured 199 seats, UPGA had 103, and there were five independents.

While these political struggles had been going on the trade unions had been demanding higher wages, and they supported their case by general strikes in 1963 and 1964. The outcome was a wage review which led to an increase of pay for lower-paid workers, but little for those who were better off.

The election gave rise to serious disturbances in the western region, and they continued through 1965. In October of that year an election was due to be held in the region, and an attempt was made to conduct it, but disorders were rife and no one believed in the validity of the results which were announced. Akintola held on to office but the factions fought in the streets and it was generally believed that arms were being supplied to the gangs by the political alliances, NNA and UPGA. The situation therefore began to look like a civil war. Criminals took advantage of the occasion, and the roads became unsafe. Federal troops were used to preserve order in the Abeokuta area.

People in Lagos seemed to be strangely unconcerned with the crisis; they were more exercised about what was going on in Rhodesia, and great dissatisfaction was expressed about what was regarded as the soft attitude of Harold Wilson's government in Britain towards Ian Smith. Could this have been an effort of the federal government to rally public opinion by the time-honoured tactic of uniting the country on an external issue? Be that as it may, Wilson was sufficiently impressed to arrange a Commonwealth conference at Lagos in the first week of 1966, and he personally attended.

It was subsequently learned that an army mutiny had been planned to take place during that period, and that it was postponed for a week in order that the mutineers might not have the British prime minister and various Commonwealth heads of state on their hands. As it was, president Makarios of Cyprus stayed in Nigeria and became involved in the coup when it took place.

Ibo officers of the federal army led the mutiny. Among those who lost their lives were the prime minister of the federation (Alhaji Sir Abubakar Tafawa Balewa), the federal minister of finance (Chief Festus Okotie-Eboh), the premier of the northern region (Alhaji Sir Ahmadu

Bello), the premier of the western region (Chief Samuel Akintola), and
seven army officers of the rank of lieutenant-colonel of higher. Of these
seven one was Ibo, two were Yoruba, and four belonged to the north. It
was a curious thing that of the four northern officers who suffered death,
not one was of Hausa origin. Three were Kanuri from Bornu in the
north-east, and the fourth belonged to Jos in the middle belt. This
became of importance later, when public opinion began to focus on the
'murder of northern ministers and officers'. The brutal slaughter of the
federal prime minister was a great shock to public opinion at home and
abroad, for he had been outstanding in keeping his hands·clean from
corruption and in placing the welfare of the country above region, tribe,
or party.

The majority of the army remained under discipline, and the general
officer commanding, Major-General Aguiyi Ironsi, brought the situation under control. The council of ministers (that is to say, the rump of
the council) met and decided to hand over the responsibility for
governing the country to the army. The acting president (Azikiwe
was in Britain, convalescent after illness) formally requested General
Ironsi to assume power. Thus· the military regime had a colour of
legality.

The officers who had engaged in the disturbances were now in a
curious position. In a sense they were the leaders of a successful coup,
but officially they were mutineers whose uprising had been suppressed.
It is not surprising that in these circumstances great modesty was shown
about having had any connection with the events of Saturday 15
January. There was one exception—Major Patrick Chukuma
Nzeogwu, whose voice had proclaimed the deed from the radio station
at Kaduna. He had led the attack on the Sardauna's house, during
which Sir Ahmadu Bello and his senior wife had been killed. Nzeogwu
was Ibo but he had been born and bred in Kaduna and he spoke Hausa
and wore northern dress. He was Roman Catholic, attended mass every
day, and abstained from drink and tobacco. On the radio he had
declared that the object of his movement was to 'establish a strong,
united and prosperous nation, free from corruption and internal strife'
and to ensure that the people had 'freedom from fear or other forms of
oppression, freedom from general inefficiency, and freedom to reach the
sky in every field of human endeavour both nationally and in-
ternationally'. Following the weekend of drama, Nzeogwu held a tiny
area in Kaduna 'for the revolution', while the rest of the country
responded to General Ironsi, able to claim a legal status. Ironsi
appointed a northerner, Major Hassan Katsina, as military governor at

Kaduna, and Nzeogwu handed over to him without resistance. Nzeogwu and other officers who had taken part in the conspiracy were arrested, but they were held under conditions of comfort, and Ironsi appeared to be embarrassed to know how he should treat them. He was anxious to convince the country that he was not acting simply in the Ibo interest, and in pursuance of this he not only appointed Hassan Katsina as governor of the north, but he invited the Sarkin Musulmi, relative of the murdered Sardauna, to visit him in Lagos, where he accorded the Sarki every honour. He also chose northern troops for his own bodyguard.

In these actions Ironsi showed wisdom, but his principal advisers were of the Ibo race. Among them was a civil servant named Nwokedi. In May Ironsi announced to the nation in a broadcast address the initiation of the second development plan, and in the same address he announced the adoption of proposals which had been laid before him by Nwokedi, namely the unification of the civil services of the federal government and the regions. The principle of this change was defensible in terms of preventing regional selfishness, and to render it acceptable to the north a public service commission was set up in which the chairman was a northerner. However, it was a bad moment to announce the change because public opinion had been brooding on the events of January, and a dangerous mood had set in. The victims of the mutiny had included several distinguished northerners, and people held their breath and waited for the north's revenge.

By May people were beginning to speak of the January revolution as 'An Ibo coup'. The unification of the civil services was capable of being presented as a device to bring the country under Ibo control, since if the top jobs were allocated in accordance with seniority, the Ibos would do better than the other ethnic groups. Much was made of this, and in northern towns students and civil servants paraded the streets in protest. The Ibos in the north occupied a high proportion of the positions in the railway, in the post office, in the public works department, in the banks, and in the accounting departments of the trading firms. It was difficult for a young Hausa recruit to feel happy in a roomful of Ibos, and attempts by local people to penetrate these occupations, though generally favoured by employers, did not succeed. This was the economic background of the tragic events which now took place. Religion also in some places influenced the situation. On a Sunday in May mobs attacked members of the eastern ethnic groups in many places while they were attending church. No distinction was made between Ibo, Efik, Ibibio and Ijaw. They wore the same type of dress and were known in the north by the generic name of *yameri*. Disorder continued for a week in some places, but the police did their best to bring the mob under control, and in Kano, where some of the worst incidents occurred, the *Sarki*, a liberal man of wide sympathies, took a strong line in restoring order. The number of deaths was variously reported. The official figure, 306, was certainly too low, but on the other hand reports that tens of thousands had suffered death were exaggerated, though widely believed in Ibo circles.

Many Ibos and other easterners living in the north now sent their families home. The bloody weekend had made them feel insecure. At this juncture the military governor of the eastern region, Lieutenant-Colonel Ojukwu, extended an invitation to the *Sarki* of Kano (who had shown such a liberal attitude to the Ibo in the recent troubles) to become the Chancellor of the University of Nigeria at Nsukka, a post rendered vacant by the resignation of Dr Azikiwe. The *Sarki* accepted the invitation and was installed as Chancellor with the usual ceremonies. It was a great gesture on both sides; it indicated that at this stage Ojukwu was seeking Nigerian unity and was not committed to secession.

Unfortunately tempers were rising and leading events in a sinister direction. In July a mutiny occurred at Abeokuta (western region) in an army unit where the troops were mostly northern but the officers were largely Ibos. The lieutenant-colonel and other Ibo officers were killed, and Ibos in more junior positions were either murdered or put in jail. The example of Abeokuta was followed in some other military depots; northern troops eliminated the Ibos either by killing them, or by giving them the opportunity to pack up and go. The head of state, General Ironsi, was at this time the guest of Colonel Fajuyi, military governor of the western region at Ibadan, and both of them were murdered.

The next most senior serving officer was Brigadier Ogundipe, also an Ibo, and he made haste to leave the country. After his departure, the most senior army officer was Colonel Gowon, chief of the army staff, and he took charge. On 1 August he broadcast to the nation a moving address, introducing himself as the new head of state, and saying, 'The basis for trust and confidence in our unitary system of government has not been able to stand the test of time . . . the base for unity is not there . . . We should review the issue of our national standing and see if we can help stop the country from drifting away into utter destruction.'

Gowon was a Christian, 31 years of age. He belonged to the Angas tribe, a small group in the Plateau province of the northern region, a group of people who had mostly embraced Christianity. His father had been an evangelist of the Church Missionary Society. Many young men of the Angas joined the army. Yakubu Gowon had been trained for his commission at Sandhurst, had served in Congo, and had completed a course in the staff college at Camberley. He possessed great charm and ready humour, and his obvious integrity won him many friends.

The north's good wishes were with him anyhow, and to win support in the south he immediately released a number of southerners who were serving prison sentences for political offences. Awolowo was released from prison in Calabar and flown to Lagos, where Gowon met him at the airport, saying that he would have need of Awolowo's 'wealth of experience'. An advisory panel of 'independent and responsible Nigerian citizens' was named to advise the military government.

The west and mid-west rallied to Gowon, but Ojukwu, military governor of the east, took a different view. Whether or not the incidents of January were an 'Ibo coup' will probably always be a matter of opinion, but there was no doubt that the incidents of July were anti-Ibo. Ojukwu refused to acknowledge Gowon as supreme commander, and indicated that his policy was now one of breaking up the federation; but at this stage it hardly appeared to involve the question of secession, for many prominent northerners were expressing the view that the north should go it alone.

In this juncture, when Nigeria appeared to be falling to pieces, Gowon made it clear that so long as he was in command there would be no tampering with the unity of Nigeria. What, then, had he intended the nation to understand when he made his first broadcast address, in which he said, 'the base for unity is not there'? Had he intended to say, 'the base is not there, but we must create it'? Or had he despaired, and now, a month later, plucked up courage? Or had he intended to say merely that the policy which inspired Ironsi's unification decree had proved unacceptable? There were people close to him in Lagos who wished to preserve the unity of Nigeria. The chief justice, Sir Adekotumbo Ademola, was one of them. They included Commodore Wey of the Navy, Kam Salem and M. D. Yusufu of the police, and three outstanding civil servants, Ayida, Asiodu, and Atta. Colonel Murtala Mohamed, a Kano man who was destined to play a great role, was of the same mind.

The opinions of this group took account of a new fact which was known to them, but which the general public was hardly yet in a position to appreciate; namely, that Nigeria was on the point of becoming a very wealthy oil producer. It was patently absurd for the north to embrace a policy of separate statehood when the oil was all in the south. The oil which had been discovered at that date was partly in the mid-west and partly in the east; but the eastern oil was all in the areas which were inhabited by the minority groups of the eastern region, and none of it was in the Ibo heartland. This circumstance was a formative element in the thinking of Ojukwu and his circle. Oil revenues were to provide the economic basis for setting up the eastern region as an independent state; but this could only happen if the eastern minorities seceded from the federation along with the Ibos, either voluntarily or under pressure.

The unification policy announced by Ironsi was cancelled, and on 12 September there assembled in Lagos a conference, consisting of a delegation from each region, to consider constitutional arrangements. Gowon led off with the view: 'We must not minimise the advantages that we will derive from our remaining together as one strong political and economic entity.' The delegations from north and east, unfriendly though they were, agreed in advocating a loose 'confederal' structure. Only the mid-west came out strongly in favour of maintaining federation, but they suggested that more states should be formed; and this now became part of Gowon's policy.

Discipline in the army presented a problem. Two battalions, one stationed between Lagos and Abeokuta and the other in Kano, had few officers left. Led by non-commissioned officers, the men put into practice their own version of 'military government', which included highway robbery. The problem was indeed tackled; the troops were martialled and brought under command, and with the idea that it would be easier to handle them if they were broken into small parties, they were divided among many towns of the north. The idea may have been well-intentioned, but it was a fatal error, for it placed these units, practised in evil-doing, in a position to organise a criminal enterprise throughout the length and breadth of the northern region. Murder and looting began early in September, and rose to a ghastly climax on 1 October.

In these September massacres many easterners died. Ojukwu put the figure at 30,000; other estimates ranged between 5000 and 10,000. The terror was such that hundreds of thousands fled away to their tribal homes in eastern Nigeria. Trading companies and banks chartered aircraft to move their employees. Many left by train, but there were tragic incidents when trains were waylaid by bloodthirsty mobs.

The Nigerian railways in Northern Nigeria lost 5800 employees and in the federal telecommunications only 450 were left out of 2000. The private sector suffered similar losses.

In August Ojukwu, military governor of the eastern region, had assembled his advisers and read a draft declaration of secession, but after discussion they had decided not to proceed at that time. However, it was decided that the region had to place itself in a position to secede from Nigeria, and to fight if challenged. In August 1966 a civil servant and an Ibo poet, who had been close to Ironsi and who were now in Ojukwu's inner cirle, had already been to France to buy arms, and at the same time an order for arms was placed in Czechoslovakia. It seems possible that the financial backing for these earliest orders came from the private fortunes of several wealthy Ibo people, including the Ojukwu family. However, in the early part of 1967 the federal military government, going to great lengths to avoid provocation, allowed the government of the eastern region to transfer £6,000,000 from the Central Bank of Nigeria to an account in London, and this was used to pay for arms.

The events of September and October 1966 caused such emotional revulsion in the east that there was no longer any room for argument. Ojukwu retaliated by forcing all non-eastern Nigerians out of the region and placed more orders for arms. Two ships loaded with weapons and munitions arrived at Port Harcourt in January 1967.

Lieutenant-Colonel Emeka Odumekwu Ojukwu was born in 1933. His father, Sir Odumekwu Ojukwu, made a fortune as a transport contractor and received the honour of knighthood for public services. The son took a degree at Oxford and entered the administrative service, but then (to the surprise of his friends) went 'back to school' by taking the Sandhurst course in order to become an officer in the army. He explained his action by saying that in his view Africa would be ruled by her armies.

The eastern region at that time was believed to have a population exceeding twelve million people. Of these, about seven million were of the Ibo tribe and the others belonged to numerous small ethnic groups. The largest town was Port Harcourt, where the townspeople were nearly all Ibos, although the original inhabitants of the area, the Edwerri, have been described as 'marginal Ibo', speaking a dialect related to Ibo but claiming a separate identity. The solidarity of the Ibos is of fairly recent growth but in the twenty years before 1966, during which Nigeria had experienced rapid growth, the Ibo people had shown an amazing response to opportunities. Their region had been the poorest part of Nigeria and that is why so many men and women sought their opportunities in the other parts of the federation. Now, driven back to their homeland, they looked to the new oil revenues and their own skills to provide the basis for independence and rapid industrialisation.

In the north, Gowon despatched a team round the country to encourage further thought about the constitutional issue, and to explore alternatives to the separatist solution which the northern delegation had supported in August. The team included Makaman Bida, who had been the minister of finance in the regional government, and he spoke for the Northern People's Congress. With him was Tarka of the Middle Belt, now out of prison, who was able to speak for the Tiv (largely Christian and important in the army). Aminu Kano of the Northern Elements Progressive Union was also a member; he had acquired standing as the establishment lost theirs. With these was an economist named Amaru Dikko, who was looked upon as the spokesman of young educated northerners. The success of these consultations was unqualified: the north rallied to the policy of Gowon, the policy of keeping the federation but creating more states within it.

The constitutional conference reassembled but the east was no longer represented. The British government sent Malcolm MacDonald, a senior statesman, to try to arrange a meeting between Gowon and Ojukwu, and at the invitation of the government of Ghana they did meet at Aburi in that country; but the Aburi meeting had no useful result – indeed, the two sides could not even agree what had taken place. On 31 March 1967 Ojukwu published the Revenue Collection Edict, by which the government of the eastern region took complete control of all revenues arising within its area, and declared it illegal for companies established in the region to pay taxes to the federal government in respect of activities within the region. During the next three weeks further edicts were published, known in the east as 'the survival edicts'. One of them cut off the courts of law in the east from the federal court of appeal. Another brought to an end all connection between the produce marketing system in the east and that which operated in other parts of Nigeria.

These actions were regarded in Lagos as highly provocative, but some weeks went by before Gowon was ready with his counter-stroke. On 27 May he declared a state on emergency, which gave him complete powers. He used them to appoint a government consisting of both military and civilian commissioners and in which Awolowo was the deputy to the head of state and commissioner of finance. The federation was declared as consisting of twelve states. The great monolithic block of the north, which had been so dear to the heart of the Sardauna and his friends, was divided into six states – an operation which has been described by John Oyinbo as 'the end of the Fulani empire, which had outlasted the British'. The eastern region was divided into three states, and this was of course a direct challenge to Ojukwu. Immediately, on 30 May, he declared the republic of Biafra to be an independent state.

25 Nigeria: the Civil War

The Nigerian Civil War stimulates interesting comparisons with other famous civil conflicts – the English, the American, and the Spanish, for instance. There are the long periods of stalemate, broken suddenly by attempts to secure a decision through deep penetration of the enemy's lines. There are the efforts of the weaker party to internationalise the struggle. The special feature for which there are few historical precedents is the clemency of the victor.

At the beginning of the war the federal forces consisted of about 8000 regular soldiers. The officers were few because some had been killed in the coups, and of the survivors a substantial proportion, being Ibos, went to Biafra. But ex-regulars were recalled to the colours and this produced a valuable reinforcement of non-commissioned officers who had performed active service in Burma, and who were delighted to be back in uniform. Volunteers were called for, and by the end of the war the size of the armed forces had increased to 150,000.

The Biafrans had some trained officers but in the opening engagements of the war casualties were heavy among this group, and the principal elements in the officer corps were university lecturers, professional men, and civil servants. The large number of refugees provided a source of recruits for the ranks; but only Ibos were accepted for the army, and many unemployed young men of the Efik, Ibibio, and Ijaw tribes were upset when their applications were refused. Ojukwu may have had reason to doubt the devotion of those ethnic groups to his conception of Biafra, but the exclusion of these elements from the army was almost the equivalent of making a present of their affections to the federal cause. In the course of the war the Biafrans may have placed as many men under arms as the federals, but many of them were in irregular units with improvised arms. When the first federal invasion took place, Ojukwu ordered every administrative division to produce 1000 men with dane-guns, matchets, clubs, stones, and knives. On the arrival at Enugu of 2000 double-barrelled shotguns which had just been imported, 2000 additional volunteers were enrolled and they were despatched to the front with a gun and four cartridges each, but without

226

any training. At the same time the police were ordered to go to the front as fighting units, and this made it difficult to maintain normal civil security thereafter.

Neither side had any tanks. The federal army was equipped with armoured cars, and the Biafrans imported a few armoured cars from France in time for the opening of hostilities. At the outbreak of the war the only artillery was on the federal side and consisted of 25-pounders which had been used for firing salutes. Both sides acquired heavier guns as the war went on.

Before hostilities opened the Eastern region government bought two B26 bombers, which were flown by French pilots; and they requisitioned several helicopters from the oil companies. The federal military government, alarmed by the news, asked the British to provide a squadron of fighter aircraft as a defence against the bombers. The British declined to comply with this request, taking their stand on the line that they would continue to supply to the federal government arms such as had been supplied in the past, but no new varieties which might 'escalate' the fighting in the event of war. The federal government then asked the Americans for fighter aircraft and again met with a refusal. These refusals provided the Russians with the opportunity for which they had long been seeking, for they had no doubts that Nigeria was the most important of the countries in Africa whose friendship was valuable to them. They supplied fighter aircraft and arranged for Egyptian pilots to fly them. They also provided heavier artillery than was available from Britain.

The Biafrans opened hostilities in May 1967 by bombing Lagos and several other places from the air. The most serious damage was done at Lokoja where a bomb exploded in a church, killing twelve members of the congregation. In August 1967 the Biafrans raided Lagos, Kaduna, and Kano from the air. They used a Fokker Friendship aircraft of Nigerian Airways for a raid on Lagos, but it blew up over the city with the Biafrans' principal arms-dealer, Oppenheim, on board. The principal result of these actions was to provoke the federal command, when at last its aircraft arrived from Russia, to carry out bombing raids on targets in Biafra. They appear to have done scarcely any military damage, but civilian casualties were numerous. These possibly did more than anything else to make the people in Biafra believe what Ojukwu's public relations people were telling them – that the federal government intended to carry out a policy of genocide, and kill them all. The air raids provided the most effective material for the Biafran propagandists, who won over many people throughout the world to the Biafran cause.

On the western frontier of Biafra was the Mid-west state. It was an area containing several ethnic groups, and those who occupied the country adjoining the River Niger spoke Ibo dialects and were generally sympathetic towards the eastern Ibos. Even more important was the fact that of the 42 officers belonging to the forces in the Mid-west, 28 were Ibos; and the military governor, Colonel Ejoor, was the only non-Ibo in the top ten. Ejoor proclaimed that the Mid-west would take no part in the fighting. It was to be neutral, a buffer state like Belgium between Germany and France. Accepting this situation, the federal military government concentrated its fighting force – the first division – on the only frontier over which it could attack Biafra, namely the border which separated the Eastern region from the Benue province of the Northern region. The distance from Lagos was 1000 miles and the last part of the route was a bad road. It was July before the federal force was deployed on the frontier. It appears that some senior officers on the federal side held that they should not attack until their Russian planes arrived, which seemed likely to coincide with the end of the rainy season. However, the rival forces had closed up to the frontier from both sides and on 5 July shooting began. By 7 July the federal command felt that they were committed to a major operation so they went forward and quickly occupied Ogoja province towards the east, a non-Ibo area which had been allocated to the South-eastern state under the arrangements recently announced (Chapter 24); and further west they took Nsukka, where the buildings of the new university provided them with a valuable fortress. The Nigerian navy, which remained loyal to the federal government and operated with great efficiency, landed a force at the mouth of the Bonny River, occupied the oil shipment terminal, and sealed off the entry to the sea from Port Harcourt. Ojukwu's seaborne link with the world now depended on Calabar.

In provoking the federal army to commit itself in this way, and to lengthen its line of communications under rainy-season conditions, Ojukwu prepared for a strategical stroke in another direction. On 9 August he despatched a force westwards across the Niger into the Mid-west state, violating the neutrality which Ejoor had claimed. The commander of the force was Major Banjo (or Colonel Banjo as he now became), a Yoruba officer whose attitude was mysterious and is likely to remain so. He had compromised himself in the January mutiny, and was under detention in the Eastern region at the time of secession. He was released and incorporated in the Biafran army; and now Ojukwu named him as commander of the force whose mission was to thrust into Yorubaland and win support there. Ejoor's Ibo officers, forewarned,

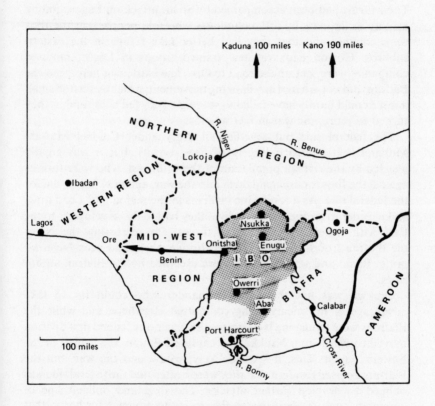

Map 5 The Nigerian civil war

arrested Ejoor and welcomed the Biafran column. The attackers moved at blitzkrieg pace, and in two days they had pressed into the Western region as far as Ore, only 135 miles from Lagos. At this moment, however, their commander Banjo seemed to lose interest in the war and wasted time by speaking over the radio from Benin, indicating that he still entertained hopes of a united Nigeria. If the troops at the spearpoint at Ore had been vigorously and resolutely commanded, they might have taken Ibadan and reached the northern outskirts of Lagos. Their thrust had been accompanied by an air attack on Lagos, and by activity in that city by fifth columnists who told people that the Ibos were coming, and that they had better take refuge in the eastern suburbs. Gowon had very few trained troops in Lagos, but two companies were sent up the road to Ore. The battle was fierce, but the Biafrans did not attempt any flanking movement, which against so small a force could hardly have failed to succeed. They fell back, and as they turned to retire, the war in fact was lost.

The federal side put together an army under Colonel Murtala Mohamed. It consisted largely of new recruits, but it was greatly assisted by the civilian population of the Mid-west, who were furious against the Ibos for dragging them into the war, and now full of zeal for the federal side. As a result, Ibo civilians in the region had a bad time, and in order to escape with their lives they had to fly, as refugees, to the East with the retreating Biafran forces. On recrossing the Niger the Biafran troops blew up the new bridge which had been Nigeria's pride. Banjo and several others were executed by the Biafran authorities.

Ojukwu was not the only commander who could try to take advantage of his enemy being committed elsewhere, and while the Biafrans were struggling back across the Niger, the federal first division moved forward from Nsukka and captured Enugu, the capital of the Eastern region. This, it seemed likely, would end the war; but the Biafrans refused to admit that they were beaten and the federal side was obliged to develop further attacks. The long and difficult line of communication made it inadvisable to try to advance further in that sector, and the attacks, when they came, made use of the short line of communication to the blown-up bridge facing Onitsha, and of seaborne communications. The navy landed a force at Calabar and after fighting in the rubber plantations near that town it was able to make the Biafrans retire to the line of the Cross River. There for a year and a half the armies faced one another without fighting, arranging to bathe in the river at mutually convenient times. A column from Ogoja made its way south and joined up with the Calabar force, thus isolating the Biafrans from Cameroon.

In 1968 the federal army stormed Onitsha across the Niger. They achieved their immediate objective and occupied the town, but it cost them dear, for many men were drowned. The Biafrans harried the federal forces behind their lines, both in Onitsha town and west of the Niger. The federal army was not able to move forward from Onitsha until the last days of the war.

The experience at Onitsha probably taught the federal army to make better preparations for their next major stroke. It took a long time to prepare, but when the blow was struck it went home. The force at Calabar had been augmented, and had been prepared for a lightning stroke. Suddenly, after all the friendly sun-bathing on the river banks (which may have lulled the enemy into false confidence) the federal army advanced over the Cross River under the command of Colonel Adekunle and in a very short time reached Port Harcourt. They were assisted by members of the local population, who were not of the Ibo tribe. The Ibo garrison in Port Harcourt devoted the brief time available to burning British property. Biafran officers warned the managers in charge (who were of course Africans) that the properties would be burned, and a small demonstration of youths then paraded with slogans and lit fires in the buildings. These fires went out, but the following day troops pumped oil into the premises and left them burning like torches. From Port Harcourt the federal force thrust to the north and took Owerri, in the heart of the Ibo country; again it looked as though the war must end, but the Biafrans counterattacked and the federal force had to withdraw. Another pause now ensued because the Biafran situation was so hopeless that Gowon hoped they would surrender, and did not want to press his advantage with the inevitable casualties and destruction. However, by the end of 1969 it had become obvious that the only way of bringing the war to an end was the complete occupation of the seceded area; so at last the federal forces advanced on all fronts and the war came to an end in January 1970 following the flight of Ojukwu and the surrender of the army commander.

That completes the summary of the military operations, but the story of the civil war must include a brief account of what was going on behind the lines.

The principal company producing oil in the Eastern region in 1967 was Shell, and under the terms of the Revenue Collection Edict (see Chapter 24) the company was required to pay its royalties and rents to the Biafran government, although by federal law the payments had to be made to the federal government. The general manager of Shell, Stanley Gray, tried to negotiate a compromise, but Ojukwu would not rest content with anything less than the full revenues, and he placed Gray under arrest. The managing director of Shell in London immediately went to Biafra and secured Gray's release. So far as the British commercial community was concerned, this spelt the end of relations with Biafra.

The Biafrans received valuable support from South Africa and Portugal, to both of which countries anything which could divide the African nations and sap their energies appeared as an advantage. Despite this, the Biafran propaganda won the sympathy of those elements in Europe and America who were most opposed to the policies of South Africa and Portugal. The Biafrans employed a public relations agency with headquarters in Geneva, named Markpress. The federal government believed that its cause was good and its conscience clear, and it did little in the way of public relations. The Biafrans on the other hand created a public relations organisation consisting of university teachers who had fled to Biafra from their posts in universities elsewhere in Nigeria. They showed skill in attracting attention and winning sympathy, at any rate in the short term; for in spite of the power of propaganda, truth will out. Anti-British newslines were considered useful, and so there were stories about British parachutists, marines, bombers, and warships. These reports were so effectively presented to the European public that they actually led to a boycott of British goods in part of Switzerland, of all places, that traditional citadel of neutrality. The news media of the world, press and television, were full of Biafran propaganda day after day for years. The films on the television news were horrific, and they were sometimes available within 24 hours of the events which they were supposed to depict. In the United States, Britain, France, West Germany, Scandinavia, and Switzerland public opinion was not merely won over, but was involved with deep emotion for the Biafran cause. It was accepted that the federal government intended to kill all the Ibos (genocide) and that its principal weapon was the blockade (starvation). The war was also presented as a religious *jihad* by the Muslims against the Christians, and this was particularly effective in Roman Catholic countries, and with the Pope.

In fact, General Gowon had issued to every man of the armed forces a booklet laying down a code of conduct. It was humane and it was generally obeyed. When Murtala Mohamed was taking Ibo prisoners in his advance through the Mid-west, employers received from one of his staff officers letters inquiring whether they would be prepared to take the captured people back into employment; yet Murtala Mohamed was, at that moment, being castigated in Biafran propaganda as 'butcher Mohamed'. When the propaganda was at its height, so that even the British government could not feel sure that it would be able to persevere in supporting the federal government in defiance of the weight of public opinion, the British foreign secretary, Michael Stewart, suggested to the federal government that they should invite a team of observers from four countries and two international organisations to go to the fighting fronts and report on the allegations of genocide. The United Nations, the Organisation of African Unity, and the governments of Britain, Sweden, Canada, and Poland sent representatives; and from the moment when their reports began to flow back, the genocide story was killed.

British opinion was much reassured by the prime minister, Harold Wilson, who paid a visit to federal Nigeria in March 1969, and came back to Britain with convincing assurances that the federal side was not engaged in genocide.

The Biafrans' most important friend in the international community was President Houphouet-Boigny of the Ivory Coast. He became deeply committed to their cause intellectually and emotionally. Ojukwu was his young friend; he regarded him as a hero defending Africa against Mohammedan penetration and against the Russian communists. Houphouet-Boigny's influence with President Bongo of Gabon was sufficient to persuade him to adopt the same course. They both accorded full diplomatic recognition. The only other countries which recognised Biafra were Tanzania, Zambia, and Haiti. The action of Presidents Nyerere of Tanzania and Kaunda of Zambia seemed strange, since they held themselves as leaders of the African campaign against South Africa and Portugal; but they were annoyed with Britain over the Rhodesian question, and as Britain was supporting the federal government they recognised the other side. Houphouet-Boigny's enthusiastic support was communicated to the French government, with whom his influence was great. France, like the rest of western Europe, was much affected by the Biafran propaganda, and General De Gaulle was not averse to seeing Nigeria fall to pieces since it would destroy the strong centre of English culture in Africa and improve the possibility that the French language and culture might establish their predominance. It has been suggested that the French government thought that by showing friendship towards Biafra they might win some advantages in the petroleum business, but it is not to be believed that the French were as ingenuous as that. The French government, while allowing the Biafrans to purchase arms, and smiling upon the logistical support furnished by Ivory Coast and Gabon, was careful to remain in correct relations with the federal government.

The Organisation of African Unity was much concerned with the war, but in this direction the federal diplomacy was much more successful than the Biafran; at the critical OAU summit meeting in Algiers in September 1968, the federal government received overwhelming support.

Leading international charitable societies sent food to Biafra, to relieve the starvation which was believed to exist. The natural route would have been overland through Nigeria, and the federal government readily agreed. However, Ojukwu could not accept the offer, because it would have destroyed the genocide story, which was the main theme of his internal propaganda by which the Ibo people were persuaded to go on fighting. For the same reason, he would not allow aircraft carrying food to fly in by day, because if they did so it would be obvious that the federal government approved. Therefore Ojukwu insisted on night flights. The charitable organisations were so deeply impressed by the Biafran propaganda that they agreed. The night flights of relief planes then provided cover for the planes which were carrying arms from Portuguese airfields in Lisbon and São Thomé, and from the Ivory Coast and Gabon. The relief organisations spent money in Biafra on landing fees (which were charged at high rates), on salaries and allowances for staff, and on the purchase of supplies (which were available in some areas) for transfer to other places where the need was more acute. The foreign currency went into the fund which the Biafrans used to pay for arms and public relations services.

Among the pilots employed by the relief organisations was a Swedish aristocrat, Count von Rosen. He was deeply affected by what he saw in Biafra, and was moved to indignation by the federal air raids against civilian targets. He therefore arranged with some friends to provide six small aircraft, which he and his friends served as pilots. On their way to Biafra they bombed the airfield at Port Harcourt, from which the federal air force was operating at that time. They carried out daring raids against oil installations in the Mid-west and against Benin airport; but this was late in the war and had no effect on the outcome.

Towards the end of 1969 one of the principal relief organisations, Joint Church Aid, reported that they had made 4361 flights, and claimed to be providing relief for 3,000,000 refugees in Biafra.

It is very difficult to secure a clear picture of the state of the Ibo heartland during the war. By the accounts of people who were there, palm oil and plantains and yams were available in sufficient quantities to prevent starvation. Yet the stories of famine, as reported by the relief organisations, came from neutral observers who were also on the spot. It must be borne in mind that the testimony of those who say that supplies were sufficient is the testimony of survivors. These were the people who had local connections. The worst sufferers were the refugees, either people from the north who had lost their local ties, or villagers who fled before the oncoming federal forces under the influence of the 'genocide' propaganda.

When the declaration of independence was made in 1967 it was not associated with any policy of social revolution, and the successful record of the Ibo people in the private sector of economic life pointed to the probability that their state would be committed to the encouragement of private enterprise. However, as the war went on Marxist theorists gained influence with Ojukwu, and in June 1969 he issued a policy statement which became known as the Ahiara declaration; it committed the government to the principles of state socialism.

Some time before the final collapse the people of the Aba area refused to co-operate with Ojukwu's government. They refused to reconnoitre or to provide food for the army. Ojukwu retaliated by arresting the Aba leader Dr Jaja Nwachuku and other prominent persons, and set up a military tribunal to govern the area.

In May 1967 Gowon had announced that Nigeria would be divided into twelve states, and these officially came into existence on 31 March 1968. Since by that time the federal forces had occupied a considerable portion of the country which was to form the East Central (Ibo) state, a state government was set up, led by an Ibo named Ukpabi Asika. He had been a lecturer in political science at Ibadan university. At the same time a government was set up for those parts of the South-eastern state (Calabar, Ogoja, etc.) which had been 'liberated' by the federal army. The governor was Michael Ani, an experienced civil servant, who made an important contribution in organising the administration of his state.

In spite of the war, life in most parts of Nigeria continued in a strangely normal manner. It is true that for some months after the flight of the eastern people from the north, the government services were very short of staff and the commercial houses had difficulty in keeping their accounts; but it was remarkable how quickly the labour shortages were made good by local people who proved able to undertake the work.

The creation of the new states provided the most exciting opportunities for local developments, and the building activity at centres like Maidugari, Sokoto, and Jos was remarkable. The oil revenues were beginning to be important in spite of the war, and they permitted the launching in March 1969 of a four-year reconstruction plan with an investment total of £1113 millions. Under military government the political consequences of creating twelve states were of course obscured, but nevertheless it rapidly became clear that there was now a far better basis for a federal form of government than there could ever have been under the previous arrangements, when the vast northern region was an uncomfortable neighbour for the three smaller regions in the south.

Cultural life also flourished, and in 1969 the Nigerian festival of arts was held at Kaduna. The most exciting part of a festival of arts is the dance competition, and among the competitors was a dance troop from the East Central state. They were all Ibos, and their brilliant performance won such public acclamation that they were obviously the winners: which the official judges quickly confirmed. Yet at this very moment the world was being told, and was largely believing, that the federal government was bent upon the genocide of the Ibo people!

When the fighting was over, the clemency of the victors was remarkable. The federal government awarded no medals for service in the war, thus indicating their view that the sores must be healed and not kept open. Ukpabi Asika, the administrator of the East Central (Ibo) state, was appointed a member of the supreme military council. Ibo property-holders who owned houses and shops in northern towns found (to their surprise) that their property was handed back to them in good order. The government of the Rivers state did not take the same view about Ibo properties in Port Harcourt, but it is probably true to say that that was the only place where hostile feeling continued to be acute after the war was over.

Following inquiries into wartime records, in 1971 several hundred ex-Biafran military, police, and prison officers were dismissed from service, including Lieutenant-Colonel Effiong, who had commanded the secessionist army in the final stage. In 1973 sixty-two more officers who had served in the secessionist army were dismissed from the federal army.

War is usually a great accelerator of social change, and this one was no exception. Whatever effect it may have had on the Ibos, it caused deep movement in the political, economic, and social structures of the north. Politically, the involvement of people with the governments of their six states was much closer than in the days of the monolithic north, when, in spite of elections, all politics took place at Kaduna, and even that was an antechamber to Lagos. Economically the employment provided by the war, and the consequent increase in wages, coincided with the boost from the oil revenues. The greatest changes occurred in social attitudes. The military governors of the new states and their associates were young men who enjoyed the company of their wives on social occasions, and who also enjoyed the conventional social indulgences of drink and tobacco. Their example was widely followed. How different from the puritanism of the Sardauna's regime. When Ibos began to return to the north in 1971, as lecturers, as students, as pump-site attendants, and as landlords, they found a social ambience which they had not known before, among people who had no longer the former reasons for disliking easterners. They had proved that they could do the jobs which the easterners had held, and they had adopted many of the social habits which in earlier days had differentiated the immigrant easterners from the indigenous northerners.

26 Nigeria after the Civil War

The ending of hostilities gave the petroleum industry the opportunity to go ahead, and growth was phenomenal. From 26 million metric tons in 1969 production increased to 112 million metric tons in 1974, at which point Nigeria overtook Libya as Africa's leading producer. Government revenue derived from petroleum was $411 million in 1970 and it increased to $8900 million in 1974. This was 83 per cent of the federal government's total income. Nigeria became a member of OPEC in 1971 and participated in the joint action of the oil-exporting states, who put up the price of petroleum by 400 per cent in 1973/4. The Nigerian National Oil Corporation was set up in 1971, and in the next three years it made arrangements with all the companies producing oil to acquire about a third of their shares. Then in 1974 by decree the NNOC's share of the equity of all producing companies was increased to 55 per cent. The government announced that its policy would be to increase NNOC's share to 100 per cent, but promised that it would not be done without paying fair compensation to the companies for their investments.

In 1971 and the following years a series of decrees transferred the ownership and management of large sectors of the economy from foreigners to Nigerians. The first decree forbade or curtailed expatriate activity in small and medium business. This was aimed mainly at the Lebanese community. Banks were compelled by law to provide more funds for indigenous enterprises. In most large businesses foreign investors were required to take Nigerian partners. The Nigerian Enterprises Promotion Decree of 1972 carried the process further. In a number of categories businesses had to be transferred into Nigerian hands. In other categories (including most of those in which expatriate companies were engaged) 40 per cent of the shares had to be sold to Nigerians, and this percentage was subsequently increased to 60, so that the control passed to Nigerian citizens. In 1975 the government acquired interests in insurance companies and newspapers which were owned by foreigners.

The compulsory transfer of ownership from foreign hands to Nigerian citizens was intended to correct a situation which dated from colonial times, and which had been intensified in the early years of independence when Nigeria relied on imported capital and skills for industrial development, offering inducements to foreign companies to come in. It was a logical counterpart, in the economic sphere, of independence in the political sphere. Nigeria had reached a position of strength, in which such a transfer seemed inevitable; but it did not have to happen in the way that was chosen by the government. It opted for a capitalist solution and declined to be impressed by criticisms from the egalitarian left. A stock exchange had been created at Lagos many years before, and a number of companies had offered shares for public subscription. The machinery for dealing in shares was therefore available, and the techniques of participation by the public as shareholders were well understood. The sale of the shares, to comply with the decrees, had to be effected at prices approved by an official body, and this body insisted that the prices should be extremely favourable to the purchasers. The sellers naturally would have liked to get more, but they were allowed to take out of Nigeria the proceeds of the sale, and Nigeria was so prosperous that the profits on the shares which foreigners were allowed to retain were still worth having: at any rate the goodwill of expatriate investors was retained to the extent that they co-operated in giving effect to the decrees. Nigerians who possessed or could borrow the means to buy the shares did very well. The operation took place at a favourable moment in relation to the development of management skills. Probably no country ever has enough good managers, but even so, Nigeria in the mid-seventies had people who could accept the opportunities which the decrees made available to them. In most of the companies which were required to transfer 60 per cent of the equity Nigerians had already for some years occupied some of the senior posts. It may be that, having no political activities, people were more inclined to attend to business.

As in nearly all wars, industrial unrest had been held in check in the interest of the national effort, but in 1971 many strikes occurred. The military government arrested a number of trade unionists but later in the year a pay increase of 30 per cent was granted – the first since 1964. Unemployment presented a grim problem; more than two million workless people were said to be in the towns in 1972.

Awolowo, who had supported the military government as commissioner of finance since he was welcomed back from prison, resigned his post in 1971.

Nigeria suffered from the drought to which attention was given in Chapter 22. The price of food rose very high. Nevertheless, the government insisted that no wages should be increased, and many strikes took place. Nigeria, rich with oil, made gifts to relieve distress in countries which were stricken by drought (1972–3).

A further development plan, 1975–80, was launched. The manufacturing sector received priority, but agriculture was to be stimulated, especially growing food. There was provision for irrigation and for large state farms. By 1976 all children of primary school age were to be at school, and this made it necessary to train many teachers.

The war encouraged bad habits, and highway robbery remained a serious problem; but the military government adopted counter-measures and no less than eighty robbers were executed.

Nigeria, like some other West African countries, witnessed unrest among students, and the universities generated a good deal of criticism of military government. In 1974 the government required all students, on graduation, to perform service for twelve months in the National Youth Service Corps. Student troubles continued and in 1978 the government appointed a commission of inquiry. Following its recommendations two vice-chancellors resigned, ten university staff members were dismissed, some students were expelled, and the National Union of Nigerian Students was proscribed.

As this story has shown, it was hazardous to enumerate the Nigerian people. However, the military government took a census in 1974. It yielded a total figure of 79,759,000, and indicated that the population in the north had increased, while in the western and east central states the figures were smaller than those which had been established in 1963. There were furious protests, and Awolowo (among others) called for the rejection of the exercise. In the the end the census was discarded and the government decided to rely on the figures established in 1963: though those had not commanded very much respect at the time.

To add to all the other troubles, the ugly subject of corruption came to a head. The military government was extremely liberal in its attitude towards public criticism, and the press had no hesitation in exposing scandals. A considerable number of public figures, including military officers, were dismissed. Public opinion tended to connect the question of corruption with two other matters, namely the permanence of appointments under the military government, and the restoration of civilian rule. Most of the governors in the twelve states, and many of the commissioners (i.e. ministers) at the centre and in the states had held their posts since 1967; it was argued that these people ought to be held responsible for allowing corruption to take place, even if they themselves had no part in it.

On the subject of restoring civilian rule, the soldiers had always made profession of good intentions. In 1970 Gowon had spoken of the possibility of returning to civil government in 1976, and had enumerated nine conditions which would have to be fulfilled before it could happen. Now however, under the challenge of public opinion, he announced that there would be no return to civilian rule in 1976, nor would he name any other year for which it could be promised; but he undertook that all state governors and all federal and state commissioners would be changed by April 1975, and that some civilians would be appointed. Sweeping changes in senior positions were in fact made in January 1975. However, the general reaction was that this was too late and too little. Serious unrest was manifest among organised workers and students, while the professional classes were disgusted at the decision not to resume political activity in 1976, which they regarded as a broken promise. Within the army discontent showed itself in indiscipline, and the officer corps complained that the high command was unable to deal with it. The main target of all complaints was inevitably General Gowon, and his credit was finally ruined by the great cement scandal.

A great deal of construction work was being undertaken, and although Nigeria had several cement factories, the demand for cement exceeded the capacity of local industry. Eager sellers came from abroad, tendering for complete shiploads, and all at once a 'custom' became established that there was a percentage for the man who placed the order. This seems to have led to many purchases being made for which there was no authority. Shipments of cement and other capital goods caused such congestion in the port of Lagos that hundreds of vessels were waiting to berth. Arrangements had to be made to unload cement at Tema and Cotonou, and carry it by road to Nigeria.

General Gowon was active in foreign policy, but it will be convenient to deal with that in Chapter 30. In July 1975 he was attending a Commonwealth conference in Uganda when the other members of the military government removed him from office and raised Brigadier Murtala Mohamed to be the head of state. The change took place without any disturbance. General Gowon did not dispute it, and went to live as a student at a British university.

There followed a drive against corruption and inefficiency and 10,000 people were dismissed or compulsorily retired. Most of the persons who had been state governors under General Gowon were indicted for corrupt practices and ordered to repay substantial sums. One of them, the former governor of the Benue-Plateau state, was executed for being implicated in a mutiny in 1976. Fifty political prisoners were released. It was admitted that the proportion of the federal budget which was appropriated for army and police (40 per cent) was excessive, and the government expressed the intention of 'releasing' 100,000 men from the forces 'following rehabilitation progress'.

The development plan 1975–80, already mentioned, confirmed a new policy which had been partially inaugurated in recent years. The diversion of a large part of the price of produce from the farmers to the state was to cease. Attention was drawn to this, and to its social consequences, in Chapter 11. All export taxes on produce were abolished. Federal boards were set up to buy produce, viz., cocoa, groundnuts, palm produce, rubber, grains, and tuber and root crops. The boards were not granted monopoly powers as buyers. They had a legal duty to purchase all produce offered (subject to quality) at their published price, but if any producer preferred to sell to a private buyer he was free to do so.

Of all the new deal which Murtala Mohamed offered, no part caused so much interest as the plan for returning to civilian government in five stages:

I 1. Restoration of confidence.
  2. Investigation of claims for new states.
  3. Drafting of a constitution by a committee under the chairman-ship of Chief Rotimi Williams.
II 1. Settling-in period for new states.
  2. Local government reform.
  3. Constituent assembly to debate draft constitution.
III   Political parties to be permitted in October 1978.
IV   Elections for state assemblies.
V   Federal elections to choose civilian government, to take office not later than October 1979.

In January 1976 Murtala Mohamed was tragically murdered in the course of a military mutiny. The Lagos mutineers had confederates at Ilorin in Kwara state, where the governor was abducted and killed. The disorders were suppressed, and 39 persons, most of whom were soldiers, were publicly executed.

Murtala Mohamed was succeeded by his close associate General Olusegun Obasanjo. He proceeded to implement the plan for restoring civilian rule. It was decided to create seven more states, so that the total number increased from 12 to 19. New administrative units described as 'local governments' were introduced in all the states, and their councils consisted mainly of elected representatives. This gave an opportunity for the country to begin again to conduct elections. Chief Rotimi Williams submitted his constitutional proposals in September 1976. He recommended that a 'national philosophy' should be adopted, defining social and political rights; that the economy should be a mixture of state and private enterprise, in which the state sector should predominate; and that the form of government should provide a strong federal centre with an executive president and a bicameral legislature, reminiscent of the USA. It was decided that a new federal capital should be built at Abuja in the Niger state.

All children of the age of six were registered to enter school in 1976, so this was the first year to enjoy universal free primary education.

Unfortunately the wonderful prosperity which had been taken for granted since the oil began to gush collapsed suddenly. At the high prices fixed by OPEC it proved impossible to maintain the volume of sales of Nigerian petroleum. It was also a year of poor crops. The expenditure on the development plan was more than the country could manage; foreign currency reserves fell sharply and inflation became serious. The government dealt with the situation by reducing expenditure on the plan by half and by curtailing recurrent expenditure. In order to reduce the dependence on imported food, Operation Feed the Nation was inaugurated.

In 1977 a constituent assembly was convened. The main element in it consisted of 203 persons who were elected by the local councillors, who had themselves been elected by the people in the previous year. No political campaigning was permitted, so that the selection of members was referable to personal merit and not to party allegiance. The federal government added twenty nominees and there were several ex-officio members including the chairman, Justice Udoma.

Inflation continued at a rate of 20 per cent, and since the wage-freeze was maintained many strikes occurred, and there was unrest among students. The government accused several trade union organisers of corruption, and withdrew recognition from more than nine hundred trade unions, leaving only seventy unions with official recognition. The importation of many classes of goods was prohibited. A brake was placed on the export of funds, and internal loans were raised. The budget of 1978 again had to face a prospect of declining revenue, and it called for heavy sacrifices: but General Obasanjo was able to report that 12,000 soldiers had been discharged after training for civilian employment, and that the appropriations for defence and police in the federal budget were down to 26 per cent.

The constitutional assembly completed its work four months ahead of schedule. The most striking feature of its proposals was that the political parties should be financed by the state. This was intended as a measure to check corruption. To qualify for registration, political parties would have to observe rules; the name, emblem, and motto must avoid any ethnic or religious note, and must not refer to any part of the country; membership would have to be open to every Nigerian, and the members of the party's executive would have to reflect the federal character of Nigeria, and the headquarters would have to be at the federal capital.

In July 1978 in a special broadcast General Obasanjo confirmed his intention of handing the country back to civilian rule on 1 October 1979, and as a step in that direction he moved back to military duties the governors of the nineteen states and also four federal commissioners who were serving soldiers. Interim arrangements were made to fill the vacancies thus created. Before the end of 1978 several political parties were formed.

27 Sierra Leone

The celebration of independence in any country should be an occasion of universal rejoicing. It was therefore sad that in Freetown in April 1961 the leaders of the All People's Congress, Siaka Stevens, I. T. A. Wallace Johnson and their associates, were in prison. Sierra Leone shared with Upper Volta the unhappy distinction of having the opposition incarcerated during the independence celebrations. The prime minister was Dr Sir Milton Margai.

The bitterness of politics was not unrelated to the spoils of office. Margai drew his main support from the Mende tribe in the south, and Stevens commanded allegiance among the Temne tribe of the north. It is difficult to know whether ethnic differences generate political intransigence, or whether cause and effect are the other way round, that is to say, whether party animosity polarises tribal feeling. It was just possible to discern a difference between the parties of a more political kind; Margai's with a background of trade and professions was the more conservatively inclined, while Stevens had trade union contracts and his attitude was more radical and egalitarian.

Fourah Bay college was West Africa's first institution of higher learning; it achieved full university status with a royal charter shortly before independence, and in 1965 a second college of the university was created at Njala, away from Freetown, where it was possible to develop programmes relating to agriculture.

As soon as the celebrations were over the opposition leaders were released from detention, but after no more than two months Siaka Stevens and his friend Kamara Taylor were convicted of sedition, libel, and conspiracy, and sent back to jail; however, their conviction was quashed on appeal.

In 1962 troops were sent to join the UN force in Congo.

A general election took place in 1962. Milton Margai's SLPP won 28 seats and Siaka Stevens' APC with allies won 20 seats; but there were 14 independents, and when it was clear who had won twelve of them declared their adhesion to SLPP. Milton Margai made a statesmanlike gesture to overcome the bitterness of the political struggle by inviting

Stevens, as leader of the opposition, to join the delegation to the assembly of the UN; and Stevens accepted.

Milton Margai died in 1964 and was succeeded as prime minister by his half-brother Albert Margai, who received the title of Sir in the following year. Albert Margai was active in foreign policy, joining with Ivory Coast, Guinea, and Liberia in a declaration of intent to work for a free trade area. He acquired a reputation as a militant at conferences, and engaged in verbal clashes with Harold Wilson, the British prime minister, at Lagos and in London on the subject of Rhodesia.

The main event of 1965 was a law restricting the activities of foreigners in the retail trade and in the construction industry.

In 1966 a proposal was brought forward for a one-party state. Naturally the suggestion was vigorously opposed by Siaka Stevens and his party. It remained a contentious issue for twelve years, until at last in 1978 it was adopted – by Siaka Stevens.

In municipal elections in Freetown APC secured a majority on the city council and Siaka Stevens became mayor. So the dangerous situation arose that the parliamentary opposition was in charge of the capital city. Irregularities were alleged regarding the process by which Stevens had become mayor, and after legal proceedings he was removed from that position in favour of Mrs Constance Cummings-John, a member of SLPP. APC showed signs of strength in country-wide elections for district councils, winning 72 places against SLPP's 68 (17 independents).

The rivalry between the two parties had become so acute that the situation began to resemble those which, elsewhere, had provoked the army to intervene to establish order; and in January 1967 Colonel John Bangura and seven other officers attempted to take action of that kind; but they were unsuccessful, and Sir Albert Margai's government survived. A general election followed in March. The parties were about equal in strength, and both claimed victory before the final results, from the most remote constituencies, were known. The governor-general, Sir Henry Lightfoot-Boston, judged that Siaka Stevens was the winner, and invited him to form a government. Thereat the military commander, Brigadier David Lansana, with a small body of troops, arrested both the governor-general and Siaka Stevens, saying that Sir Henry's action was unconstitutional. However, Lansana's personal relationship with Margai was too close to permit his motives to stand above suspicion. Although he was a man of culture and charm, his military qualifications were not held in great respect by the officer corps. He had not taken the precaution of rallying their opinion behind him, and they were not prepared to allow him to use the army to keep Margai in power. They arrested him, together with both Margai and Stevens, suspended the constitution, and set up as government a National Reformation Council, consisting of eight officers under the chairmanship of Lieutenant-Colonel (later Brigadier) Andrew Juxon-Smith. They set about correcting the extravagances of the politicians, and they secured international support in the form of loans from the International Monetary Fund, the British and West German governments, and the Standard Bank of West Africa. However, Juxon-Smith was not well endowed to command loyalty and affection as head of state. He spoke as though he had supernatural powers, and he refused to contemplate leading the country back towards civilian government.

With an officer corps devoting much of its time to civilian affairs, the NCOs took charge of the army and they also took their own view of political matters, which was not very different from that which was associated with the name of Siaka Stevens. In 1968 they overthrew the NRC, and set up the Anti-corruption Revolutionary Movement, which later changed its name to National Interim Council. Eighty-four officers of the army and police were arrested, but the NCOs invited Colonels Bangura and Genda, who had left Sierra Leone in the course of the recent troubles, to çome back and occupy senior positions. All the members of parliament elected in the controversial elections of 1967 were summoned to Freetown, and a national government was set up under Siaka Stevens (he had recently been living in Conakry under the protection of Sekou Touré). A number of SLPP members were then unseated for irregularities, leaving APC with a workable majority. Albert Margai fled the country. In his absence SLPP fell into factions, and there was serious political violence. A new opposition party, the United Democratic Party, was formed in 1970, but almost at once it was proscribed by law. The army was stirring again, and to forestall a mutiny numerous officers and men were arrested. A number of people were placed on trial and condemned to death, including Brigadier Lansana and Brigadier Juxon-Smith.

The government acquired a majority shareholding in the diamond mine. It had no money to pay for its shares, but an arrangement was made that the company should receive compensation over a term of years, out of the profits which were expected to accrue to the government.

In 1971 the army commander, Brigadier Bangura, with a small party of troops made an attempt on the life of the prime minister, but the majority of the army remained loyal to the government. The plotters were arrested and Brigadier Bangura with two others were tried and executed. The prime minister signed a defence pact with Guinea and two or three hundred troops arrived in Freetown from Guinea to act as a bodyguard for Siaka Stevens. They behaved with great discretion. In the following month the constitution was amended and Sierra Leone became a republic with Siaka Stevens as executive president.

The year 1972 was not a happy one. The leaders of SLPP (which was legal) were sent to prison to join the leaders of the United Democratic Party (proscribed). The economy suffered from inflation. In 1973 a general election was held but SLPP boycotted it so APC won all the seats save five. After the election the Guinean troops went home, all political detainees were released, and charges of murder against several SLPP members were withdrawn. A customs union with Liberia was inaugurated under the terms of the Mano River Agreement (Chapter 30).

In 1974 a new five-year-plan was announced, and it was to concentrate on the production of food. The iron ore mine closed as its reserves were becoming exhausted. The trade deficit was serious, and inflation continued. A census was held and yielded a figure of 3,002,426, which was an increase of 40 per cent over the previous census, held in 1963.

A bomb exploded at the house of the deputy prime minister, Kamara Taylor, and following this eight people, sentenced to death in various trials between 1970 and 1975, were executed.

In 1978 the country was consulted in a referendum regarding a one-party constitution. President Siaka Stevens said that it was necessary 'if the country is not to disintegrate into tribal factions'. According to an official announcement, 2,152,454 votes were cast in favour of the one-party constitution, and only 63,132 against.

28 The Gambia

The Gambia celebrated independence in 1965, and although the British government had felt unable to believe that it could be successful as a sovereign state, in the following thirteen years this country had a record equal to the best in Africa for stability, prosperity, and political freedom. The prime minister, Dauda Jawara, had organised the Progressive People's Party (PPP) with disciplined branches throughout the land. His followers occupied 24 seats in the legislature and the other eight were won by the United Party, led by Peter N'jie. The UP co-operated with the PPP in celebrating independence, and took up a position in opposition shortly afterwards.

Sir John Paul, who had been the last colonial governor in Africa, remained as governor-general of the sovereign state. Towards the end of the year 1965 a referendum was held as to whether the country should become a republic, or retain the Queen of England as head of state. By 61,568 votes to 31,921 the people decided to stay with the Queen. In the following year Sir John Paul relinquished the position of governor-general to Alhaji Farima Singateh, who represented the Queen as governor-general. At the same time the prime minister received the honour of knighthood, and became known as Sir Dauda Jawara. In 1970 the proposal for a republic was again placed before the people, and this time it was accepted. Sir Dauda became the executive president.

The country benefited from a British grant-in-aid of £360,000 a year, but in 1967 there was a record harvest of groundnuts, the purchasing power of the farmers increased by 50 per cent, the revenue exceeded expenditure by £500,000, and the government dispensed with the British grant-in-aid. A four-year plan was adopted.

The long discussions with Senegal about a federal union had ended with the signature of three agreements under which the two countries undertook to co-operate in foreign policy, in defence, and in controlling the river Gambia (1965). President Senghor of Senegal visited Banjul in 1967 and a treaty of association between Senegal and the Gambia was signed. A secretariat was set up to facilitate inter-state activities. The requirement of visas for passing the frontiers was abolished, and an outline agreement was reached regarding the development of the river. In spite of this, two years later Senghor made his angry outburst regarding smuggling (Chapter 19). That phase of strained relations was overcome, and in 1970 it was agreed that Senegalese diplomatic posts should represent the Gambia everywhere except in Commonwealth countries; and that a bridge should be built across the river to facilitate traffic between the northern and southern parts of Senegal.

The Gambia's climate from November to March is sunny, dry, and not too hot: very attractive to Scandinavians, whose countries in winter are the ice-box of Europe. A tourist industry developed, providing visitors with sun and sea on the ocean beaches pounded by the Atlantic rollers and on the placid golden sands of the tidal estuary.

The Gambia had in colonial times a strong trading organisation described as a co-operative, though it was closely controlled by the government. Sir Dauda Jawara's government followed a policy of extending state trading, largely through the co-operative formula, in commerce, groundnut processing, and hotel-keeping.

The groundnut crop was a little less than usual in the drought year 1973, but buoyant prices ensured good incomes for the farmers. The number of tourists doubled in that year. In 1974 the groundnut harvest was the largest ever, and the price was the highest on record. In 1975 the government celebrated ten years of stability, tolerance, and prosperity. Generous aid was received from Russia, communist China, and Libya, and a West German company built a brewery. In 1976 Senghor again visited Banjul, and it was agreed to set up a Gambia River Development organisation. In the following year it was settled that a barrage combined with a bridge should be built across the river at Yelitenda. Unfortunately in 1976 and 1977 drought struck again, and the Gambia suffered more severely than in 1969–73. It became necessary to distribute free rations of rice in the upper river region, and aid was received from the FAO, the EEC, Britain, Canada, the Netherlands, West Germany, Japan, Ivory Coast, Togo, and Sierra Leone.

Expenditure on navies (and armies) is often criticised, but in 1977 the Gambia made a wise investment, buying a coastal patrol boat from Britain. In its first sixteen weeks of service, it earned a million pounds in fines imposed on foreign fishing vessels, which it arrested for poaching in territorial waters.

29 Guinea-Bissau

After the tragic death of Amilcar Cabral his brother Luiz Cabral became president, and as prime minister he had Francisco Mendes, who brought the freshness of youth to his duties, for he was born in 1940; but he was a veteran of the struggle for independence. His death in a car accident in 1978 was a grave loss to his country.

Guinea-Bissau was a one-party state, but that did not eliminate opposition, and in 1975 a dissident section of the party attempted to overthrow the government. No less than 188 persons were accused on capital charges. In 1977 there was more trouble, and a former president of the party's central committee, Barbosa, was pronounced guilty of treason and condemned to death; but the sentence was commuted.

The government declared that it would not become involved with ideological blocks. Close relations were established with Russia and communist China, and aid was received from the EEC, Britain, Sweden, and the Netherlands. An agreement was concluded with Portugal for technical co-operation, but this did not work well and after about a year the Portuguese technicians were deported and a Portuguese newspaper was banned. An agreement for mutual assistance was concluded with Senegal. The president attended the Franco-African summit conference in 1976.

Amilcar Cabral was himself a Cape Verdean, and the party which he founded, PAIGC, was devoted to the liberation not only of the mainland territory but also of the islands. In 1975 the Cape Verde Islands became independent, and the question was posed what mode of union should be adopted between Cape Verde and Guinea-Bissau. In 1977 a Unity Council was inaugurated, but opposition against Cape Verdeans manifested itself in Bissau, and at a party conference towards the end of the year it was announced that unification was a 'long-term goal'.

A measure of land nationalisation was adopted.

In 1977 Luiz Cabral was re-elected as president for a four-year term, although he was opposed by the marxists.

PART IV

CONCLUSION

30 Wider Groupings

Africa was littered with abortive treaties and institutions supposedly designed to promote co-operation, said Dr Adebayo Adedeji, chairman of the United Nations Economic Commission for Africa (ECA), speaking in Lagos in 1976. It would be of small interest to devote attention to that litter, but the purpose of this chapter is to identify the initiatives which hold promise for the future.

The critical starting-point was the need for sixteen African countries, including the francophone states of West Africa, to renegotiate their association with the EEC. They had become associated with the EEC in 1957 but at that time they were not sovereign states. When the date for renewal came, they had to negotiate as independent states; but how independent is it possible to be in such a situation? Obviously they had to form a league. This was the dynamic behind the group which formed OAMCE and UAM in 1961 (see Chapter 20). The group was much more extensive than West Africa. No ex-British colonies were involved, because they had not become associated with EEC in 1957.

In 1962 Olympio initiated negotiations for the purpose of arranging an economic group of Togo, Dahomey, and Nigeria. This was the first attempt to form a group on a basis logical for West Africa, abandoning the old colonial division between French and British. It produced a meeting of foreign ministers at Cotonou, and they agreed to set up a Benin Union; but Maga of Dahomey upset the plan by trying to bring Ghana in, and it was impossible at that time for Ghana and Togo to be accommodated in one organisation.

The meeting of UAM at Bangui in 1964 was an occasion for rejoicing because the war in Algeria had ended. The francophone states of sub-Saharan Africa had been trying to give moral support to Algeria without adopting a position which might cause France to modify her generous treatment in aid and trade. The cease-fire solved that problem, and permitted a new beginning in relations with France. There were two outstanding achievements before the end of the year. The West African Monetary Union (UMOA) was formed, by which Ivory Coast, Dahomey, Upper Volta, Niger, Togo, and Senegal agreed with France to

255

continue to use the franc CFA (now standing for *Communauté financière africaine*) as their currency, and France undertook to support that currency and to maintain its value, whatever imbalance of payments the members might incur.

In December 1964 negotiations with the EEC were successfully concluded, and the oversea associates secured terms which were acceptable to them. The agreement was for five years, during which the EEC undertook to pay $800m in aid to the associated countries. The former French territories, which had enjoyed prices subsidised by France for cocoa, coffee, groundnuts, and some other items were to have the subsidies phased out through the five-year period, eventually coming down to world prices. For exports from associated countries to EEC countries, valuable tariff protection was secured.

OAU was formed in 1963 and it was expected that other African groups would be discontinued. UAM, which was political in character, hesitated, but after about a year it formally dissolved. Its economic counterpart, OAMCE, however, was not easy to disband. It had various functional activities, among which was an airline. Senghor was anxious to keep it alive and in September 1964 he journeyed to Ivory Coast to call on Houphouet-Boigny, to try to persuade him to adopt the same view. It was the first meeting of the two since independence. After the meeting Houphouet-Boigny was extremely coy about making any statement. However, in the following months Ivory Coast and several other francophone states became acutely aware that Ghana was giving aid and comfort to people who wanted to raise rebellions in their countries. This was a reason for re-forming a political association of French-speaking states, and it happened in 1965 at Nouakshott, where OCAM was formed. OCAM provided a political forum and took over the functions performed by OAMCE.

In 1963 a new influence entered the field. The ECA, masterminded by secretary-general Robert Gardiner, began to advocate economic co-operation between the states of West Africa. At first it was a voice in the wilderness, but Gardiner persisted, and made an impression. In 1965 President Tubman of Liberia responded to the ECA initiative by calling a meeting at Monrovia. Later in the year, ECA brought fourteen countries together at Niamey in Niger, and persuaded them to discuss a proposal for a West African Economic Community. Various committees set to work, which resulted in two conferences in 1967. The first of these brought civil servants together at Accra in April. They made sufficient progress to lead on to a council of ministers at Dakar, in November, when twelve states agreed to form the West African

Economic Community, with the aim of establishing a West African common market. A further meeting was held in Monrovia in 1968.

These were the years of civil war in Nigeria, and for that reason they were unpropitious for carrying the project further. Ivory Coast had recognised Biafra as an independent state and had broken off relations with Nigeria. Some other countries, though still in relations with Nigeria, were not anxious to cultivate a closer connection. Against this background, early in 1970 seven francophone states signed a protocol declaring their intention to form an organisation described as *Communauté Economique de l'Afrique de l'Ouest* (CEAO). It looked like a move of hostility towards the WAEC. However, it was three years before the proposal was drawn up in the form of a treaty, and by that time the international image of Nigeria had improved. Dahomey and Togo withdrew from CEAO, and other members voiced assurances that nothing in the CEAO treaty was inconsistent with membership of groups including anglophone countries.

Nigeria and Togo had in 1972 made an agreement for close economic co-operation which they described as ECOWAS, to which they invited other states to adhere. This was the fruit of negotiations between General Gowon and General Eyadema, and it heralded the entry of Gowon into international affairs. He lent a million pounds to Dahomey (Chapter 23) and Dahomey withdrew from CEAO. Gowon was the chairman of OAU this year, and he took the opportunity of the meeting of OAU in Lagos to make it clear that Nigeria would play a leading part in the next round of negotiations with EEC. With the entry of Britain into EEC and the dismantling of commonwealth preferences in the British market, association with EEC became important for Nigeria. Fifteen African countries met at Lomé in December 1973 to discuss the matter, and it was inevitable that at such a meeting Nigeria, with its immense superiority in economic strength, should stand out as the leader. The African associates and would-be associates joined with countries of the West Indies and of the Pacific to constitute one negotiating body, known as ACP (Africa-Caribbean-Pacific). ACP negotiated with EEC all through the year 1974, and the negotiations led to the Lomé Convention of 28 February 1975, which settled the terms on which the 46 ACP countries would be associated with EEC for the ensuing five years. The ACP countries secured virtually duty-free access for their exports to the ECM without giving any reciprocal undertaking. They were to receive aid totalling $4000m. They received assurances of co-operation in industrial and technical matters. Also they secured Stabex, a new arrangement to 'stabilise' their export earnings from many raw materials and some semi-manufactured products: if the revenue from an exported commodity were to fall below the average revenue of the previous four years, the affected country would qualify for a money payment equivalent to the shortfall; but if that country subsequently were to earn more than the average for the preceding four years, it would have to refund the payment.

These long negotiations brought the West African countries together under the effective leadership of Nigeria, and led on three months later (May 1975) to the enlargement of ECOWAS, which now had fifteen members. This realised the vision of Olympio, Gardiner, Tubman, Gowon and Eyadema. The fifteen countries declared their intention of creating a customs union which should be fully effective by 1990. It was agreed that the headquarters should be at Lagos, and that the first executive secretary should be Dr Aboubakar Ouattara of Ivory Coast. His deputies were from Ghana and Guinea. Among the first acts of ECOWAS was the establishment of the fund for co-operation, compensation, and development. Its income was to be derived from contributions from member states, from the income of community enterprises, and (hopefully) from subscriptions from outside the community. The fund would finance community projects in member states, in particular the less developed states. It would pay compensation to members who suffered as a result of trade liberalisation or 'as a result of the location of community enterprises'. It would guarantee foreign investment made in pursuance of the treaty's provision for 'harmonising' industry. Though ECOWAS's headquarters were at Lagos, the fund's place of business was Lomé, and its first director-general was a Liberian, Dr Alexander Romeo Horton, who had been largely responsible for the establishment of the African Development Bank (see below). The location of the principal institutions of ECOWAS and the choice of senior executives demonstrated that the barrier between the francophone and anglophone parts of West Africa had been bridged.

Nigerian foreign policy displayed forthrightness and vigour. In New York at the UN, in Brussels at the EEC, and at meetings of OAU and OPEC, Nigeria made her influence felt in the problems of the African continent and of world trade. In West Africa Nigerian influence was reinforced by the development of a programme of bilateral aid. The original intention was to supply petroleum at reduced prices, but this was found to be contrary to the rules of OPEC, so the programme was changed to granting loans on easy terms. The Nigeria Trust fund of $80m was placed at the disposal of the African Development Bank, to be used in aid to poorer African countries. Gifts were made for the relief of distress in the Sahel countries during the drought. In 1978 a detachment of the Nigerian army formed part of the UN peace-keeping force in Lebanon.

ECOWAS held a summit meeting at Lagos in April 1978. Sixteen states were represented. They were the fourteen with which this book is concerned, and also Mauritania and the republic of the Cape Verde Islands. They adopted a protocol of non-aggression, agreeing not to attack each other and to recognise as definitive the frontiers between them. This can be regarded as a declaration of intent by ECOWAS to deal with political as well as economic matters. Still dealing with politics, the heads of state congratulated the presidents to Togo, Liberia, and the Gambia of settling the differences between Guinea and its neighbours Ivory Coast and Senegal. Commentators posed the question whether ECOWAS was taking over the functions of OAU in respect of its region. The heads of state agreed that as from 28 May 1979 no state within the community should increase its customs tariff on goods originating from any other member state. This is regarded as the first step towards abolition of customs duties on goods originating in the community. It should end the practice by which countries have protected infant industries with prohibitive tariffs. The heads of state also decided to adopt an agreement on the free movement of persons within the community, and requested the council of ministers to prepare an agreement for adoption at the next summit meeting, planned for 1979. This had been described by Dr S. K. B. Asante as 'the first real effort at African unity'. It is an attempt to achieve on a larger scale what Houphouet-Boigny so signally failed to achieve within the Entente in 1965.

The Chad Convention was concluded in 1964. It brought Nigeria, Niger, Chad, and Cameroon into association for developing the resources of Lake Chad – an interesting and perplexing area of water, sometimes very large and in other years much smaller, sometimes receiving water from its affluent rivers and at other times discharging water into them. Good progress was made by the Chad group in studying the behaviour of the lake and in using its resources.

The Niger River Commission also was set up in 1964. It consisted of nine states – Nigeria, Niger, Mali, Guinea, Benin (which possess parts of the river) and of four other states whose interest was more remote. In fourteen years there was little sign of useful activity, but the conception of a regional treatment of the great river for purposes of water supply, navigation, electricity, irrigation, and fish culture offers exciting possibilities, which might have improved prospects of realisation within the framework of ECOWAS.

The Senegal river presented possibilities of development if agreement could be secured between the four riverain states, Guinea, Mali, Senegal, and Mauritania. An organisation was brought into existence for this purpose in 1963 but it achieved nothing and was dissolved in 1971. In 1972 Senegal with her neighbours Mali and Mauritania – without the quarrelsome Guinea – set on foot the Organisation for the Development of the River Senegal (OMVS). This organisation set to work on the construction of two dams, one of which (Manatali) was intended to generate electricity for the working of iron ore deposits in Mali and Senegal. The conservancy of the dammed river was to render it navigable from the sea to the Malian border.

The Mano River is the frontier between Liberia and Sierra Leone, and the Mano River Union, concluded between these two countries, began to yield results in the late seventies. An impressive bridge was completed, and in 1978 a common external tariff became effective; it was of interest that the new common tariff involved considerable reductions in import duties by both countries.

The African Development Bank was founded in 1964. With 48 members, all independent African states, its range extends far beyond the west. In 1978 it took the decision to invite non-African states to become subscribers to the capital stock of the bank. It is an important channel for mobilising funds for development in Africa.

The annual summit meetings of the heads of francophone countries are attended by the heads of several West African states. General De Gaulle and his successor President Pompidou took much trouble in cultivating personal relationships with the heads of francophone countries in Africa, and President Giscard d'Estaing institutionalised the idea. In 1975 he went to Bangui and met there the heads of all the francophone states of Africa. The following year a similar summit meeting was held in Paris. It proved to be more than an occasion for consolidating cultural connections, for it set up a fund to pay interest on loans on behalf of the least favoured countries, to which France would subscribe 5000m CFA and the other countries would contribute 2500m CFA. Surprisingly, Guinea-Bissau, Cape Verde, and São Thomé attended this meeting. In 1977 the Franco-African summit meeting took place at Dakar, and in 1978 it was again in Paris. On both these occasions attention was directed to military questions, for French troops were engaged in the defence of three African countries (Mauritania, Chad, and Zaire) and in the logistical support of those operations the French garrisons and transit facilities in Senegal and Ivory Coast had been employed. The desire to preserve links with France was strong in some parts of West Africa, and these meetings appeared able to provide a method of achieving that aim without involving regional organisations which could get in the way of more logical combinations uniting francophone and anglophone states.

31 Fourteen Ways to a Continental Destiny

The theme of the period covered by this book is the change from a general acceptance of the supremacy of white rulers to a confident assertion of the equality of black people. The substitution of fourteen sovereign states for three colonial empires and one independent settlement of repatriates must rank as a revolution. Europeans and Americans tend to think that revolutions are about freedom; and that freedom means either avoiding the interference of authority, or taking part in choosing the government. Freedom, however, has been defined in many ways, and for this revolution it meant the vindication of the Africans. It was not precisely a question of race, for there was no racial affinity between Twi and Tuareg, nor between Tiv and Temne; but the occupiers of a certain space – sub-Saharan Africans – achieved a sense of shared identity.

In the minds of Nkrumah and some of his African contemporaries, the purpose of their new states had little to do with individual liberty. Perhaps its neatest definition was provided by Sekou Touré, with whom Nkrumah had such a curious love-hate relationship: 'The total rehabilitation of African man'. Nkrumah's definition was a little longer:

> The peoples of the colonies know precisely what they want. They wish to be free and independent, to be able to feel themselves on an equality with all other peoples, and to work out their own destiny without outside interference, and to be unrestricted to attain an advancement that will put them on a par with other technically advanced nations of the world.

There are two foundations on which governments may base their authority; force and consent. In West Africa at the stage of colonial expansion (1880–1910) force was used; but by 1940 the colonies had become very peaceful areas, where people could wander about without being molested, and the consent which was accorded to the authority of the government was remarkable.

The French encouraged consent among Africans by identifying the leaders and treating them with respect, inviting them to adopt French culture. By welcoming Africans to the parliament in Paris, and by promoting black men to senior positions in the civil service, they produced an impression of equality and fraternity which served well for a time. The constitution of 1946 did not provide a successful form of government for the Fourth Republic, but it offered considerable advantages to the African members of that republic. Colonial status ended with the incorporation of the African territories in the republic. This resembled the method adopted by the Russians for dealing with their possessions in Asia, which were made parts of the Union of Socialist Soviet Republics; and Paris is closer to Dakar than Moscow to Kamchatka. The USA made comparable arrangements for Alaska and Hawaii.

It may have appeared in 1946 that the African areas were not equal partners in the French republic, because the franchise was more restricted in Africa than in Europe; but it was inevitable that African citizens should have the same voting rights as those of the metropolitan country, and it took just ten years for that to happen. In those years however other important changes occurred. Indo-China and Algeria refused to be incorporated in the French republic, and opted for the nationalist solution. In Africa people had begun to talk about African personality and Kwame Nkrumah was showing the way to independence. In 1956 dwellers in metropolitan France had to consider facts which had been unknown in 1946. Then it was not appreciated that Africa was in a state of demographic explosion. By 1956 it was clear that if population continued to increase at the rate of 1 per cent per annum in France and at the rate of $2\frac{1}{2}$ per cent per annum in Africa, the republic would have an African president before long.

The reasons brought forward by De Gaulle for the constitution of 1958 were of course rather different. The Fourth Republic had failed to deal with its problems, and it was thought necessary to provide greater power for the president and a correspondingly reduced role for the legislature. That was the proposition to which the African parts of the republic (except Guinea) voted 'Yes', and in so voting they accepted that they would no longer send deputies and senators to Paris. Membership of the French community remained available to them, but after two years of debate they all preferred the road to independence.

Did they however achieve something less than independence? Close links with France remained, through the monetary union, through subsidisation of crop prices, through defence agreements, through the comprehensive character of French aid, and through the well-organised cultural connections of the francophone areas. This complex relationship was much criticised as neo-colonialist, and both France and the African states were sensitive about that criticism. Several African countries requested the removal of French troops, and in each case the French complied. All the francophone states widened their international contacts and diversified their sources of aid. Thus African countries demonstrated that the link with France did not weigh heavily upon them. The monetary union however remained. Under its rules, members accepted limitations on the widening of avenues of trade – that is to say, on the use of certain currencies; but the advantages which the African financial community provided for its members – especially for those with adverse trade balances – were so manifest that the rules were accepted. The situation raised, in specific form, the general question of the relationship between aid and independence. Was the continuing receipt of substantial aid from the ex-colonial power consistent with independence? Aid and independence were discussed at a conference of 110 non-aligned countries at Dakar in 1975. The conference asked industrialised countries to supply food, technical aid, and credits to less developed countries, but called on the LDCs to make themselves less dependent on 'imperialism' and to 'obtain economic emancipation [by] . . . controlling their resources and national wealth'. It appeared to be agreed therefore that aid was consistent with independence provided that the recipient state controlled its resources. Was it permissible to exercise control over resources of foreign currencies by entering into agreement with the financial community to abide by the rules of that organisation in regard to exchange control? Clearly six West African countries took the view that it was permissible.

In the sixties regret was expressed, in various quarters, that the French possession had split into so many parts. However, as years went by, the ex-French colonies developed such contrasting political features that it became difficult to imagine them as willing participants in one federation. Sekou Touré wrenched the initiative not only from De Gaulle but from the federalists with his famous 'No' in 1958, for with Touré independent no leader could accept less and remain credible. Yet there was an attempt to bring the other places together in the federation of Mali. It was Houphouet-Boigny who prevented that union from combining more than Senegal and Soudan. De Gaulle, agreeing in 1959 that Mali might opt for independence, made his contribution to strengthen the only federal nucleus which was available; but it fell to pieces. This was entirely consistent with the chapter-theme. If there ever was an article of European manufacture, it was the federation of French West Africa. Its bases were a European language and a European culture. The small units were much more accessible to Africans who wished to assert their leadership, and eight votes in UNO looked far more prestigious than one. Natural groupings of West African states – alliances around river valleys, or the total association of all – could only be hindered by a political expression of francophony.

The British ruled with a very small number of officials and military officers – far fewer than the French – and they relied almost entirely on prestige. They assumed that Africans would consent to be ruled. This assumption was offensive to Africans of quality – to educated men who had passed the same examinations as their rulers, and to chiefs who were proud of their inheritance. No qualities of good government could compensate for such an assumption of superiority. Good government cannot redeem a colonial relationship. On the contrary, as the Portuguese proved, he who rules worst rules longest.

In 1947 few Africans wished colonial rule to end. As Awolowo wrote in that year (*Path to Nigerian Freedom*),

> Given a choice from among white officials, Chiefs, and educated Nigerians, as the principal rulers of the country, the illiterate man, today, would exercise his preference for the three in the order in which they are named. He is convinced, and he has good reasons to be, that he can always get better treatment from the white man than he could hope to get from the Chiefs, and the educated elements.

Nevertheless, as Awolowo went on to say, it was inevitable that the educated people should become the leaders of the country.

In the decade 1940 to 1950 lively political activity developed in most parts of West Africa, as explained in earlier chapters. The number of educated people was increasing, and new technology provided them with radio receivers and airmailed newspapers, placing them in contact with the world, a world which reverberated with declarations of national emancipation and human rights. The educated élite who were working to make an end of colonial rule were reinforced by the African troops who returned from distant battlefields, where they had formed their own conclusions about race relations.

The nationalists believed that it was necessary to destroy the prestige of the white man with the uneducated people. Azikiwe and Nkrumah deliberately set to work to do this. Both were basically well disposed towards Britain, but that did not deter them from dragging Britain's image through the mud in the interest of the nationalists' cause. Both were educated in America, a land of colour-consciousness and anti-colonialism. The cinema helped them; the urban population became accustomed to see white people on the screen engaged in criminal activity and promiscuous love. The war of 1939 to 1945 also was damaging to the prestige of the colonial powers, for France was overwhelmed by the Germans, and Britain suffered reverses from the Japanese.

There was little in the performance of the colonial governments that could be effectively attacked. Individual rights were protected by the law and were more secure than in many of the states of UNO. Material progress, if it was stagnant in the thirties, was very rapid in the fifties. However, apologists who put forward these arguments to justify the continuance of the colonial regime missed the point. Individual liberty and material progress were not enough. It became intolerable to Africans to be ruled by white men. In this they had the support of world opinion, and of many people in Britian and France. The dynamic of the independence movement was not in protest against oppression, nor in complaints against economic exploitation, but in the idea that Africans were equal to Europeans, and that the colonial system had to be ended to prove it.

It was common in Britain and France to speak of self-government being 'granted'. Militant Africans preferred to believe that they had won their independence in a struggle. Newspapers in West Africa occasionally referred to the bitter fight against imperialism and even mentioned pools of blood. In fact there was not much struggle, except in Guinea-Bissau. In Ivory Coast and Gold Coast people made it clear that they were prepared to create disturbances and go to prison. When that had been made clear, the contest was won, because it takes two to make a fight, and in West Africa neither the British nor the French were prepared to have one. Indo-China and Malaya, Algeria and Kenya, were quite enough. The blood flowed elsewhere, and there was a grim foreboding that more might flow in southern Africa.

In the early fifties it was felt that there was a problem, whether the élites of educated Africans could communicate with the illiterate masses. They seemed to have made themselves remote from the people. For conservatives it was the perfect argument against going too quickly – it would never do to hand the African peoples over to a tiny unrepresentative minority! For liberal people it was a genuine anxiety, and among these some African nationalists might be counted. Kwame Nkrumah faced this problem and solved it. His CPP proved that the educated élite – at any rate a section of it – could communicate with the mass; also that a meaningful election could be held among illiterate voters. Proof was provided during the same years in Senegal. Sekou Touré's success in Guinea in 1958 added corroboration.

Among the forces which pushed the colonial powers to liquidate their positions was the influence of USA and USSR, both opposed to colonialism. Pressure from USA was intense during the war and continued afterwards, reaching its most specific expression in the resolution of the House of Representatives of 1955 '. . . that the United States should administer its foreign policies and programs and exercise its influence so as to support other peoples in their efforts to achieve self-government or independence'. Russia demanded the end of the British, French, and Portuguese empires, and in 1955 at the Bandung conference China became a major influence in the same direction. The example of India was also important.

The victory of the Labour party in the elections of 1945 in Britain was favourable for African nationalists. Creech-Jones became secretary of state for the colonies, and he and his wife were friends of many African leaders. They belonged to the Fabian society, committed to the aspirations of the educated élite. Creech-Jones gave directions to colonial governments to stimulate local government by encouraging elected units, and this disposed of the policy of developing native authorities, which had been the alternative to handing over power to the educated élite. However, in most parts of West Africa native authorities could not be wiped away. The result was a combination of elected councils and traditional authorities, and the politicians of the urban centres had to court the votes of country people who wished to know what views candidates held on matters such as chieftaincy disputes, local boundaries, and the allocation of stalls in markets.

The foregoing reasons were propelling West Africa towards the transfer of power from colonial governments to sovereign states, but it would not have happened so soon without the faith and drive of Kwame Nkrumah. He set the pace.

As a publicist he questioned whether independence had really been secured. Ghana, he said, was independent because Ghana understood how to deal with foreign investors, but many African states had merely exchanged colonialism for neo-colonialism. This word had to work hard. It had a specific meaning in Marxist dialectic, where neo-colonialism was an advanced form of capitalism, and colonialism in its 'neo-' form would not be ended until capitalism had been ousted. The equation of neo-colonialism with capitalism may be left to those who wish to write or read dialectic. For those who prefer the historical method, neo-colonialism bears other meanings. It was applied to any situation which Africans found disagreeable. One such, the situation of France in Africa, has been considered. Another such situation arose when the inhabitants of a country saw that their opportunities of investment were blocked because important sections of the economy were occupied by foreigners. This problem was dealt with by several governments (Chapters 24, 26, 27). Another situation described as neo-colonial related to the heavy load of debt service which weighed on some LDCs which had accepted too much 'aid' on 'easy loan' terms. In the early days of aid, such loans were associated with the thought that if adequate capital were provided for LDCs, their economies would 'take off' and be able to service the loan charges. However, it did not happen. This led Britain, and other aiders, to cancel debts due from poor LDCs, and to grant aid in the form of gifts. Debts owing by Sierra Leone and the Gambia to Britain were cancelled in 1978. France's measure to deal with this problem was mentioned in Chapter 30. The behaviour of developed countries which sold manufactured goods to LDCs and bought raw materials from them was frequently described as neo-colonial, and the same opprobrium was applied to countries whose citizens controlled advanced technology. The interest expressed by human rights enthusiasts in the internal affairs of some West African countries earned the same obloquy.

In this revolution political liberty was not a major consideration, and provided that a government asserted African prestige, restrictions on political liberty were accepted; for instance, the single-party system. At the end of 1978 four of the fourteen states had civilian constitutions in which only one party was legal. Liberia, though not officially a one-party state, had evolved a method of ensuring that one party stayed in power. In three countries military governments had formed a single party, and in three countries military governments permitted no parties; though in one of these, Nigeria, the government had declared its intention to permit parties and to provide them with funds from state coffers. In Senegal the formation of parties was controlled by licence. In Upper Volta, where civil government had recently succeeded military, there were several parties. Upper Volta and the Gambia might be paired as countries in which political parties were freely permitted; but in the Gambia one party had held an impregnable position ever since independence. No example had occurred of a government peacefully changing from one party to another in response to an expression of the people's will.

As to why the one-party formula was adopted, Marxist teaching counted for much, for communist countries are one-party states, and although few African leaders accepted communism, many adapted much from communist methods. In organising parties some African leaders followed the communist model, with cells in localities and democratic centralism for the high command. That sort of party is not intended to be a constitutional opposition; it is to seize power and keep it. Secondly it must be said that in several states civilian governments fell prey to corruption. A corrupt politician could not part with power. His venality would be exposed and he would be punished. Therefore the one-party system was necessary in corrupt regimes. However, that was not the explanation for all cases. Africans had traditional procedures for settling arguments in tribal gatherings; discussion continued for a long time but in the end the chief announced the consensus of opinion, and the matter was settled. The single party in Ivory Coast reanimated those ancient practices. Officially, Ivory Coast maintained that the single party was necessary for a limited period while the country was becoming a nation. Siaka Stevens' statement when Sierra Leone went over to one party reflected that opinion. Licensing parties in Senegal was based on refusal to permit political activity to those who declined to accept the principles on which the state was based; and the Nigerian government, declaring its intention to encourage the formation of parties, made it clear that no party would be permitted which did not support the concept of Nigeria as one nation. Nation-building was held to justify the suppression of separatists. This recognised the fact that the spirit of nationhood was brittle and needed nurture – unlike the feeling of Africa as a continent, which was spontaneous.

At the end of 1978 six governments were military, and two countries had resumed civil rule after periods of soldierly power. The principal cause of military coups was the example of those who had done it before. Togo started, and coups became a habit. A government which declined to give the electors a fair chance to judge it gave away the basis of its authority and opened the way to soldiers who would say that they had been trained to devote their lives to their country and that that they were better qualified to rule. One of the causes of military takeovers was the endeavour of civilian governments to reduce the cost of the armed forces. Military governments always provided generous funds for 'defence', under which description they increased their emoluments.

The fourteen countries, about twenty years after independence, were all different, vastly different. The diversity made it all the more noteworthy that they came together in ECOWAS.

One solemn fact however united all people of West Africa in spirit and it joined them with all other Africans: the fact that in southern Africa black people were still governed by white people. As Kwame Nkrumah had eloquently spoken and written, every African felt that his human dignity was impaired so long as any Africans remained unfree. The determination to make an end of this was a major influence on public opinion and on foreign policy. Non-alignment might serve as a guide for African states in their relations with the rest of the world, but the rest of the world was expected to be fully aligned in regard to southern Africa. The racial conflict in that part of the continent placed a strain on friendship between African countries and states which continued to maintain relations with the republic of South Africa. An example of such strain occurred in connection with the Commonwealth games in 1978, when the Nigerian government refused to allow its athletes to participate, as a protest against the behaviour of New Zealand citizens in visiting South Africa to take part in sporting fixtures.

While the spirit of continental solidarity had grown, talk of 'African personality' had fallen out of fashion. These words were used by J. C. Bruce, a New York journalist, as long ago as 1907, but they were not mentioned in Nkrumah's *Autobiography* (1957). Sekou Touré spoke of them in 1958, repudiating the notion of interdependence between Africa and Europe, and the phrase entered current argument as a protest against that. Nkrumah employed the phrase in 1960, still with diplomatic connotation, when he spoke of 'the projection of the African personality in the international community'. That did not explain what sort of a state the African personality would inspire, nor where it would find the borderline between freedom and authority. Some Africans repudiated the concept of African personality on the ground that it was a cult which cut them off from the eternal truths which great thinkers of the past had established for common humanity. With all the urge for change, Africans betrayed a 'powerful prepossession towards antiquity': the names Ghana and Mali prove it. Nkrumah did not seem happy with the phrase 'African personality'; in 1963 he equated it with 'deep-rooted unity' which expressed itself as Pan-Africanism. He used the words 'African genius' as an alternative. In 1964 he described his personal philosophy as 'the map in intellectual terms of the disposition of forces which will enable African Society to digest the Western and the Islamic and the Euro-Christian elements in Africa, and develop them in such a way that they fit into the African Personality'.

Bibliography

INTRODUCTION

Fage, J. D., *Atlas of African History* (Edward Arnold, 2nd ed., 1978)
Harrison Church, R. J., *West Africa: a study of the environment and of man's use of it* (Longman, 6th ed., 1968). Recommended for a detailed description of each country with maps.
——, *West Africa; Environment and Policies* (Van Norstrand, 2nd edition, 1977).
Lipschutz, Mark R., and Rasmussen, R. Kent, *Dictionary of African Historical Biography* (Heinemann, 1977).

CHAPTER 1

Cary, Joyce, *The Case for African Freedom* (Secker & Warburg, London, 1951).
Colonial Development and Welfare Acts 1929–70: A Brief Review (HMSO, London, 1971) Cmnd 4677.
Hailey, Lord, *An African Survey* (OUP, London, 1938).
——, *Position of Colonies in a British Commonwealth of Nations,* Romanes Lecture (OUP, 1941).
——, *Great Britain, India, and the Colonial Dependencies in the Post-war World* (University of Toronto Press, 1943).
——, *Future of Colonial Peoples* (OUP, 1943; Princeton University Press, 1944).
Macmillan, W. M., *Africa Emergent* (1938; Pelican, 1949).

CHAPTER 2

Austin, Dennis, *Politics in Ghana 1946–1960* (OUP, 1964).
Boahen, Adu, *Ghana, evolution and change* (Longman, 1975) chs 16–19.

Crowder, M., and Ajayi, J. F. Ade (eds), *History of West Africa* (Longman, 1974) Vol. II, chs 17 and 18.

Gann, L. H., and Duignan, P. (eds), *Colonialism in Africa 1870–1960* (CUP, 1970) Vol. II, chs 1 and 10–14.

Hailey, Lord, *Native Administration in the British African Territories* (HMSO, 1951) Part III.

Keay, E. A., and Thomas, H., *West African Government for Nigerian Students* (Hutchinson, 3rd ed., 1977); also covers other West African countries.

Nii Bonne III, *Milestones in the History of the Gold Coast.*

Nkrumah, Kwame, *Autobiography* (Nelson, 1957).

Price, J. H., *Political Institutions of West Africa* (Hutchinson, 3rd ed., 1977); also deals with Nigeria, Sierra Leone, Liberia and Gambia.

Report of the Commission of Inquiry into the Disturbances in the Gold Coast 1948 (HMSO, 1948, Colonial no. 231).

Statement by HMG on the Report (foregoing) (HMSO, 1948, Colonial no. 232).

Gold Coast: Report by Committee on Constitutional Reform 1949 (HMSO, 1949, Colonial no. 248).

Gold Coast: Government's Proposals for Constitutional Reform 1953 (Government Printing Department, Accra, 1953).

CHAPTER 3

Ajayi J. F. Ade, and Tamuno T. N. (eds), *The University of Ibadan 1948–73* (Ibadan University Press, 1973).

Azikiwe, Nnamdi, *My Odyssey* (C. Hurst, London, 1970).

Burns, Sir Alan, *History of Nigeria* (Allen & Unwin, 8th ed., 1972) ch. 20.

Crocker, W. R., *Self-government for the Colonies* (Allen & Unwin, 1949) ch. 6.

Crowder and Ajayi (eds), *History of West Africa*, Vol. II: Aluko, Olajide, ch. 18, 'Politics of Decolonisation in British West Africa 1945–60'.

Fry, Richard, *Bankers in West Africa* (Hutchinson-Benham, 1976).

Gann and Duignan (eds), *Colonialism in Africa*, Vol. II, chs 1 and 10–13.

Hailey, Lord, *African Survey Revised 1956* (OUP, 1957) chs 4–6, 8, 10.

——, *Native Administration in the British African Territories*, Part III.

Heussler, Robert, *The British in Northern Nigeria* (OUP, 1968).

Ike, V. Chukwuemeka, *University Development in Africa, the Nigerian Experience* (OUP, 1977).

Niven, Sir C. Rex, *Nigeria* (Benn, 1967) chs 22–3.

Pedler, F. J., *West Africa* (Methuen Home Study Books, 2nd ed., 1959) ch. 5.

——, 'Universities and Polytechnics in Africa', The Twelfth Lugard Lecture, *Africa*, xlii No. 4 (1972).

Post, K. W. J., *The Nigerian Federal Election of 1959* (OUP, 1963).

Yesufu, T. M. (ed.), *Creating the African University* (OUP, 1973).

CHAPTER 4

Crowder and Ajayi (eds), *History of West Africa*, Vol. II: Aluko, Olajide, pp. 644–9, 659–60.

Foray, Cyril P., *Historical Dictionary of Sierra Leone* (Scarecrow Press, 1977).

Hailey, Lord, *Native Administration in the British African Territories*, Part iii ch. 9.

Hailey, Lord, *African Survey Revised 1956*, pp. 324–6, 532–6, 668–9, 794–5.

Kup, A. P., *Sierra Leone, a concise history* (David & Charles, Newton Abbott, 1975).

MacKenzie W. J. M. and Robinson K.E. (eds), *Five Elections in Africa* (Clarendon Press, 1960).

CHAPTER 5

Crowder and Ajayi (eds), *History of West Africa*, Vol. II: Aluko, Olajide, 'Gambia', pp. 649–53, 660.

Hailey, Lord, *African Survey Revised 1956*, pp. 327–8, 536–9, 669–70.

——, *Native Administration in British African Territories*, Part iii ch. 10.

Hazlewood, A. (ed.), *African Integration and Disintegration* (OUP, 1967): Robson, Peter, ch. ii. 4.

Hopkins, A. G., *Economic History of West Africa* (Longman, 1973) p. 283.

CHAPTERS 6 AND 7

Carter, G. M. (ed.), *African One-Party states* (Cornell University Press, New York, 1962).
Crowder and Ajayi (eds), *History of West Africa*, Vol. II chs 15 and 19.
Gann and Duignan (eds), *Colonialism in Africa 1870–1960*, Vol. II: ch. 7, Delavignette, Robert L., 'French Colonial Policy in Black Africa 1945 to 1960'; Vol. IV (CUP, 1975): ch. 4, Thompson, V., and Adloff, R., 'French Economic Policy in Tropical Africa'.
Hailey, Lord, *African Survey Revised 1956*, pp. 206, 328, 542, 616, 670, 1338, 1369, 1476.
MacKenzie and Robinson (eds), *Five Elections in Africa*.

CHAPTER 8

Cornevin, R., *Histoire du Togo* (Berger-Levrault 1969).
——, *Histoire de l'Afrique* (Payot, Paris, 1975) ch. xvii.
Gann and Duignan (eds), *Colonialism in Africa 1870–1960*, Vol. II ch. 7, op. cit.
Hailey, Lord, *African Survey Revised 1956*, pp. 324–43.
Pedler, F. J., *The Lion and the Unicorn in Africa* (Heinemann Educational Books, 1974) pp. 108 to 110 for more about the family and commercial background of Sylvanus Olympio.

CHAPTER 9

Crowder and Ajayi (eds), *History of West Africa*, Vol. II, pp. 526–8.
Bienen, Henry, 'State and Revolution: the work of Amilcar Cabral', *Journal of Modern African Studies*, Vol. 15 no. 4 (1977).
Blackey, Robert, 'Fanon and Cabral: a contrast in theories of revolution for Africa', *Journal of Modern African Studies* (1974) p. 191.
Chilcote, Ronald H., Political thought of Amilcar Cabral, *Journal of Modern African Studies* (1968) p. 373.
Gann and Duignan (eds), *Colonialism in Africa 1870–1960*, Vol. II: ch. 4, Duffy, James, 'Portuguese Africa 1930 to 1960'.
Handyside, Richard (transl. and ed.), *Revolution in Guinea. Selected texts by Amilcar Cabral* (New York, 1969).
Hailey, Lord, *African Survey Revised 1956*, pp. 228–33, 353–7, 378–9, 562–4.

CHAPTER 10

Buchanan, K. M., and Pugh, J. C., *Land and People in Nigeria* (University of London Press, rev. ed. 1958).

Capet, Marcel: the work cited in the text is quoted by Hopkins, A. G., in *Economic History of West Africa*, p. 245.

Caldwell, J. C., and Okonjo, C. (eds), *Population of Tropical Africa* (Longman, 1968) esp. pp. 155–224.

Caldwell, J. C. (ed), *Population Growth and Socio-Economic Change in West Africa* (Columbia University Press for the Population Council, 1976).

Cornevin, Robert, *Histoire du Togo* (Berger-Levrault, 1969) pp. 273–7 for registration of births and deaths in Togo.

Hailey, Lord, *African Survey Revised 1956*, ch. IV.

Hamilton, W. B., Robinson, K. and Goodwin, C. D. W. (eds), *A Decade of the Commonwealth 1955–1964* (Duke University Press, 1966): T. E. Smith, ch. 18, 'The Population of the Commonwealth'.

Marris, Peter, *Social Consequences of the Lagos Slum Clearance Scheme* (Institute of Community Studies, Nigeria, 1959).

Singer, H., and Asani, J., *Rich and Poor Countries* (Allen and Unwin, 1978).

World Bank, *Trends in Developing Countries* (1973) and *Atlas: population, per capita product, and growth rates* (1973).

CHAPTER 11

Bauer, P. T., *West African Trade* (CUP, 1954).

——, *Dissent on Development* (Weidenfeld & Nicolson, 1971).

Bauer, P. T., and Yamey, B. S., *Economics of Under-developed Countries* (CUP, 1957).

——, *Markets, Market Control, and Marketing Reform* (Weidenfeld & Nicolson, 1968).

Colonial Development and Welfare Acts 1929–70 (HMSO, 1971), Cmnd 4677.

Farer, T. J. (ed), *Financing African Development* (MIT Press, 1965).

Gann and Duignan (eds), *Colonialism in Africa 1870–1960*, Vol. IV, 'The Economics of Colonialism'.

Geiger, T., and Armstrong, W., *The Development of African Private Enterprise* (National Planning Association, Washington D.C., 1964).

Hamilton, Robinson and Goodwin (eds), *A Decade of the Commonwealth 1955–1964*, Part VI.

Hamrell, S., and Widstrand, C. G., *The Soviet Block China and Africa* (Scandinavian Institute of African Studies, 1964).

Hazlewood, A., *African Integration and Disintegration*.

Helleiner, G. K. *Peasant Agriculture, Government, and Economic Growth in Nigeria* (Homewood, 1966).

Hevi, Emmanuel J., *The Dragon's Embrace; The Chinese Communists and Africa* (Pall Mall Press, 1967).

Hodder, B. W., *Economic Development in the Tropics* (Methuen, 1968).

Hopkins, A. G., *Economic History of West Africa*.

Lee, J. M., *Colonial Development and Good Government* (Clarendon, 1967).

Mikesell, R. F., *Economics of Foreign Aid* (Weidenfeld & Nicolson, 1968).

Myint, H., *Economics of the Developing Countries* (Hutchinson, 4th ed., 1973).

Onyemelukwe, C. C., *Economic Underdevelopment, An Inside View* (Longman, 1974).

Robson, P., *Economic Integration in Africa* (Allen & Unwin, 1968).

Saylor, R. G., *The Economic System of Sierra Leone* (Duke University Press, 1967).

Stevens, Christopher, *The Soviet Union and Black Africa* (Macmillan, 1976).

Thomas, M. F., and Whittington, G. W., *Environment and Land Use in Africa* (Methuen, 1969).

Report of the Commission on the Marketing of West African Cocoa [the Nowell Report] (HMSO, 1938) Cmd 5845.

CHAPTER 12

Ewing, A. F., *Industry in Africa* (OUP 1968).

Gann and Duignan (eds), *Colonialism in Africa 1870–1960*, Vol. IV: Kilby, Peter, ch. 12, 'Manufacturing in Colonial Africa'.

Geiger and Armstrong, *Development of African Private Enterprise*.

Hodder, B. W., *Economic Development in the Tropics* (Methuen, 1968).

Kilby, Peter, *African Enterprise: The Nigerian Bread Industry* (Hoover Institution, Stanford University, 1965).

Pedler, F. J., *Economic Geography of West Africa* (Longman, 1955) ch. 8.

Reader, W. J., *Metal Box, A History* (Heinemann, 1976).

CHAPTER 13

Carter, G. M. (ed.), *African One-Party States*: Liebenow, J. Gus, ch.
VI.

Clapham, Christopher, *Liberia and Sierra Leone* (CUP, 1976).

Wreh, Tuan, *The Love of Liberty* . . . (C. Hurst, 1976) gives the view of
a hinterland man critical of Tubman's policies.

CHAPTERS 14 AND 15

Alexander, H. T., *African Tightrope* (Pall Mall Press, 1965).

Apaloo, F. K., *Report of the Commission to inquire into the Kwame
Nkrumah properties* (Ghana Ministry of Information, 1966).

Austin, D. and Luckham, R. (eds), *Politicians and Soldiers in Ghana*
(Cass, 1976).

Beckman, Bjorn, *Organising the Farmers* (Scandinavian Institute of
African Studies, Uppsala, 1977).

Boahen, Adu, *Ghana: evolution and change* (Longman, 1975).

Busia, Kofi A., *The Challenge of Africa* (Praeger, New York, 1962).

——, *Africa in Search of Democracy* (Routledge & Kegan Paul, 1967).

Davidson, Basil, *Black Star: a view of the life and times of Kwame
Nkrumah* (Allen Lane, 1973).

First, Ruth, *The Barrel of a Gun* (Allen Lane, 1970) deals with military
coups in Ghana and Nigeria.

Genoud, Roger, *Nationalism and Economic Development in Ghana*
(Praeger, 1969).

Jones, Trevor, *Ghana's First Republic 1960–1966* (Methuen, 1976).

Kesse-Adu, Kwame, *Politics of Political Detention* (Ghana Publishing
Corporation, Tema, 1971).

Killick, T., *Development Economics in Action* (Heinemann Educational
Books, 1978).

McKown, Robin, *Nkrumah* (Doubleday, New York, 1973).

Moxon, James, *Volta: Man's Greatest Lake* (Deutsch, 1969).

Nkrumah, Kwame, *Autobiography* (Nelson, 1957).

——, *Africa Must Unite* (Heinemann Educational Books, 1963).

——, *I speak of Freedom* (Heinemann, 1961).

——, *Challenge of the Congo* (Nelson, 1967).

——, *Axioms of Kwame Nkrumah* (Nelson, 1967).

——, *Neo-colonialism* (Nelson, 1965).

Ocran, A., *A Myth is Broken: an account of the Ghana coup d'état of 24th
February 1966* (Longman, 1968).

Omari, Peter, *Kwame Nkrumah* (C. Hurst, 1970).

Thompson, W. Scott, *Ghana's Foreign Policy 1957–1966* (Princeton University Press, 1969).

Woronoff, Jon, *West African Wager: Houphouet versus Nkrumah* (Scarecrow Press, Metuchen, NJ, 1972).

CHAPTER 16

Adamolekun, Ladipo, *Sekou Touré's Guinea* (Methuen, 1976).

Camara, Sylvain Soriba, *La Guinée sans la France* (Presse de la fondation nationale des sciences politiques, 1976).

Carter, G. M. (ed.), *African One-Party States*: Cowan, L. G., ch. IV.

Gigon, Fernand, *Guinée Etat-pilote* (Tribune libre Plon, 1959).

Rivière, Claude, *Guinea*, translated by Thomson and Adloff (Cornell University Press, 1977).

CHAPTER 17

Cornevin, R., *Histoire du Togo*.

—— *Histoire de l'Afrique* (Payot, 1975) ch. XVII.

Decalo, Samuel, *Coups and army rule in Africa* (Yale University Press, New Haven and London, 1976).

CHAPTER 18

Bennett, Valerie P., 'Military government in Mali', *Journal of Modern African Studies*, vol. 13, no. 2 (1975).

Ernst, Klaus, *Tradition and Progress in the African Village: the non-capitalist transformation of rural communities in Mali* (Hurst, 1977).

Ewing, A. F., *Industry in Africa* (OUP, 1968) p. 28.

Imperato, Pascal James, *Historical Dictionary of Mali* (Scarecrow Press, 1977).

CHAPTER 19

Ba, Sylvia Washington, *The Concept of Negritude in the Poetry of Leopold Sedar Senghor* (Princeton University Press, 1973).

Carter, G. M. (ed.), *African One-Party States*: Milcent, E., ch. III.

Hymans, J. L., *Leopold Sedar Senghor; an Intellectual Biography* (Edinburgh University Press, 1971).
Irele, Abiola (ed.), *Selected Poems of Leopold Sedar Senghor* (Cambridge University Press, 1977).
Mezu, S. Okechukwu, *The Poetry of Leopold Sedar Senghor* (Fairleigh Dickinson University Press, 1973).

CHAPTER 20

Ewing, A. F., *Industry in Africa* (OUP, 1968) p. 39.
Woronoff, Jon, *West African Wager: Houphouet versus Nkrumah.*

CHAPTER 21

Fischer, Wilhelm, *Ober-Volta* (Kurt Schroeder, Bonn, 1962).

CHAPTER 22

Dalby, David, and Harrison Church, R. J. (eds), *Drought in Africa* (SOAS, London, 1973).
——, Harrison Church, R. J., and Bezzaz, Fatima (eds), *Drought in Africa 2* (International African Institute, London, 1977).
Kountche, Lieutenant-Colonel Seyni, *Discours et Messages* (Secretariat d'Etat à la présidence chargé de l'information et du tourisme, Nyamey, 1975).
Laya, Dioulde, *Le projet de mise en valeur des cuvettes de Kutukale et Karma en pays Songhay* (Etudes Nigeriennes No. 24, IFAN, Paris and Nyamey, 1973).
Mayer, Reinhold, *Die französische Politik der Cooperation Culturelle et Technique und die nationale Entwicklung* (Helmut Buske, Hamburg, 1973).
Niger, periodical published by the government of Niger, 1968–73.
Nyamey, Université de, *Handbook 1975–6.*

CHAPTER 23

Decalo, Samuel, *Coups and army rule in Africa* (Yale University Press, New Haven and London, 1976).
Ronen, Dov, *Dahomey; between tradition and modernity* (Cornell University Press, Ithaca and London 1975).

CHAPTER 24

Arnold, Guy, *Modern Nigeria* (Longman, 1977).

Awolowo, Obafemi, *Autobiography* (CUP, 1960).

Bello, Alhaji Sir Ahmadu, *My life* (CUP, 1962).

Decalo, Samuel, *Coups and army rule in Africa* (Yale University Press, New Haven and London, 1976).

Oyinbo, John, *Nigeria: crisis and beyond* (Charles Knight, 1971).

Panter-Brick, S. K. (ed.), *Nigerian politics and military rule* (University of London, Athlone Press, 1970).

Wolpe, Howard, *Urban politics in Nigeria* (University of California Press, 1977).

CHAPTER 25

Akpan, N. U., *The struggle for secession 1966–70* (Cass, London, 1971).

Beer, C. E. F., *The politics of peasant groups in Western Nigeria* (Ibadan University Press, 1977).

Hunt, Sir David, *On the spot* (Peter Davies, London, 1975) ch. 9.

Luckham, Robin, *The Nigerian military: a sociological analysis of authority and result* (CUP, 1971).

Niven, Sir Rex, *The war of Nigerian unity* (Evans Brothers/Nigerian Publishers, 1970).

Oyinbo, John, *Nigeria: crisis and beyond* (Charles Knight, 1971).

Panter-Brick, S. K., *Soldiers and oil* (Cass, London, 1977).

Stremlau, John, *The international politics of the Nigerian civil war 1967–70* (Princeton University Press, 1977).

CHAPTER 26

Beckett, Paul, and O'Connell, James, *Education and power in Nigeria* (Hodder & Stoughton, 1978).

CHAPTER 27

Cox, Thomas S., *Civil-military relations in Sierra Leone* (Harvard University Press, 1976).

Foray, Cyril P., *Historical Dictionary of Sierra Leone*.

Kup, A. P., *Sierra Leone, a concise history*.

CHAPTER 30

Mazrui, Ali A., *Africa's international relations* (Heinemann/Westview 1977).

CHAPTER 31

Burke, Edmund, *Reflections on the Revolution in France* (1790).
Coleman, J. S., 'The emergence of African political parties', in Haines, C. Grove, *Africa Today* (Johns Hopkins Press, Baltimore, 1955).
Crowder and Ajayi (eds), *History of West Africa*, Vol. II, chs 18 and 19.
Louis, W. Roger, *Imperialism at bay 1941–45; the United States and the decolonisation of the British Empire* (OUP, 1977).
Nkrumah, Kwame, *Africa Must Unite, Autobiography, Axioms of Kwame Nkrumah, Consciencism* (Heinemann, 1964).
Perham, Dame Margery, *The Colonial Reckoning*, Reith Lectures (Collins, 1961).

Index